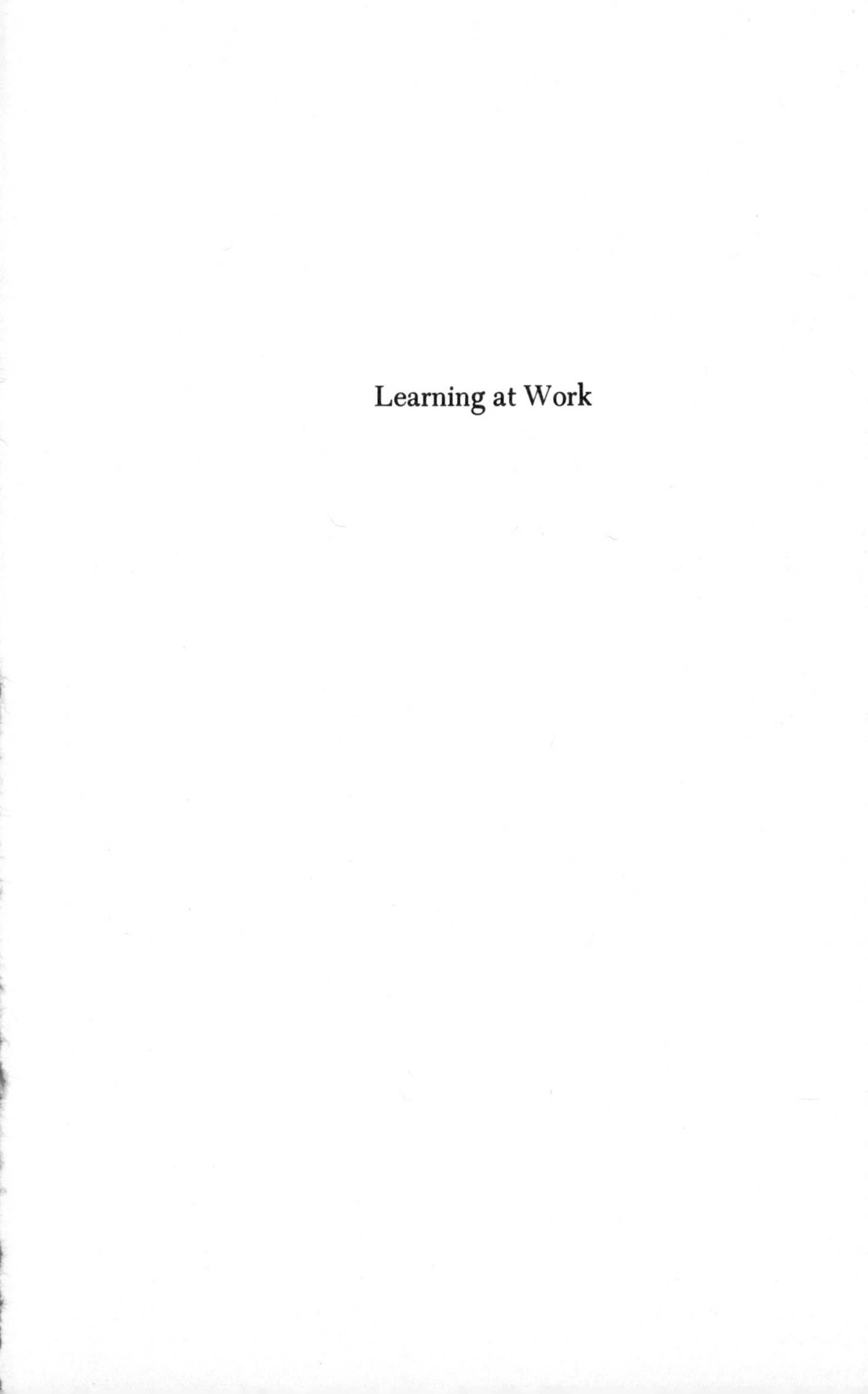

Learning at Work

Avice Saint

Learning at Work

human resources and organizational development

Professional-Technical Series

Nelson-Hall Company, Chicago

ISBN 0–911012–22–2

Library of Congress Catalog Card No. 73–81275

For information address
Nelson-Hall Company, Publishers, 325 W. Jackson Blvd., Chicago, Ill. 60606

Manufactured in the United States of America

Contents

Acknowledgments

My initial experiences as a training practitioner raised questions about whether training and learning within an organization could be productive. These experiences sparked an interest in examining prevalent but often inconsistent assumptions about what constitutes "training" within organizations: What are the basic issues that need to be understood if training-learning processes are to help organizations and their people learn and adjust to changes in work in order to accomplish their goals and resolve their problems?

During this time, leadership demonstrated by two executives of an organization in which I worked led me to realize that management practices make an enormous difference in the learning process and its outcome. I am especially grateful for the way in which Norman Arrighi directed a task force which involved both managers and workers in the analysis and improvement of their instructional and learning efforts. I owe much to Robert Tobias for the way in which he incorporated training activities as part of management planning, preparation, and execution of an organization's conversion to an automated supply system.

Continuing work as a training and development practitioner, I turned to the University of California to learn how to do more systematic research on "learning within organizations." My tentative conclusions showed that learning is a function of the conditions provided by the organizational environment and by the qualities of the training-learning processes. I am deeply indebted to Dr. Jack London for his continuing guidance and support; to Dr. Martin Trow for helping me gain fresh insights into the issues that arise when training and learning are within organizations whose primary goals are other than educational; and to Dr. Anselm Strauss for teaching me his strategies of qualitative research, without which I could not have learned the methods of comparative analysis that made this research fruitful. My gratitude goes to Dr. Bernice Fisher (now at Columbia University) for critiques that helped evolve further research.

Extending the original research, I sought to learn more about the training and learning practices of different organizations. This book has grown out of this extended study. It now seems clear that what makes training worthwhile is the result of internal conditions of the organization's environment that spark and reinforce learning and the designs that build learning into the work operations.

Organizational leadership, then, in its effort to keep its people competent, up to date, and productive, must not merely increase conventional training activities; nor should it simply make a choice between the newer strategies of organizational development, management by objectives, job enrichment, or transactional analysis. We go in the wrong direction if we attempt to "paint on" a strategy that succeeded elsewhere. Rather, each organization, each group, each individual, must be involved in learning as it relates to doing in order to become aware of the need for adapting to change. When this happens, learning makes an enormous contribution to the well-being of both the organization and its workers.

The central task of management today is creating an organizational climate that evokes human growth and training-learning processes that integrate learning with work. In this way training can help an organization and its people accomplish what they need to do.

I am deeply indebted to many professional colleagues in the training field, to those in university departments, and to those involved in the extended survey of organizational training practices. I am especially grateful for the initial interest and the stimulating insights of Dr. Marvin Berkeley of Texas Instruments, who provided strong encouragement.

I owe an enormous debt of gratitude to the five organizations who agreed to participate in the extended survey and allowed me to discuss with their managers and employees the issues of training and learning: Western Electric, Chase Manhattan Bank, Raymond Corporation, the Western Region of the Internal Revenue Service, and the White Sands Missile Range of the Department of Army. As it became clear that each of these organizations was getting productive results by integrating training with the action needed to solve problems on the job, I obtained permission from each to present a case study illustrating one of their productive training patterns.

It is impossible to acknowledge the help of every individual who has participated in this survey, although a list appears in the Appendix. There are key figures, however, to whom I wish to express my special gratitude.

I owe much to George G. Raymond, President of the Raymond Corporation, for sharing insights gained from his successful experience with the "learning" of his organization and his workers to resolve organizational problems. I wish to thank Robert Cline, assistant to Mr. Raymond, for making arrangements, providing introductions to managers and workers, and for helping me to understand how their intradepartmental task groups applied the team techniques they had learned.

At the local level of Western Electric I am deeply grateful to James Etheredge, Jr. for his continuing and thoughtful coordination of Western Electric's corporate, regional, and installation participation. I appreciate his commentaries and critiques, reflecting as they do his competence in and commitment to the field of training and development. To James Martin, manager of a local installation of Western Electric, I wish to express gratitude for his incisive recounting of the Team Effectiveness experience of his group, and for his sharing of the entire record of the case. At the corporate level of Western Electric, I owe much to Arthur G. Foster for making it possible to analyze the Team Effectiveness program; and to Matt Lynaugh for sharing his professional experience and for his review of technical concepts.

At Chase Manhattan Bank I wish to thank Albert S. Woodhouse, who guided me through their organization and outlined the principles upon which their training and development practices are based. Without the continuing assistance of Ben Roter the case study could not have materialized. I owe much to him for his helpful review, commentaries, and critiques. Mark Loftin made me aware of the productiveness that can be gained when the planning and design of training links the learning process with work operations.

At Internal Revenue's Western Region I wish to express my indebtedness to Paul O'Rourke, who indoctrinated me in the principles and practices of their training programs, guided me through their organization, made it possible to participate in the organizational development process at the Ogden Service Center, and provided helpful critiques. My deepest thanks go to members of the Blue Group, one of the teams at the eighth Organizational Development seminar at Ogden's Service Center. They graciously accepted me as one of their group and demonstrated to me how effective a group can be once it has learned to work together. My special thanks are due to Mike Jones, Maxine Bills, Dick Nelson, Eula Stringfellow, and Eli Yearsley, and their resource man, Fred Berry.

At the Department of the Army I am grateful for the continuing professional leadership and assistance of Ben B. Beeson, Director of Civilian Personnel. At Army's White Sands Missile Range, I wish to express my appreciation to Roy Autry and James Patton for making the survey possible and arranging for the discussions with their managers and employees. I particularly wish to thank Carl Clifft for his professional help in understanding the background, principles, and practices of their Cooperative Education Program, and for his meticulous review and critiques of the case study on that program.

The United States Civil Service Commission has provided invaluable assistance. At the federal level, I wish to express appreciation to James R. Beck, Jr., Director of the Bureau of Training, and to Dr. Edward Jones and Dr. James Lau, for helping me to understand the productive learning approaches of the Federal Executive Institute at Charlottesville, Virginia. To Harry Wolfe, Al Beller, and LaVor Neuenswander my gratitude is due for making available the resources of the Executive Seminar Center at Berkeley, California and the San Francisco Regional Training Center of the U.S. Civil Service Commission. My appreciation goes also to Phil Jiminez of the Commission's Intergovernmental Programs.

I owe much to Robert Mager, Peter Pipe, and Barbara Wachner for their professional help. Their leadership in the field of educational technology has been stimulating and has borne fruit, as this book witnesses.

And finally I wish to express my debt of gratitude for the friendship, understanding, and continuing encouragement of Ruth Beales; for the cheerful patience of Elizabeth Tollmann in her editorial assistance, and for the efficiency with which Grace O'Connell typed the manuscript. Without their teamwork this book would never have become a reality.

Avice Saint

Learning at Work

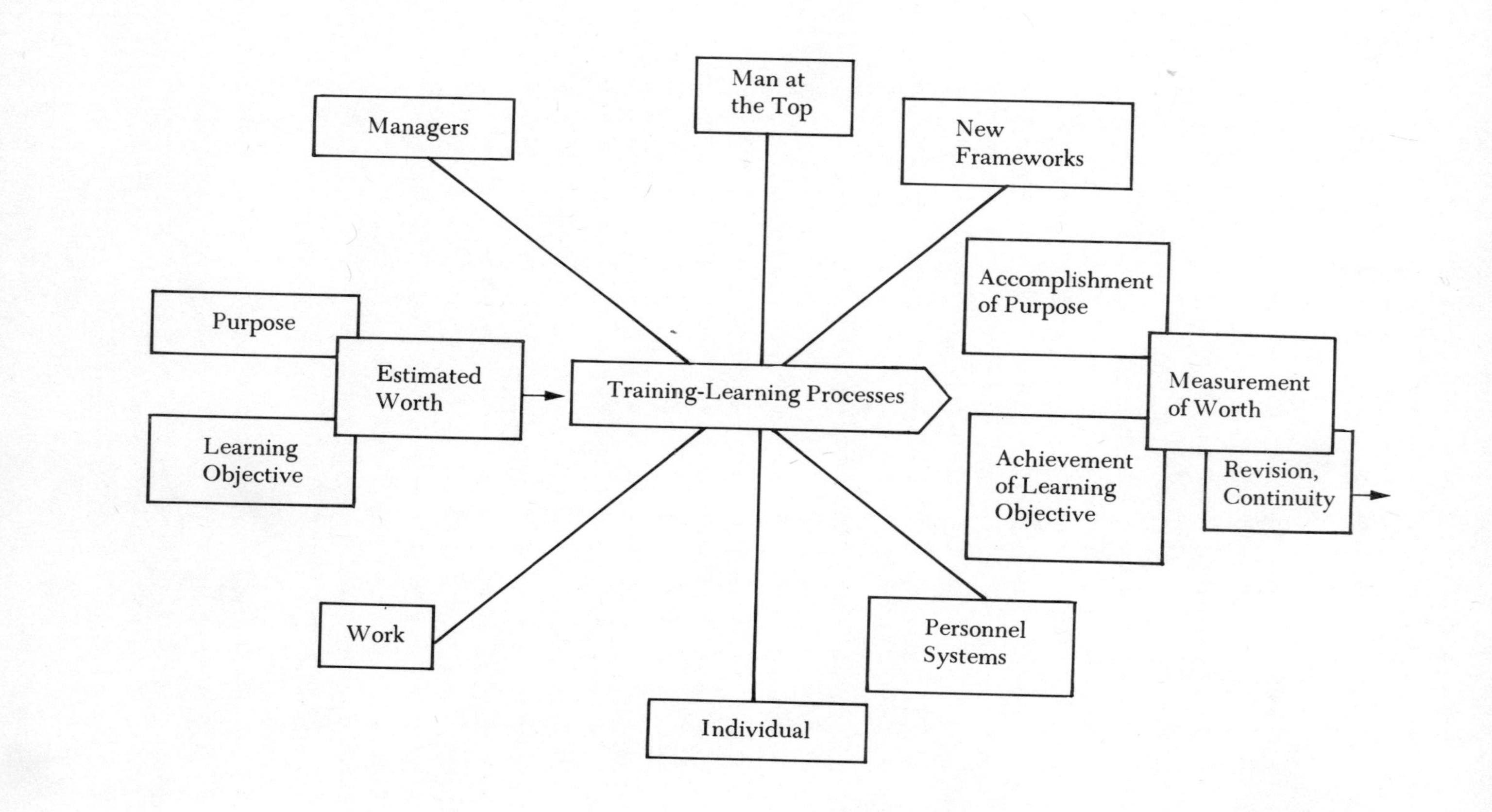

Managers
Man at the Top
New Frameworks
Purpose
Estimated Worth
Learning Objective
Training-Learning Processes
Accomplishment of Purpose
Measurement of Worth
Achievement of Learning Objective
Revision, Continuity
Work
Individual
Personnel Systems

1

Learning Can Be Productive

The purpose of training within an organization—whether it be a government agency, a business, a hospital, an industry, or a research organization—is to contribute to that organization's effectiveness. The function of learning is to help an organization and its employees acquire knowledge and to use it to produce progress. Until we know and understand the meaning of the training-learning process, its functions, and its purpose *within* the context or organizational activities, we shall be uncertain and most likely deprived of productive results. The findings of a comparative study of many contemporary training and development practices within large organizations, and the examples described in this book, show that where training and learning are *understood,* are *wanted,* and *action* is taken to apply and use them in work, productive results do occur.

The objective of this book is to describe what must happen within an organization, both to its framework and its operations and to its instructional-learning processes, if the organization and its employees are going to learn and adapt to their work tasks and roles. The observations on which this book is based show that the way an organization is constituted influences the outcome of the instruction-learning processes and that the qualities of training and development programs affect the competence of the organization to produce.

The major finding was that productive results occur primarily when training and learning are integrated with action needed to solve real organizational problems and accomplish work goals. The book aims to discuss the organizational environment and the training-learning process as they interrelate in real life. One cannot be understood without a grasp of the other, since learning to be productive is not separate from but a part of the whole realm of work operations. Its wholeness is found in the employees' performance, in their achievement of competence in the work of the organization.

The organizations whose training and learning systems are compared and analyzed in this book are all large-scale organizations. Although their explicit purposes differ, they are essentially alike in their basic characteristics: a hierarchy of authority, specialization, and division of labor into the functions of comptrollership, budget and accounting, procurement, management information systems, production, marketing, personnel; rules and regulations; and systems for the recruitment, utilization, and recognition of human resources. A newer feature is their adaptation to changing external environment and internal technology.

The members of the organizations described herein are: managers—including executives, middle managers, and supervisors who make decisions, organize the work and manage personnel; and employees—including staff and line workers. They represent a wide range of occupations: clerks, semiskilled and skilled craftsmen, administrators, scientific and research technicians, professionals, managers of various technical fields.

The variety of distinctions made between training, education, and learning suggests that many people have something different in mind. Quite often training is used to denote practical, vocational experience, and education is used to denote the broader process of preparation or discipline of the mind or character through study or instruction. However, attempts to split hairs in making distinctions are likely to be too artificial and usually fail. The definitions I plan to use are the following:

1. *Training* includes any effort *within* the organization to teach, instruct, coach, develop employees in technical skills, knowledge, principles, techniques, and to provide insights into and attitudes toward the organization. Essentially, training enables managers and employees to learn and adapt to the tasks of their work and the roles of their positions.

2. *Learning* is the individual's adaptive process through which he comes to understand and respond to the requirements and demands that his work and his position make on him. Learning may be a change in what he knows, what he likes, or acquires the habit to do, what skills he can perform, or how he identifies with the group or the organization.

3. *Training-learning process* as used in this book is more than the two-way instructor-learner relationship. It is a continuum which includes: the *situations and problems* that give rise to the need for learning; the *actions required* on the part of those responsible to establish conditions and activities which enable workers to learn and adjust to new tasks, concepts, and roles; and the

changes in behavior and *operations* resulting from the application and utilization of knowledge.

Can Learning Be Productive?

The question persists whether learning and training within organizations can be productive. Although considerable research has been done in university psychological labs to understand learning techniques of industrial tasks, comparatively little research has focused on the learning processes that occur within large-scale organizations. One study by Porter describes Rand's development of an Air Defense Warning System, during which the research team discovered system training concepts and their relationship to the behavior of different components of an organization.[1] Another study in this field was done by David King.[2] He describes his experiences as consultant to three Norwegian firms, using case analyses of systematic training for operators, supervisors, and work reorganization, pointing up fundamental issues in the establishment of training systems within organizations.

The work of behavioral scientists, particularly those in the field of organizational development, points up the need for managers to gain insight, knowledge, and techniques that result in increased effectiveness for their organizations.

In an earlier study, I described the uncertainties of productivity from training endeavors in a large organization.[3] The findings of the research showed that: (1) organizational realities influence learning and instructional efforts both positively and negatively; (2) the training-learning continuum as it extends throughout the organization requires attributes different from those of the more simple two-way instructor-learner relationship; (3) the purpose of the training is more than the acquisition of knowledge and more than change in behavior since it is functional toward accomplishment of work, whether it is the completion of a report, the making of a product, the supervision of an operation, or whatever the task.

The original study was extended to the comparison and analysis of current training practices in other kinds of organizations. It was found that the *major factor of effectiveness* was the *incorporation of training and learning with the action* needed to accomplish work, to solve operational problems on the job. Because the teaching-learning continuum exists within and throughout the organization, the profitability of training must be built into all its interrelationships as well as the relationship of the instructor (whether it is a teacher, a programmed device, a manager, or a problem-solving group) and the learner. If learning activities are to be productive, they cannot be separate from the organizational structure, its systems, and the workers they seek to help.

Throughout this book, examples are given to illustrate that the organizational framework, within which the learning goes on, affects the learning process and its outcome. Little may be done by managers to help their workers develop because managers are rewarded for production and cost reduction efforts, and not for development of their employees. Some lip service may be given to development, and training may be handled through standardized programs administratively convenient for handling large numbers of employees. Employees may lack the opportunity to learn, or may not even be aware that they *need* to learn in order to become productive. Excellent training programs and courses may be conducted in the same organizations, but they are appendages to the corporate body rather than interrelated with its operations; under these circumstances, training efforts bring little in the way of productive results. Comparison and analysis of the more productive training practices have shown certain elements common to organizations that use their operations, problems, and situations to stimulate the reaching for knowledge, to make its need more obvious in order to complete certain tasks and to build the confidence and competence of employees.

Training Policy and Practices

Organization executives have become increasingly skeptical of training programs. Managers do not seem to manage better as a result of participating in management development programs, and employees do not demonstrate improved competence.

Policy and practices toward training are often paradoxical. We profess that it is organizational policy to train employees for their jobs; nevertheless, on-the-job training is often a myth. Although management seems to accept in principle the value of employee training, often this is not evidenced in their practices; nor is this principle always valued in the lower levels of the organization. Just as supervisors are responsible for the organization, delegation, and control of work, they are also responsible for seeing that subordinates are helped to acquire the skills and knowledge they need. We read of the increased importance, costs, and amounts of training, and at the same time we hear reports of the precariousness of training programs and their vulnerability to budget cuts.

Today, educational technologies and their materials flood the market, but they are far more sophisticated than the organization's readiness to integrate them into the mainstream of day-to-day operations. The increased importance given to training by the commercial world is not matched by the second-rate status accorded the training function in organizations. What is generally not recognized is that integration of these learning technologies into the organization's operations is generally more problematic than their original development. Acquiring knowledge is one thing, and using it to produce progress is another, but both are needed for productivity.

Skepticism and inconsistencies of current learning practices of organizations should encourage us to become aware of changes in the meaning, the functions, and the purpose of training-learning processes within organizations. Although organizations profess interest in training and development activities, not enough attention has been paid to the basic issues. We need to pay attention to whether our assumptions about learning within organizations are valid in view of the action needed to keep organizations updated and productive.

Traditional Assumptions

The failure to recognize that many of the current training practices are outmoded or incomplete is evident in examining some traditional assumptions on which training learning processes in organizations are based.

For years the practice of on-the-job training has been accepted as a legitimate way for employees to learn. But the long period of time required, such as apprenticeships, is no longer necessary or practical. Furthermore, many operations today have a knowledge base, and the challenge to the organization is to provide work opportunities in such a way that employees can apply what they have learned in their work.

The costliness of errors in the present technological age makes trial and error methods obsolete as well as unbusinesslike. Accurate and timely information on results must be given to the employee in order to increase confidence and lessen possibilities of error.

We oversimplify the purpose of training when we say that things would run smoothly if each employee used his knowledge and skills to improve his performance to its peak. It is no longer merely the gap between an employee's skills and the requirements of his job on which training systems must focus. It is also the gaps in the relationships between departments, between units, and between individual employees. The procedures of today's technologies require new liaisons and teamwork. To focus on gaps in individual knowledge is not enough. We need also to focus on errors that result from procedural breakdowns.

We commonly think of the instructional learning continuum as a two-way relationship, the success of which is dependent upon the instructor having taught well and the learner having successfully acquired the knowledge. This notion must give way to recognition that there are many factors within organizational life that aid or constrain the learning process, making it more complex and thus affecting its outcome and its productivity.

When organizations establish training courses, the underlying assumption is that there will be a consequent increase in productivity and that workers will better be able to adjust to job changes. But the completion of courses has never been a guarantee that new ideas and concepts will be incorporated into work. Even simulation of the real operation does not insure transfer of what has been learned to the job. The rapid changes in knowledge and the needs of workers for job-change assistance make formal classroom systems and methods outmoded. What is needed now are new ways to transmit laterally recently developed techniques and knowledge from those *who know* to those who *need to know*. The old assumption that traditional and time-consuming production of subject matter courses and development of expert instructors will accomplish the passing on of information to the younger generation of workers is no longer feasible. This assumption has led to an overemphasis on academic certificates and degrees, as well as on the organization's system of training records. Too much attention to credits and quantitative measurements obscures the purpose for which organizations have the training-learning function. The knowledge base alone is not enough. Organizations need new ways to help workers integrate what they know into what they do.

Basic Issues

Enough has been said here to show that any training system that is simply superimposed upon, but not really incorporated into, the operations of the organization holds little promise of productivity. In the midst of the skepticism and discussion as to possible routes for the maintenance of competence, not much attention has been paid to the basic issues. We seem to be moving in the direction of increasing the amount of training and educational activity without questioning the patterns of instruction and learning within organizations. It is important to understand this, because the examples discussed in this book show that those organizations that have been successful in making knowledge productive to their firms have established new patterns.

The basic issue we need to comprehend, in order to make learning productive for organizations and their people, concerns understanding what happens to educational functions when they become embedded in an organization.

Extension and Adaptation of the Training-Learning Process

The training-learning process extends throughout and adapts to the organization of which it becomes a part; if productive results are desired, it must take on practical attributes (initiation, methods, design, feedback, continuity) that interrelate the learning to the objective and integrate the knowledge with its use in work operations.

There has been a tendency for organizations to establish separate training or educational units which, although they are "attached" to the organization, do not function differently from those in most educational institutions. Their courses are usually directed toward subjects that are related to that particular organization; and, normally, course completion is recorded in career development records as evidence of completion of certain required content or subject matter training. What should be realized, however, is that the training-learning practices within an organization cannot remain as separate entities, but must become part of a whole training-learning process related to work requirements and employees' needs to learn. They are a part of a total process in which the needs for the learning have roots in the organization's work and in which the learning results affect workers' actions and organizational operations. Training-learning within an organization cannot be defined without relating it to the organizational setting.

The emphasis is on the working environment, the setting of goals, the understanding of responsibilities for their achievement, the feedback of information on progress, and the application of what has been learned to other projects and problems. These comprise the primary or fundamental training-learning process, while external training programs are supplemental. Thus it is a new concept of training and learning integrated in action which is needed to meet operational goals, and to solve real problems on the job. The training-learning continuum begins with work situations that *give rise to the need* to learn and adjust to new tasks; it extends to the *application* of knowledge and creative approaches to work.

Influences of Organizational Realities on Instructional and Learning Efforts

The organizational environment is bound to affect the process of learning. We, therefore, need to be concerned with day-to-day realities and the degree to which they influence learning positively or negatively:

1. Work pressures make "time off" to participate in training activities seem impractical.
2. Routinized procedures prescribe ways that work must be done. This limits opportunities for trying out different approaches to accomplish work objectives.
3. Training activities tend to be directed in ways and at times administratively convenient to the organization.
4. Managers, concerned with handling activities piecemeal in nature, often "wash their hands" of training. They fail to develop the capacities of their people through delegation of responsibilities. Thus, employees often receive guidance through improvisations that fail to provide the continuing help needed by employees in learning and adjusting to changes in their tasks.
5. Changing technologies create needs for job-change assistance. New systems, which cut horizontally across department lines, require workers to gain insights into how other components function.
6. Reorganization and the addition or deletion of missions affect the existence of jobs, force the shifting of workers, and require their adjustment to new tasks.
7. Prevalent is a built-in resistance to change. Large organizations stubbornly cling to long-established ways that worked in the past.

Training Is Functional Toward Achieving the Goals of the Organization

Training—in addition to enabling people to learn new tasks and roles—needs to be functional toward the purposes of the organization. What happens to the training function when it is embedded in organizations whose major function is other than that of education, such as making products, providing services, and selling goods? Does the training function differ when it is within an organization? It *must* differ if it is to function productively. Members of the organization participate in training activities to learn *in order to* improve their performance, to fulfill their responsibilities, to solve problems, or to achieve work objectives.

We need to examine the relationship between functions and purpose. For example, the function of the circulatory system is to deliver blood through the body, but its purpose is to nourish and to maintain the organism. The question is not only whether the circulatory system is delivering blood, but also whether that blood is being utilized and is producing the desired result. This holds true for an organization. Is the function contributing to its purpose? Training enables people to learn and adjust to new tasks and new roles, but its purpose is to improve productivity, develop manpower, assist in the socialization of its employees, aid the mobility of its workers, and induce self-development. In this case, the question is not only whether a training activity is helping people learn but whether what they have learned is being utilized to achieve the desired results?

If training is functioning, then it is contributing to the activities of the organization in a number of different ways:

1. It improves products, services, sales by strengthening performance through the application of what has been learned.

2. It creates new knowledges, helps organizations learn from their experiences, puts new knowledge to work, and develops new techniques.

3. It helps to develop the flexibility and capabilities of manpower, and from an economic standpoint, provides maximum productivity from human resources.

4. It provides a built-in means of preventing obsolescence in times when many professionals and technicians become outdated a few years after graduation from college.

5. It is functional toward the socialization, or resocialization of employees, since socialization is no longer thought of as "preparation for life" for the young but rather as a continuing life process for adults. Accelerated change exerts pressure on institutions of work to become institutions of training.

6. It is functional toward mobility of personnel. It aids the advancement of employees by providing knowledge and skill required for higher level jobs.

7. It is functional toward helping organizations remedy certain "dysfunctions." Because of their closely defined directives, rules and regulations, systems and procedures, and narrow specializations, organizations produce conformity and rigidity of action. Training can provide fresh outlooks and eliminate old techniques that literally have become "trained incapacities" since the conditions that originally required those techniques no longer exist.

8. It is functional toward individual self-development. When organizations transfer to individuals the desire to learn and to apply what they have learned, they provide a continuing process which brings constant renewal and updating. This hedges against men going to seed and builds into the organization the foundations for keeping men's minds active and productive.

Our examination of the relationships of organizational realities to learning processes within an organization calls for new ways to regard learning and work, new places, new times, new involvements and partnerships of workers, to the end that learning may be closely related with productive results. Recognition of what is happening in training-learning systems leads us to the realization that many underlying assumptions are no longer valid. The functions and purposes for which training and learning exist within organizations demand that we think in new ways. We need innovations in: (1) leadership and direction of programs for job-change assistance; (2) organizational frameworks that provide conditions and relationships that influence training and learning positively—that clarify and differentiate authority and responsibilities throughout the entire organization, and build new combinations of expertise; (3) roles for managers with a new spirit of sharing their knowledge and a new concern for the development of their subordinates as well as learning from subordinates; (4) methods for transmission of knowledge; and (5) ways of fitting in the learning process with work operations.

Instead of patching up old training practices which have not been successful, we need innovation and change in training-learning systems that will convert knowledge productively into the operations of the organization. Throughout this book examples will show that *productive results occur where new frameworks and patterns integrate training with action needed to meet operational goals, and solve real problems on the job.*

Is Learning Worthwhile to an Organization?

The practical payoffs resulting from new training and learning approaches show that they are worthwhile to both organizations and their people. The productive results of the many cases and incidents described in this book and its appendix will provide an impressive picture of the benefit side of the ledger. They include increased productivity, such as profitable product changes, increased sales, growth of profit rates, smoother processing of orders and shipments, improved performance, more effective mobility of people, reduction of cost-incurring items, lower turnover, and many others.

What causes these training and learning efforts to be worthwhile? It is the design that interrelates the learning process with the mainstream activities of planning, servicing, and producing. One becomes aware of the need to learn in order to accomplish the job for which he is responsible, or to advance to the job to which he aspires. And it is the application of what one knows to what one does that truly makes knowledge productive. Thus, training is integrated with the action needed to achieve work goals and solve problems that impede progress in work. Once the work objective is determined, then the training experiences function toward its achievement. The learning process is thus systematically engineered into a more secure, time-space relationship with the management of work where it can be productive.

How do management and the work force estimate the worth of training and learning activities? They find them worthwhile when and where systematic designs make learning an integral part of their jobs, making the job easier and advancement more certain. In a sense, the worth of training equals the benefits minus the costs. When organizations are successful in engineering the work environment and the qualities of the learning process so that they facilitate the utilization of learning, then both managers and employees realize the benefits. If something is vital to what the employee does, he will consider it worth knowing and interesting. Job immediacy of learning builds connections that help in the retention of what the employee learns. Management's concept of the worth of training comes as the result of being directly involved in the determination of both work and learning objectives as well as making progress reviews on performance that help subordinates learn.

The measure of worth depends upon no single factor. It results from the total systematic and collaborative process. If the executive's behavior shows that learning is a mainstream activity in that organization, the subordinate manager makes the effort to develop his people, especially where the executive inspects the results.

The models for productive learning are designed to fit individual organizations' needs. No one perfect model exists. But the comparison of successful examples of training-learning strategies shows elements common to all that make the difference between productive and nonproductive learning. These are: top leadership that shows learning is a mainstream activity; managers that do manage the development of their people; special frameworks and structures interspaced in the regular organizational structure, and provided with sufficient authority and combinations of expertise to engineer the productiveness of learning; work that makes obvious the need for learning; individuals aware and desirous of learning and capable of adaptation to change; personnel systems that are linked to growth and development; and ways of learning with high relatedness to work objectives, time and space flexibility, and participative methods.

Learning must be integrated with action if knowledge is to produce progress. Benefits such as the following often cause both management and the workers to change their estimates of worth: helping both organizations and people hedge against obsolescence; strengthening of performance; giving the firm a competitive edge through superior utilization of people's abilities; preventing the dissipation of what has been learned; lessening of gaps between technological advancement and worker abilities; improving the quality of work life.

When one experiences the worth of learning, the estimate of its cost decreases and there is a change in values. One's estimate that his own worth depends upon his need to learn and to contribute to the group results from participation in learning to work together to achieve group goals. Managers' estimates of the value of their human resources and the need to help them remain alive, up-to-date and productive, results from integrating their training responsibilities with their total management job. The design of systematic training engineers the integration of learning and work, making it well nigh impossible to resist change and stay with what has always been done. Throughout the book we shall see that efforts to enable employees to learn and adjust to changes in work merely by increasing the conventional training and educational resources are no longer enough. Examples will show why we need to understand the interrelationships of learning and doing and devise new ways of learning and doing and new patterns for the use of what has been learned so that day-to-day operations will improve. The genuine development of employees comes from the natural interweaving of training and learning with work operations. This is what makes learning come alive as part of—not apart from—what the worker does.

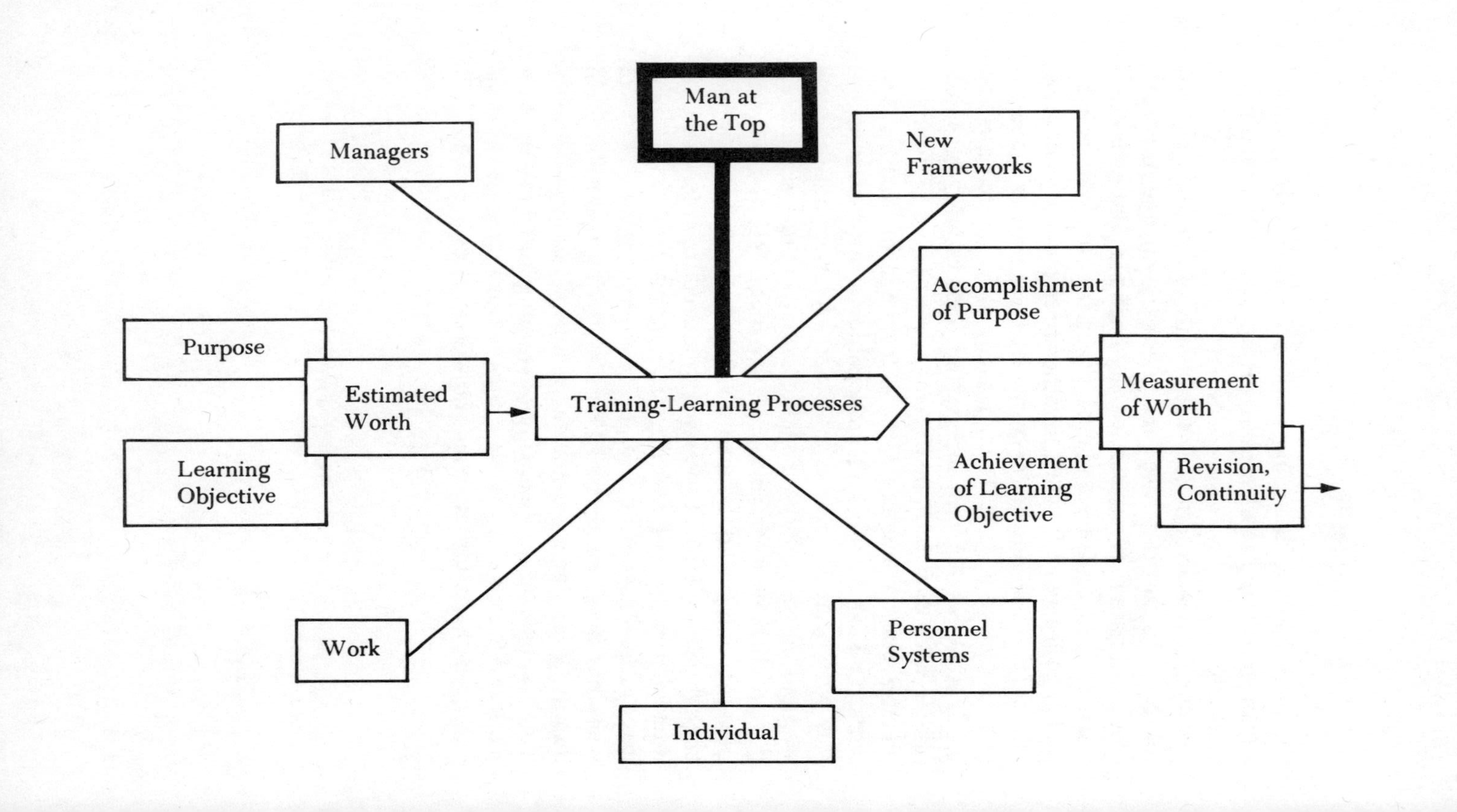
Man at the Top
Managers
New Frameworks
Purpose
Estimated Worth
Learning Objective
Training-Learning Processes
Accomplishment of Purpose
Measurement of Worth
Achievement of Learning Objective
Revision, Continuity
Work
Individual
Personnel Systems

2

The Man at the Top

Where organizations have instructional and learning practices that are productive, their executives demonstrate the capacity to bring about integration of growth and development processes with day-to-day work operations; to them developmental means learning the work, applying knowledge to the work, using it to improve the work, or learning from the work experience.

What is the most distinctive feature of executive practices in organizations which succeed in making their training-learning systems worthwhile? The executive integrates the development of his employees with the effective management of his organization. He *trains* through the establishment of goals and the evaluation of specific progress accomplished to achieve those goals. Thus he is both an instructor and a learner; he is a group leader and a coach of individuals. He finds no conflict between his instructional role and his management role. In fact, they are one.

In comparing organizational training-learning efforts, it becomes clear that the role of the executive is changing from that of passive support and approval to active leadership and participation in the learning processes. It requires the man at the top to see that learning goes on all through planning, budgeting, production, marketing, and management information systems. The man at the top has full supervision over the growth and development of his people.

The questions appropriate for the man at the top—and which have been asked by executives of organizations whose learning efforts are productive—are: What do our organization and its people need to learn if we are to be successful? And how can we operate day in and day out so that we can continually learn and adjust to internal and external changes?

The man at the top must first learn that training must not be set apart as an added function; rather it must be incorporated with and contribute to the functions and activities of the organization. The strength of the learning process lies not in its additive qualities—such as more knowledge, more information, more skill—but in its capacity to contribute productively to the mainstream operations.

Observations show that the learning process has positive impact when the man at the top demonstrates that training-learning activities are part and parcel of mainstream operations. We can learn from them what executives have done to make training function productively. These examples suggest to executives routes to follow when they desire (1) conditions that prompt the initiative and persistence to apply learning to work; (2) innovative learning processes; and (3) interrelationships between the conditions and the processes.

Sparking Examination of Instructional-Learning Processes

The man who heads the organization—or a segment, operation, or function of it—is best able to initiate an examination of its instruction-learning processes. An initial push, direct from the executive, signifies top interest and concern. Where the executive manages the development of his people directly through his managers, even though he may delegate portions of the training activity, the feeling permeates the organization that learning is a mainstream activity. This is in sharp contrast to a popular notion that the training function can be turned over to a staff training department and that development is something that can be left to each individual.

When the man at the top initiates an examination of what his organization needs to learn, and when the initial push comes from him, it makes an enormous difference. An example will illustrate this point:

> A task force was appointed by the top manager of a large government agency to discover what learning programs were needed by the organization and its people to help adjust to extensive technological changes in the automating of its inventory and warehousing systems. The executive at the head of the task force set up a process using the normal supervisory-subordinate channels through which to analyze group and individual performance and find indicators of learning needs.
>
> The task force chairman visualized the goal as increased organizational effectiveness, and therefore the process of determining what action was needed must be a part of organizational activities. Surveys of training needs are common to organizations, and people are accustomed to the fact that the training staff conducts them as part of their functions. But this case was different. This was no routine paper process turned over to a training staff. It was department heads conferring with their managers, managers discussing with their supervisors, and supervisors with their workers. A subtle yet extremely important difference exists between filling in a form and discussing with your superior what you feel you need to learn.

The task force chairman arranged briefings for the top department managers and their supervisors on how to carry out this survey. He worked for understanding of the process and an awareness of its objectives and benefits. He pushed for target dates when some departments lagged, and got them to agree. When the total job was complete, together with analysis of the needs and what action could be taken, he followed through to get each department started on its share of the total plan. He bolstered the training staff with the resources they needed to develop training that must be sponsored centrally. He arranged for the task force to monitor employee participation in outside training activities as well as utilization of ideas gained from such participation to improve operations within the organization.

Leadership of this caliber raised the sights of the entire organization. The results were impressive. The feeling that training and learning efforts were worthwhile was contagious. There was a significant increase in the number of individuals initiating their own learning agenda. Improved training opportunities for advancement portrayed the attractiveness of the organization for recruitment purposes. Both lateral and upward mobility was augmented as the result of internal training plans. Collaborative teams worked out solutions to costly internal problems. The organization was well on its way to a total learning environment.

What brought about this productiveness of learning effort? Probably most important, although not the only factor, was the initiation of the examination of learning processes and needs by action from the top man. The integration of the search for what the organization and its people needed to learn with its normal superior-subordinate relationships focused attention on internal work problems. The executive's follow-through in monitoring and reviewing managerial actions brought managers and subordinates closer in their efforts to improve operational effectiveness.

The impact of top leadership was later demonstrated in a negative way. When the task force chairman left the organization, he was not replaced. The task force was immobilized for some time. The training staff, although it continued to administer the central training opportunities that had been developed, was returned to a place of isolation from the major thrusts of organizational activity. Thus the most significant advances—the departmental ongoing activities which strengthened the integration of growth and development with the managerial job—began to decline.

At a time when information processing systems "filter out all sensory impressions not readily expressed in words and numbers" such as emotion, feeling, and intuitive judgments, there is reason for concern that top executives need to take a "long unflinching look at unprocessed reality."[1] This applies to the area of human development, learning, and growth. Training reports, studies, and surveys that concentrate on the numbers of people trained, hours of training, categorical kinds of training, and cost models are not only expensive to set up but are costly to maintain. Worse, they are most often an unreal picture compared with the executive-sparked examination of instructional-learning processes that we have just discussed.

The significance of top leadership in providing the initial push to look at what an organization needs to learn is discussed in the Internal Revenue Service case study (see Appendix, p. 279).

The capacity of men at the top to spark an examination of instructional-learning processes includes an ability to get down among managers of middle and lower echelons to discover the extent to which they are developing their people. The man at the top who asked the question, "What do you and your people need to learn to make our organization more effective?" learned how to participate with his managers in answering the question. It brought about productive learning in mainstream activities on the job.

Building Intra-organizational Frameworks To Create and Share Know-how

Some executives have designed frameworks that combine talents and energies of diverse groups, departments, and interests of their organizations in production of individual growth and organizational development. Such executive insight has recognized that traditional organizational designs yield systems operationally suited to an environment more stable than that of today with its rapid rate of technical change. The building of collaborative structures whose strength is contributed by parts of the organization removes the obstacles of departmental vested interests which often block the learning needed both for individuals and the organization.

Not all examples of this trend are identical. Some structures have been set up to initiate new systems that change work procedures affecting the entire organization. Others have been devised to make departments share in manpower development. Employees need guidance not only in learning their current jobs but to prepare for position moves within the organization. In some cases, executives have recognized the need for frameworks that make possible the harnessing of internal resources for the purpose of developing and transmitting knowledge so that it can be used, shared, and made a productive part of work operations.

Collaborative Conversion to New System

Worth analyzing is the success of executives who, facing overhaul of old procedures and getting new ones into the operational bloodstream, have incorporated the training aspects of the task in the total design and action. See Charts 15 and 16, pp. 189 and 190. Visualizing the role of the executive in the following illustration, together with the results, may be instructive:

> A large government organization was faced with the need to convert its requisitioning, inventory, and stock maintenance systems to a new world-wide system of automatic data processing being implemented by its headquarters. Local applications of the system had to be planned, developed, and implemented. A governing board representing the major departments and staff groups affected or involved in the changeover was given authority to direct and coordinate the conversion.
>
> Along with other tasks, the board's chairman tackled the problem of how to help an organization learn what it needed to learn to make the conversion effective. He included the Training Director in planning meetings and requested that a comprehensive training plan be submitted to the board. He requested the members of the board to review the plan and suggest changes.
>
> The plan integrated training with each phase of the conversion. The training staff became temporarily a part of a special training unit for the conversion to the automated procedures. This unit was part of the total framework to implement all phases of the conversion. Twelve key technical managers were temporarily loaned to this special training unit from other departments. They were groomed to design and prepare the

training material and programs. The procedure writers in the Planning Department, who were preparing the new procedures, were linked to this special unit, providing the new knowledge to the course developers who organized it into teachable units.

Another phase of integration of training into the total conversion was the analysis made by the automated systems analyst and a member of the training staff of the impact of the new procedural requirements on the workers' need to learn in order to correctly process their work under the changed system.

Further integration into the mainstream operations was accomplished by designating key supervisors to transmit the new system to groups of workers. The supervisors were groomed in how to conduct training sessions for the workers through: (1) their participation in workshops they felt they needed, such as Instructional Techniques, Audiovisual Aids; and (2) those sessions (prepared by the key trainers) which provided help in specific procedures they needed to know in order to transmit them to their employees.

The board chairman managed to keep reluctant department heads contributing to the total team effort, although some threatened to withdraw their technicians from the special training unit. And on the eve of the instructional workshops, department directors indicated they would withdraw support because they did not want their supervisors to become involved in the instruction of subordinate work groups. But the chairman and the board held fast and the plan continued.

The conversion, although it had, as the experts said, some debugging to be done, went smoothly. The quality of the training was acknowledged to be excellent. The morale of the special training unit was particularly high, and its spirit was contagious to the supervisory-instructors as well as to their worker-learners.

The crucial element that made this training-learning effort both effective and productive in helping the organization convert to a new automated system was the leadership of the board's chairman. He took the steps to incorporate the training plans and efforts into the total planning and total project of conversion. He created the temporary training unit, staffing it with the combined expertise of the technical experts and training staff. He secured contributions from the departments to staff it, and helped the department managers to overcome their bias in favor of their own interests, and learn to support the organizational goal. He reinforced the supervisory-subordinate relationships by educating department managers through the Governing Board to their training responsibilities as part of their managerial duties. The reluctance and signs of opposition by some of the department managers were held under control, indicating the importance of the executive to hold groups together in a common cause.

A Framework for Manpower Development

An excellent illustration of executive leadership in building an intra-organizational framework is found in a case study on Chase Manhattan Bank's Manpower Planning and Development Program (see Appendix, p. 249). Its Central Manpower Planning and Development Committee interlocked components of the Head Office with the branches in making the manpower development program work.

Shared Contributions to Central Training Resources

The Internal Revenue Service, Western Region, provides an example of executive leadership in the establishment of a framework to which member organizations of the region contribute personnel on a temporary basis (see Appendix, p. 279). The employees on loan to this central regional training center learn to create and share instructional units on needed knowledges. They also act in a variety of training capacities, as instructors, consultants, moderators, and observers, serving the entire region when needed.

Top Man Instructs His Managers and Reviews Their Development of Subordinates

Where executives of organizations have assumed their instructional role, it makes an enormous difference in the effectiveness with which people in the organization learn and adjust to changes. Although the top executive is not normally thought of in this light, he is an "instructor" to his subordinate managers in many ways. He sets goals and gives assignments, makes progress reviews giving his managers feedback, and reinforces their development. He reviews the ways in which his subordinates develop their employees and watches for progress in their development and growth.

An example will illustrate this point:

> A government agency had sponsored an after-hours program to provide support to the general educational development of its employees. With instructors provided through the cooperation of the public schools, participants were helped to review math, reading comprehension, and other fundamentals. The quality of the instruction and its helpfulness to participants in passing promotional exams usually attracted sufficient participation. However, managers for the most part did not encourage their employees, nor did they recognize their improvements in work.

Then the top executive reviewed a progress report on this program and learned that over 60 percent of the participants mentioned the help the classes had given them in their work, even though most had originally enrolled to increase ability to take promotional examinations. The executive described the benefits to his department managers and suggested they encourage their workers to take advantage of them. He personally visited the classes, talked with participants, and pressed the matter with his department managers.

Apparently the listening level was high. As a result, the number of participants and number of classes tripled. Managers began to notice improved performance of those who received help in the classes. Improved skill in mathematical calculations helped them improve their work on discounts and in estimating cube content and weights. Improved language skills helped them to handle phone orders and write memoranda more efficiently.

Thus, as the result of the executive's instructing his men, managers became aware of their responsibility to encourage their employees to get help and apply it on their current jobs as well as to prepare for the future. Not only was an impact felt on the quality of the work, but employees increased their option on learning and capacity for upward mobility. The key role was that played by the executive. A considerable number of employee evaluations indicated that when they became aware of the top executive's efforts to bolster classes on their behalf, they decided to enroll.

The instruction-giving responsibility of the top executive has not gone unrecognized. Jacques made a study of one factory and the interaction of its organizational structure, its customary way of doing things, and the behavior of its members. Of interest here is his finding that *the executive's behavior with respect to his subordinates is the main factor in training.*[2] The top executive is the most powerful training influence in the whole organization, since the behavior of managers toward their subordinates is influenced by their superiors' behavior toward themselves. To the extent that the top executive uses alternatives to detach himself from the job of instructing, he weakens the entire training and development function. By the way in which he integrates the development of his managers with the total executive role, he sets the pattern for making learning and growth a mainstream activity of his organization.

Alfred P. Sloan, Jr., former head of General Motors, illustrates an executive who developed his top managers to arrive at decisions by discussions in governing committees and policy groups.[3] He says:

> These were not the creation of a single inspired moment but the result of a long process of development in dealing with a fundamental problem of management, that of placing responsibility for policy in the hands of those best able both to make the decisions and to assume the responsibility.[4]

The story is told of Mr. Sloan that when all his technical advisors had voted unanimously for a recommendation, he asked them whether they saw anything wrong with it, to which they replied negatively. He then said he didn't either, but proposed that they postpone for a month the final decision to give themselves a chance to think. What he wanted his managers and advisors to realize was that if there is no case against a recommendation, there is no case for it. He wanted to teach his men the need for conflicting opinions. A month later the proposal was turned down. He felt that much of his effort in General Motors was devoted to providing the right framework for decisions and worked to instruct his managers in the "sometimes onerous process of discussion."

> The group [he said] will not always make a better decision than any particular member would make; there is even the possibility of some averaging down. But in General Motors I think the record shows that we have averaged up. Essentially this means that through our form of organization, we have been able to adapt to the great changes that have taken place in the automobile market in each of the decades since 1920.[5]

There is considerable evidence to show that it is not simply by chance that many top executives are superb educators of their subordinates; in fact, their capacity to bring people along often pushes them to top positions. An example is General Marshall, who performed one of the greatest educational feats in military history.[6] After he became Chief of Staff of the United States Army, he developed the largest and ablest group of general officers in American history.

Top Man Participates in Learning and Sets an Example

Actions are more convincing than words. Therefore it is not surprising that top executives who themselves participate in learning activities accomplish more by example than by exhortation. People know whether what one professes is real or fake. Thus, participation means more than an executive speech acknowledging the importance of learning and development.

What does executive participation mean with respect to

learning and development? The pattern of executive practice in organizations with successful learning programs is moving the organization into a growth and learning posture that keeps it up to date, alive, and able to compete. Going off to an executive workshop, although it may serve to show others that the executive is never too old to learn, does not bring about the acceptance of new ideas, concepts, or techniques. Nor does it help people learn to work together. Those executives who are successful in keeping their organizations growing are themselves learning with and from their subordinates. When they participate with their managers in the determination of the objective of the learning experience, they learn and help their managers to learn how to work to achieve their objective. They are learning, too, when they are facilitating and encouraging the growth of their managers.

Is it reasonable and possible for executives to participate in programs where they learn the importance of creating an environment in which the people will grow and produce, and then help their own organizations to plan and manage change? "Yes" is the answer that several examples will provide.

The President's Role in Organizational Development

George Raymond, President of Raymond Corporation, was seeking an approach to create a culture that would enable his people to grow and out-produce the giants in their field—materials handling. He attended organizational development laboratory training sessions and requested a consultant to work with his top team. As the result of his managers' confrontation with facts about their managerial styles, the entire group became convinced that they needed to plan an extensive program to learn how to negate the issues that were impeding the organization in its efforts toward effectiveness. As a result, they have been continuing week-long managerial Grid Labs and other tools to develop team building, using their own line managers as trainers. This case is discussed in more detail in the study of the Raymond Corporation (see Appendix, p. 263).

The Federal Government also believes that it is reasonable and possible for executives to participate in programs, and that after having learned the importance as well as the ways of keeping their organization up to date, alive, and productive, they can help their organization develop.

Federal Executive Training

With the help of the U.S. Civil Service Commission's Federal Executive Institute, the top executive of a federal activity brought about productive results in his organization through planned and managed change and the help of an organizational training and learning process. This executive participated in an eight-week learning experience at the Federal Executive Institute in Charlottesville, Virginia. With a top-notch staff and a well-prepared learning program motivating top executives, the Federal Executive Institute has in its few years of existence built a new type of "learning community for top executives." It aims to give them awareness of changes that are constraints on the effectiveness of their organization and provides guidance for new strategies. It discards the "narrowness of the conventional classroom and the pouring in of more information." Rather it provides an open climate for self-directed learning and experiences in learning how to work together.

Having participated in these new learning approaches, the top executive of this organization understood its needs better. On his return, he commenced to build an entire organizational learning unit by helping his people discover through co-active teams how to get more satisfaction through their achievements and become more productive. With the help of the agency's training consultant, he first arranged for his top team of managers to participate in an Organizational Development Grid Lab. The entire team thus became aware of the benefits of learning to work in these new directions.

The top managers continued to participate in a series of organizational development sessions for all managers and supervisors; they instructed, consulted, moderated, and observed. At the close of each session, teams that had learned how to work together to become effective in solving simulated problems then selected an organizational problem they felt needed attention in their work units.

Returning to their jobs, the participants also continued to meet in these team structures, resolving the problems they had identified during the session and thus continuing to put into practice the skills they had learned.

The results of these team-building sessions show benefits such as increased cooperation and strengthening of internal learning processes, which in turn suggests ways to make better use of outside training; constructive solution of problems; increased delegation of responsibility and opening up of communications between different parts and levels of the organization.

These benefits are adding daily evidence that the top man's participation in learning provides a live example to his organization; and the quality of the learning experience is such that it helps him to initiate and manage changes through helping his own organization learn and grow.

Today the role of the man at the top is changing with the times. His responsibility is to design and build a learning organization, to heighten the entire level of learning, making it possible for individuals to perform above previous levels. This means designing a learning organization that can adjust to change, integrate learning with its operations, and use internal know-how productively. As we have seen in organizations successful in their training and learning efforts, the responsibilities of the executive clearly require more integration of the development of people with his management role.

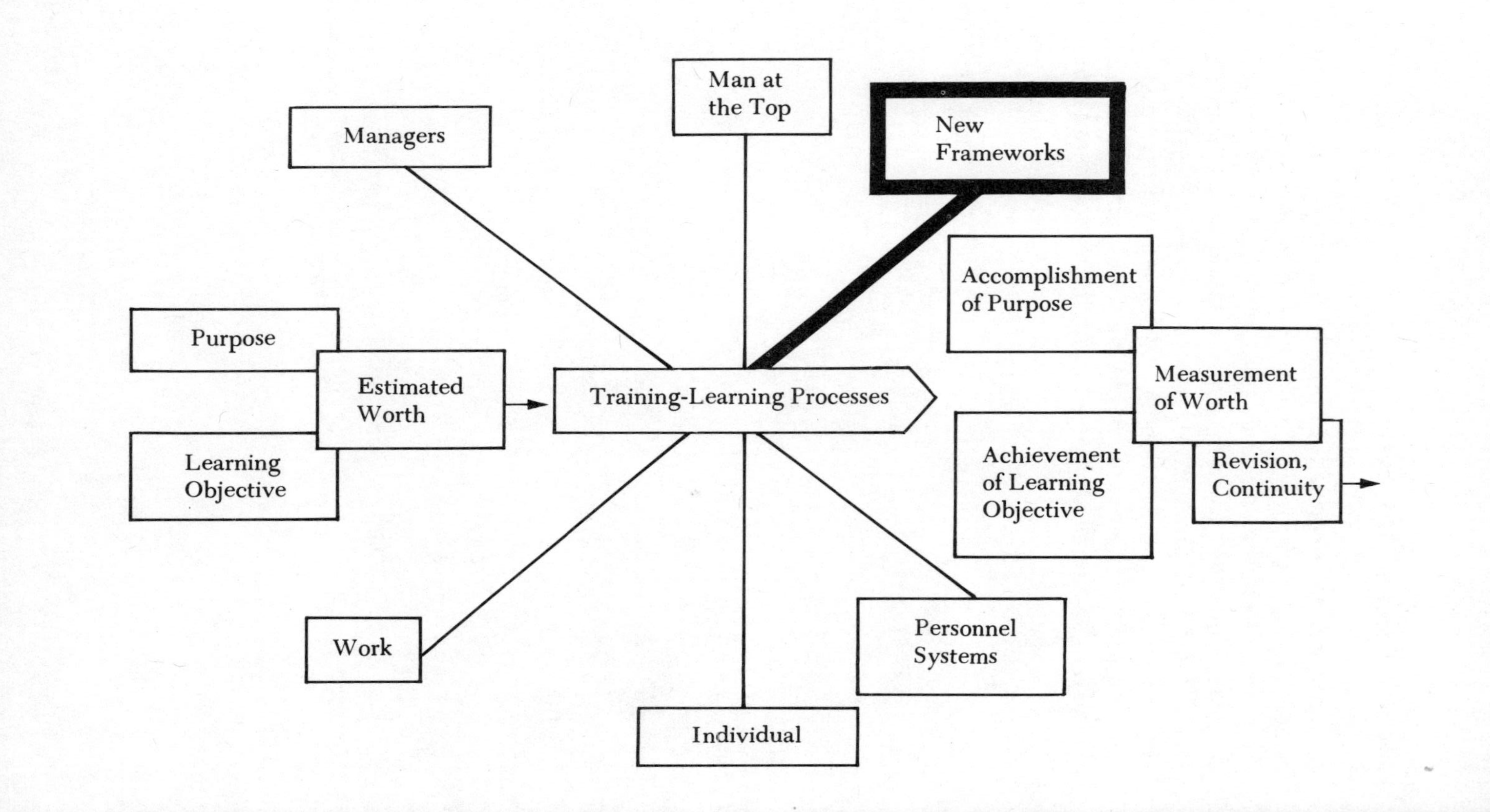
Managers
Man at the Top
New Frameworks
Purpose
Estimated Worth
Learning Objective
Training-Learning Processes
Accomplishment of Purpose
Measurement of Worth
Achievement of Learning Objective
Revision, Continuity
Work
Individual
Personnel Systems

3

New Frameworks for Learning

Patterns for learning in organizations whose training and development efforts are productive show that, in addition to the normal organizational structures, new frameworks have been added. The specific purpose of these collaborative groups, whether they are temporary or permanent, is the achievement of an objective to which the organization is committed. The new framework has the responsibility, the authority, and the resources to design and put into action those learning-training processes which will function to achieve the objective.

Why doesn't the traditional organizational pattern provide the kind of structure that will produce progress from training and learning activities? For one thing, the traditional two-way relationship—the instructor teaching the student in the classroom—has literally exploded in the face of the rapid rate of change of systems and processes. The training-learning process has been extended in a continuum that spreads throughout and across organizational lines, thus requiring new relationships and new co-action to achieve the ultimate purpose. In order for many training-learning processes to function in ways that they can be fully utilized by the organization, special frameworks are needed to pull the diverse interests, personnel, and units into harmonious and productive co-action.

The formation of collaborative frameworks to oversee the functioning of training-learning within an organization thus meets a gap in the traditional organizations in several ways. First, a collaborative framework can design and implement systematic training processes based on the analysis of the impact of organization-wide systems on the operations of different units and their personnel, making it possible for each person involved in the total process to learn specifically what he needs to learn in order to accomplish his job and also to see the relationship of his part to the total process. Secondly, such a framework can interrelate centralized planning in large-scale organizations with the local training and learning efforts, making it possible for central resources to adapt to and support more closely genuine learning and development needs generated by local management and supervisory requirements. Thirdly, it can link the supervisory-subordinate relationship with the training expertise and educational technology of a staff training and development unit. The success of any organizational training effort rests on the integration of development of personnel *with* the whole job of supervisors and managers. Fourthly, collaborative effort can, by combining technical know-how with training expertise, make knowledge available, in teachable and learnable ways, for sharing with the entire organization.

It is no longer enough to say that training is a line responsibility and that the training staff advises and assists the line. It has been demonstrated that special frameworks are needed to remedy the inertia that results from the ambiguous division of responsibilities.

Teams That Learn To Solve Problems

More and more companies are pushing forward in their use of temporary teams to attack troublesome situations. The strategy of developing problem-solving teams, a difficult and important challenge, is being demonstrated by a number of the organizations described throughout this book and in the case studies in the Appendix. Bennis sees this strategy as one of the training requirements of "organizations of the future."[1] Although it is far easier to permit individuals and separate units of the organization to function in isolation, the demands of our technological systems are forcing organizations to find collaborative ways of building "synergetic teams." Bennis has described synergy as "where individuals actually *contribute more* and *perform better* as a result of a collaborative and supportive environment."[2]

The formation of problem-solving and training teams is seen in organizations that are successfully meeting the basic issues of the training-learning processes within organizations today. These organizations understand that training-learning practices within an organization cannot remain as separate entities but must become part of a whole training-learning process which interrelates work and performance requirements and employees' needs to learn. They also understand that a stable framework with responsibility and authority to get the job done must be able to withstand the pressures of organizational forces that would take higher priority if allowed to. They clearly see that training and learning efforts must be functional toward achieving an objective or purpose desirable for and needed by the organization or one of its components. The incorporation of a training group into what is primarily a working group to achieve a needed solution moves the learning process into a more secure time-space relationship, where it can be effective and productive.

Consideration of the following example will illustrate the points under discussion:

> A departmental work-team was appointed within a large warehousing and supply company to study and improve a serious work situation. Increasing backlogs, a large number of errors, and confusion in paper work flow had resulted from the failure to implement properly a new inventory system. The team was instructed to locate the sources of error and confusion, to work out improved procedures, and was given authority to put them into action subject to approval of the top manager.
>
> The team sampled documents, followed through on procedures to determine errors, breakdowns, misunderstandings, and gaps in the system. It interviewed supervisors and workers and analyzed all the facts bearing on any given problem. It developed improved procedures that would remedy the errors, recommended changes to the top manager, and once its proposals were approved, it validated the new method or procedure and then installed it.
>
> The team's attitude was objective. It avoided placing blame and worked to find "soft spots" in the system itself and get agreement as it went along, initiating changes during the process. It avoided the tendency to locate the sources of all problems in individuals. Rather, it diagnosed situations as symptoms of malfunctioning systems. After verifying the effectiveness of the new procedures, it put them into effect and then went throughout the department, instructing all those needing to learn and use the changed procedures. The results were impressive. As procedures were corrected and the soft spots reinforced with additional safeguards, the team instructed workers, insuring the continuity of the correct processing. The backlog was eliminated, the

number of errors dropped enormously, and the confusion of workers was replaced by confidence.

Analysis of the accomplishments of this work team and their impact on the learning-training process that was interwoven with their action should be instructive. As one of the members put it, "The team, without initially being aware of it, developed one of the best training programs that could have possibly been designed. By virtue of our mission and the need to accomplish it, we developed the qualities and characteristics a good training program needs." In their effort to achieve the purpose, the revision of the processing systems, they studied and learned causes of breakdown, and by exploring the possible actions they discovered workable solutions. Feedback and progress reports to the team by individuals working on different parts of the system helped the group learn what their next actions should be. Once they acquired knowledge of the correct system, they organized the transmission of this knowledge to those who had the need to know. They learned how to gain cooperation throughout the branches of the department, and how to coordinate their efforts with the operators.

Did the team meet today's basic issues of organizational learning and training?

1. The learning-training process was seen as part of the total work production effort. Learning objectives and needs originated in the work situation. First, the team responsible for action needed to learn what was fouling up the processes, causing the errors, increasing the backlog, and causing failures in the meshing of the system. It also needed to learn how these procedures could be corrected. Once this was accomplished, their next training task was to instruct those who needed to learn the revised procedures as well as unlearn the old ones. When the learning process is extended, such as this was, throughout

the productive operations of work, traditional notions of "instructors" and "course content" are replaced by newer and broader concepts. The instructors in this case were the managers and supervisors who were placed on the "team." They were learners as well as instructors, since they first had to discover and create workable processes in order to teach others. The content was not subject matter or a curriculum in the old-fashioned sense, but it was the substance and structure of what the workers needed to learn.

2. Organizational realities such as work, pressures, and the feeling there was not time enough to train were replaced by a readiness to absorb instruction in the changed procedures. Conflicts of interest and outright resistance were reduced or eliminated through integration of the training with the action. "Time off or lost time" was not an issue. Those participating in the solution of problems had the responsibility, felt its challenge, and received the satisfaction of achievement.

Managers became involved; they were part of the problem-solving efforts. They saw themselves fulfilling their training responsibilities in a different way than when called upon to lose manhours for training that did not help them accomplish their goals.

3. The learning and training efforts in this case were functional toward the finding and correcting of causes for excessive errors and backlogs. What the team learned to do was to eliminate obstacles in the nature of "bugs" and gaps in the systems processes. The malfunctioning procedures became the basis for discovery of ways to correct the failures. And the revised and improved systems that the team created became the content of training that helped employees learn how to change their operations. Thus, the learning and training process functioned to improve the effectiveness of the production effort.

When critics of training within organizations say that training efforts are not productive, they may not only be applying the wrong measurements of worth, but quite possibly they have not discovered that they are using the wrong learning processes for individual and organizational improvement. The teams that find solutions and make them work, such as the one we have just reviewed, are replacing the stereotyped training activities of yesterday. Their process is not the passive listening to talks and lectures or the storing away of knowledge acquired from books. It is an active, productive learning process because the workers learn what they do, thereby using their know-how to produce progress. The training content is about their work. The team of instructors is created by pressing managers and technicians into learning and training activities. This approach produces both individual and collective learning which enhances the workers' abilities and satisfaction in achievement. As Chapter 8 will discuss, the collaborative team process produces the qualities for effective and productive learning: focus toward accomplishment of a common purpose, self-directed learning efforts, continuing feedback combined with trial tests and checks for feasibility, examination and exploration of a range of alternatives, and critical examination of mistakes.

A notable example is that of Western Electric's Team Effectiveness Program, a continuing team-building and problem-solving learning process in which training is integrated into action needed to solve troublesome work situations (see Appendix, p. 229).

Interrelating Central and Local Training-Learning Efforts

In speaking to the problems that organizational structures create in training efforts, we cannot ignore a special feature of the large-scale national, and often international, corporation: its hierarchy of various levels above the local or field operation and their relationships with the corporate or central level at the top of its organization. The large-scale organizational structure, as well as the ways in which personnel see their roles at various levels, do provide some formidable obstacles to the achievement of productive learning. All too often the setting apart of the educational and training efforts of large organizations in centralized schools hinders the very process of integrating the learning and development of people into the productive processes for which they have been created. This is particularly true where the learning process needs to be closely related to the participants' work.

The training centers generally emphasize subject matter disciplines, the acquisition of information, and providing the worker-participants with more knowledge about systems and techniques, the principles of which may be related to their work. But the very separateness of the central schools, their approximation to and modeling after academic life, sets up barriers that make it difficult to transfer knowledge to work operations and incorporate it to the benefit of both the employee and his organization. Often the acquired knowledge and the returning worker's desire to apply it make difficult his re-entry into work surroundings unprepared for and resistant to change. The findings here may go counter to what seems to be a current trend in the training business: the establishment of the training center. It all depends upon the conditions under which the training center is founded, and the processes by which it keeps itself linked with the mainstream of learning and growth on the job. The problem arises when an organization invests primarily in a centralized institution, thus providing an illusion that something is being done, but which really contributes little to the productiveness and renewal of the organization's vitality.

The description of two illustrations and a comparative

analysis of their productive results should serve to help clarify the point being made:

A national agency established a Methods Engineering Program throughout all of its activities. In the case of one of its local activities the supply of qualified methods engineers was not adequate to fill the need. The answer was to develop them. The corporate headquarters arranged for the design and preparation of a course which would provide techniques in methods-time-measurement, skills and know-how to set standards, the ability to create methods improvements, and techniques for the development of standard data and time formulas. A first-rate course with competent instructors and relevant and usable techniques, it was presented yearly at each of the agency's activities.

Although the seven-week course of instruction was repeated each year, an evaluation of the contributions and productiveness of the newly trained engineers was disappointing. Some questions were raised as to the quality of the instruction, but the heart of the problem was found to be the uneven quality of the supervisory coaches of the new methods engineers. Some of the newly trained men said that the objectives of their work were not explained and that by the time they understood what was really expected of them they had lost much time. In other cases, supervisors failed to link work projects so that the new men could apply what they had learned. Some mentioned the lack of feedback on their work and felt they did not know whether they were proceeding correctly or not.

The Methods Engineering Chief, with the help of the training staff, provided guidance to the supervisory coaches. Suggestions were made on the development of individualized plans outlining specific work projects

> that provided opportunities for the new men to try out techniques learned in the course. Ideas were provided on how to delegate responsibility, make progress reviews, and incorporate the continuation of their learning process into the day-to-day operations.
>
> The situation improved, although not all of the supervisory coaches were able fully to assume their training role, and the Methods Engineering Chief increased his efforts to strengthen the work and learning experiences of the new methods engineers. But overall performance improved and the productive results were gratifying to management, who saw increased savings in manpower and costs that resulted from improved methods and time management.

In this case we see the complementary efforts of the central agency and the local activity to develop an effective training-learning process. The central agency put the requirement of the methods engineering function on the local activity, and it helped to the extent that it contributed a highly relevant course of instruction. But the local activity had to bridge the gaps between the course and getting its techniques into the mainstream operations. The fact that the national agency had made a mandatory requirement upon the local activity to complete periodic methods surveys of every department was a strong factor in providing an organizational environment receptive to these surveys. But no system or no knowledge transfers itself, even when regulations make strong requirements. It took the local effort to make the training-learning process live.

Relationships between central and local training processes are not always as productive. Staff at headquarters level are considerably removed from the day-to-day operations of local activities and are not aware of the organization's negative influences on training. Conversely, local activities that have initiated and maintained worthwhile training efforts may be deluged by requirements for data or for participation in programs that seem only distantly related to the real needs of the local activity. Large organizations often provide centralized training activities on the ground that if such training were left to the local activities, the training would not be accomplished. It is also claimed that centralized training is more efficient, that better training is secured at less cost, and that one professionally prepared course is better than a rash of locally prepared efforts of less quality.

But *efficiency in the production of courses and participant achievement of high scores do not guarantee effectiveness of the application or productiveness of the learning.* If training centers are to keep in tune with all we know about what helps people to learn and adjust to change, the centralized school may be an outworn concept as it now stands. The functional role of any training-learning effort—which is helping people to learn in order that a productive purpose is accomplished—needs to be firmly cemented into application and use. The central schools with their subject-matter-centered approach can pose serious obstacles to motivating members of a work force to integrate their learning with their work. The more impersonalized and institutionalized administration of these central schools and the problems standing in the way of carry-over of school concepts to work operations seem at odds with helping an organization keep its people alive and productive, learning and adjusting to change. A case study illustrates this point:

> Over a period of several years, the field activity of a large national agency developed a local procedure for the selection of participants to attend outside training. An Education Selection Committee looked closely at all proposals for evidence that the outside training was sup-

plemental to the plan of the individual and his superior for development, that what they hoped to accomplish was feasible and worthwhile for both the organization and the individual's development. Managers were thus encouraged to use care and judgment in their selection and nomination of people. The committee followed through and reinforced positive benefits through having participants personally report on their experiences and make suggestions for utilizing them. The improvement of the selection process was directly related to the improved incorporation of new ideas and productive results to the organization.

Then the national agency mandated a centralized system for surveying requirements for its centralized courses. The highly formalized survey overshadowed the local procedures completely. The prescribed preciseness of the procedure, its imposed sequence of dates, the mandatory forms and data required caused a flood of red tape. Managers did not take too seriously requests for quotas since this was a selection of "courses" only, not involving selection of personnel. No one was sure what quotas they might receive, if any, and whether the funds would be available when the time came, and for that matter, whether the same personnel would be on the rolls.

Although the neatly ordered list of "courses required" appeared "efficient," the results were disappointing. Managers and employees became irked at the delays, uncertainties, and the increased processing required. A maze of paper work was created. The increased cost of travel and daily subsistence for attendance at schools primarily in the eastern United States was questioned, and not always supported, by local management. Poor timing was forced by receipt of quotas for dates not requested and the consequent scheduling of participants before they had sufficient background to benefit from the course.

If we analyze what happened in the preceding example, we see that the most serious result was the weakening of the supervisory-subordinate foundation for learning: thinking through how an external course could beneficially supplement the ongoing internal training and learning processes. Although the organization could point to its compliance with the annual survey of requirements and acceptance of assigned quotas, this mandated inventory of requirements for its central school courses crushed the initial interest and vitality of the earlier plan with its conscious selection of an external resource sorely needed and with its high potential for productive assimilation. Such centralized systems may be administratively more convenient and may present a visible picture of educational and learning activities. But they tend to take away much of the essence of what truly makes learning worthwhile to both an organization and its people.

Two case studies, that of the Western Region of the Internal Revenue Service and that of Chase Manhattan Bank (see Appendix, pp. 279 and 249), illustrate highly integrated and productive relationships between central and local levels of their organizations. The central training activities of both are geared toward the application of learning at the supervisory-employee foundation at local levels.

Combining Managerial, Technical, and Training Expertise

In many of the companies receiving productive results from their training efforts, and in all those represented by the case studies in the Appendix, we find the use of special organizational frameworks that provide for collaboration and blending of different kinds of expertise to provide the learning needed to achieve an objective, whether it be the improvement of a service, the implementation of a system and its procedures, or whatever.

It is generally thought that those with technical expertise lack the tutorial abilities to instruct; and, on the other hand, the training staff, although skilled in instructional technology, lacks technical expertise. Some would solve this dilemma by turning the responsibility for all training over to a central training unit. They argue that a training staff with time and resources can learn the technical know-how. Another solution is to coach those with technical expertise in the tutorial role. This solution has to find ways to meet the problem of releasing technical and operational people for long enough periods to provide them grooming in instructional skills, as well as the time to present the training.

Organizations, successful in their training efforts, have found several ways to combine technical and instructional expertise. In doing this they have taken cognizance of special features of the training-learning process when it is extended and adapted to an organization of which it becomes a part. They have demonstrated that in order for learning to be productive for the worker and the organization the simple two-way relationship between instructor and learner is not enough. Relationships and connections must be made between all the parts and the people involved in the process from the determination of the need—what is worth knowing—to the making of the knowledge gained usable in work. They have linked managerial responsibility for training with these new combinations of technical and training expertise. As we shall learn in Chapter 8, training incorporated in action needed to accomplish a work goal and solve a work problem will demonstrate those qualities that make the learning productive: relatedness of content, participativeness of learning by doing, flexibility of sequence, appropriateness of instructor and coaching guidance.

To illustrate the points being made, an example that was introduced in Chapter 2 is appropriate here, but for a different purpose. This is the case of the organization (see p. 25) that converted its requisitioning, inventory, and stock maintenance systems to a new world-wide system of automatic data processing implemented by its headquarters. In that chapter, we emphasized the executive's role in building an intraorganizational framework. Now our attention is focused on the integration of management, staff, and technical expertise. Together they were able to contribute more and perform better. See Charts 15 and 16, pp. 189 and 190.

The integration of different parts of the organization was brought into this framework: (1) by the combined efforts of the top systems analyst and the training staff to analyze where and who in the total organization (which departments, which branches, which units, which personnel) would have their work affected by the new system changes and what the new job requirements would be; (2) by the interlocking of procedure writers (who designed the way the uniform procedures would be applied to their local activity) with the supply technicians (who prepared and presented the training sessions) with the coaching help of the training staff in methods of preparation and presentation; (3) by the involvement of the supervisory-subordinate relationships in transmitting the new knowledge to the work force. Supervisors selected to train employees in the new procedures were given coaching in how to instruct and how to adapt the institute's programmed presentations to their own groups.

As we saw in the previous discussion, the results were successful in effecting a comparatively smooth conversion to the new procedures.

This special framework by combining the strengths of several groups and different expertise accomplished what no one group could have accomplished alone. The expertise was drawn from seven departments. No one group could have produced what was useful and needed by nearly one-half of the entire work force. The performance of each expertise was improved by its blending with the others. For example, the quality of the procedures being written was improved. The supply technicians who had been placed in the role of "key trainers" suggested the use of words that would be understood by all instead of a sort of procedural jargon understood only by systems and procedures people. The trainers also pointed out flaws and inconsistencies in the procedural processes. The instructional process thus forced a clarification in order to make the procedure teachable and learnable. The technical procedure writers and the supply technicians acting as key trainers gained insight and skill in how to prepare, design, test, validate, and present learning materials. Training staff enlarged their understanding of how the systems and procedures functioned.

A new type of framework had been invented. It was interspaced within, not added to, the normal organizational structure. For approximately a year, the collaborative efforts were directed toward the conversion to the new automated procedures under the leadership of a special Governing Board and its chairman. By combining their expertise, these groups were able to create new knowledge—the new principles and procedures for operations in requisitioning, inventory, and stock maintenance—and transmitted it successfully through the productive processes of the organization by interrelating both the learning and the productive processes.

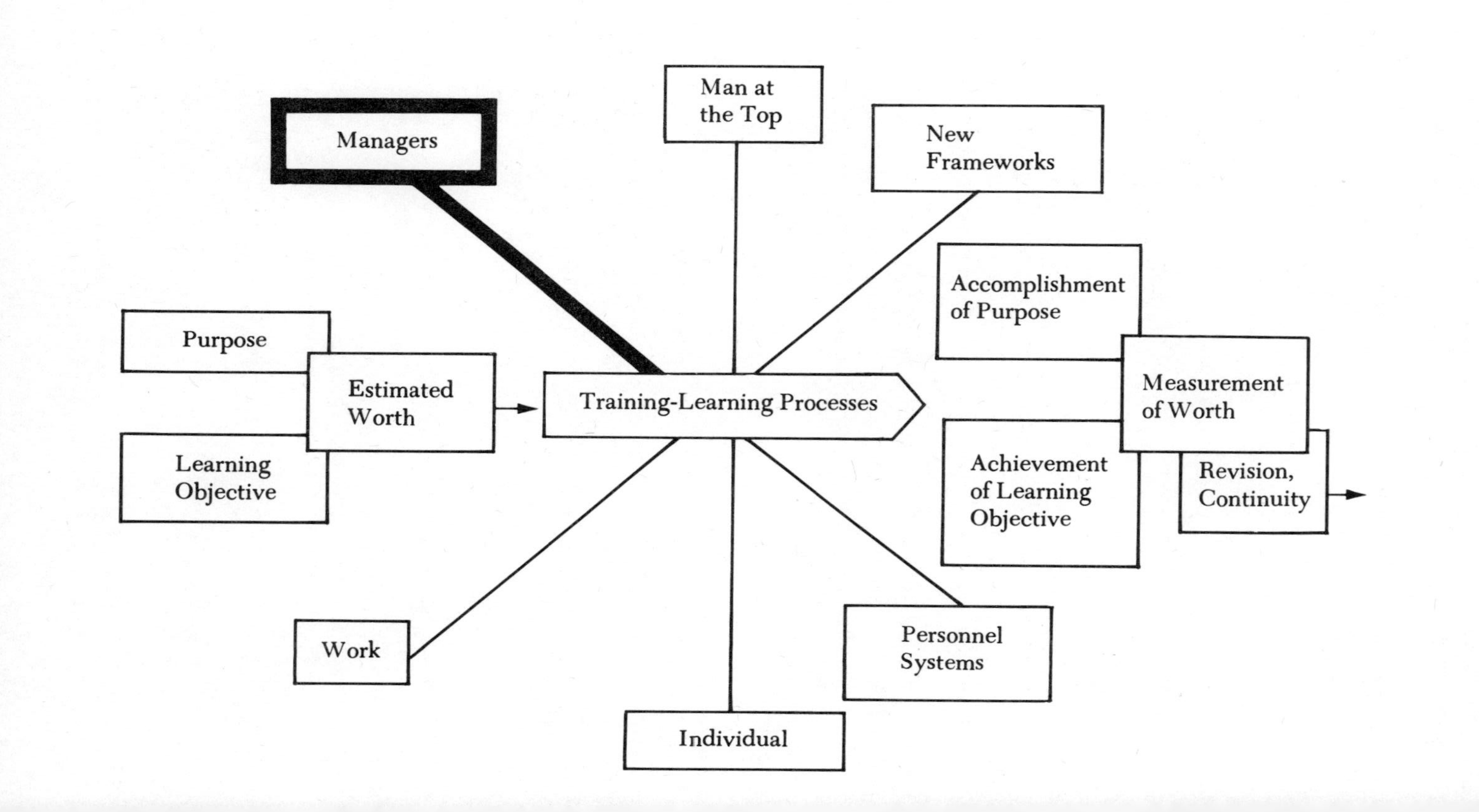
Managers
Man at the Top
New Frameworks
Accomplishment of Purpose
Measurement of Worth
Achievement of Learning Objective
Revision, Continuity
Purpose
Estimated Worth
Learning Objective
Training-Learning Processes
Work
Individual
Personnel Systems

4

Managers Make Learning Productive

When managers have integrated the development of their subordinates and themselves with their overall managerial job of planning, executing and controlling work, they have made learning and training productive. What has been evident in the successful organizational strategies for growth and development is that managers develop themselves through helping their people learn. When a manager participates with his subordinates in a group problem-solving activity, he is learning as well as helping his subordinates learn.

Let me try to put the manager's role into a perspective which will clarify the discussion that follows. The learning process is a complex pattern of interlocking tasks within an organization. The role of the manager in this pattern rests on the fundamental supervisory-subordinate relationship which is the foundation and major channel for making training productive.

In Chapter 1 we discussed the failure of the traditional assumption that increasing the amount of participation in learning activities would somehow produce increased competence and progress. And we saw that any training system that is simply superimposed upon an organization, and not really incorporated into its operations, holds little promise of productivity. This means that training-learning practices can no longer remain as separate entities, but must become part of a whole learning process. The learning needs of employees take root in the work of the organization. And what employees learn must be incorporated into work to make it productive. Since the supervisor must bear responsibility for the performance of his subordinates, the supervisory-subordinate relationships are at the heart of the training and learning process.

Managers' conception and execution of their training tasks as a part of their total job is the key in making knowledge productive. The fundamental basis for employee growth and development lies in the ways that supervisors: (1) set operational goals with their employees; (2) discuss progress made and provide feedback on their productivity; (3) recognize achievement. Thus, learning is an integral part of the day-to-day operation. The supervisory feedback and positive recognition helps employees to learn from their experience.

In organizations where managers are making learning productive, a number of environmental factors are strong and positive influences:

1. The development of subordinates is a high organizational priority.

2. Managers are accountable to their superiors for development of employees and are recognized for their accomplishments in this field.

3. Planned organizational programs help managers learn more about training and development through participation in programs where training is integrated in the accomplishment of operational goals.

4. Managers are helped to eliminate the fear that training will expose their shortcomings, weaken their

job security or threaten their departmental autonomy.

We will examine several aspects of the managerial task of making learning productive.

Setting the Climate and Conditions for Learning

The desire to learn is strongly influenced by the work climate established by managers and supervisors. *The job environment is the most important influence affecting the development of the individual in an organization.*

In organizations whose strategies are improving the productiveness of learning, managers do create the climate that sparks learning; they understand that it is their responsibility to provide conditions that encourage productive learning. The work operation is the place where employees are stimulated to inquire, experience, experiment, discover, create—in short to learn and grow.

In his "Note to the Presidential Task Force on Training" (see Appendix, p. 307), Marvin Berkeley has presented three premises directly concerned with climate on the job which adds up to a trim synthesis of management's responsibility for an environment that sparks learning. Dr. Berkeley says that

> development cannot be externally forced on the individual; it must spring from the person's inner desire to grow, initiative to begin, and persistence to achieve.
>
> The governmental institutions wherein development takes place bear the responsibility to their employees to foster those conditions, as a natural part of the working environment, whereby the need for self-development becomes obvious, personal efforts are enchanced, and appropriate talent and achievements are rewarded.[1]

Here are some observations from managers and workers

in firms which have successfully established new approaches to employee development. "The managers in this department," said one worker, "pull their people into the operations in a way that makes them feel a definite part of the organization." Others noted how their managers "made time for them" and listened to their problems. Others told of the interest shown by their bosses, particularly when they had learned to accomplish a difficult piece of work. One manager expressed his feeling about the creation of work climate by saying, "I see it as part of my job to create the best atmosphere I can, no matter what blocks may occur in the rest of the organization." Many of them repeated the point that unless you "encourage people to be active, try to raise their sights, and stimulate them with questions pertaining to their projects, they can easily become disinterested and listless." "People don't learn much, or develop either," some said, "when they're bored." The best way to create interest in learning then is to see that it is needed beyond the situation in which it occurs. *To organize work that requires learning is to make the learning worth knowing.*

The following illustration exemplifies a manager who worked to create the climate for learning and growth:

> A manager of an inventory control branch in a government agency found that the number of procedural changes continued to increase, resulting in confusion among workers and an increase in errors. He found that most people were reading the changes in the regulations, but the long, wordy, and often ambiguous directives in and of themselves did not make clear the course of action to be taken. Customarily the procedures were sent to the various branches whose interpretations often conflicted.
>
> The manager wanted to encourage individual initiative in analyzing the changes as well as under-

standing and coordination between branches. He set up a committee to review the changes, whose members were selected by branch supervisors on a monthly basis. Within one or two days of the receipt of changes, the committee reviewed and discussed each change and its effect on their operations. It then analyzed, agreed upon, and accomplished the training needed for people to learn and apply the changes. The group in fact analyzed what different workers now needed to know in order to make the changes, and how they could best be helped to learn. In short, this group built the connections between the changed written procedures and what each employee was required to do because of the change that he had not done before.

The committee discarded the more conventional training approaches such as talks on all the procedural changes given for everyone (whether they needed them or not). Instead they set up the following pattern for their actions: (1) where the new procedures did not affect any of the branches, they took no action and did not route them; (2) where the new procedures required minor changes, guidance was given in a simple checklist; (3) where the new procedures required major changes, a desk guide was designed to provide a flow chart and directions for changes to be made; and (4) where the changes were too complex for the desk guide, training sessions were held which offered demonstrations of the new procedure and an opportunity to practice them.

What were the results? The manager's approach increased the interest of the entire branch in adapting their work to changes. Supervisors became more confident. Confusion disappeared and errors declined. The manager established a climate for change that sparked workers' interest in learning. The guidance was what they needed, and it was incorporated with their work. The process that had been worked out automatically sorted out those items highly important and related to their success on the job. It sparked the interest as well as the effort of individuals to learn.

But not all managers demonstrate the qualities that encourage favorable conditions for learning. Take the following example:

> The services manager of a purchasing department took no responsibility, other than that of routine distribution of information, for helping his people learn. It might be said that his notion of instructing his people and helping them to adjust to changes could best be described by the phrase "route to all concerned." The requirement that each worker should initial the form, indicating that he had seen and read a procedure, was somehow a protection to the manager in the event of any question as to whether he had done his part in giving the information.
>
> The purchasing department changed its entire procedure for processing purchase orders. A staff group, the planning division, prepared a manual outlining the new procedures. The department director distributed advance copies of the manual to his division managers in a staff meeting, advising them that the date of implementation was but a week off. Several division chiefs demurred at preparing their people for these changes on such short notice.
>
> However, the manager of the servicing division remarked that his branch chiefs were "paid to supervise" and this included keeping their employees informed about any changes in the procedures. "They've kept abreast of things so far . . . and they'll handle this too." When he returned to his office, he told his secre-

tary to "route these procedures to all concerned." She asked whether this was to include all employees, and he replied, "That's up to the branch chiefs—they'll know what to do with them."

The manual was routed "to all concerned" and the resulting confusion caused a large number of errors. Quality control engineers discovered most of the errors were in the service division and reported that employees either did not understand the new procedures or showed a disregard for them. When the Department Director asked the manager of the service division what the problem was, he replied, "I don't know what's the matter with these people. They were given the opportunity to read the changes—we routed them to everyone concerned. But they don't seem very enthusiastic about making changes. I spend half of my time answering their questions and looking things up for them. But they'll catch on in time. They just have to make up their minds to live with the system."

The conditions established by this manager were discouraging to any learning effort by the members of that division. His passive attitude toward the changes discouraged both the branch chiefs and their people. The manager failed to understand that what was needed were conditions to encourage individual effort to learn. It was not surprising that no one took the initiative to implement the new regulations.

Integrating Worker Performance with Learning

In many of the firms having increased success with their training and learning efforts, managers are using a new approach with individual employees that integrates learning with their day-to-day work performance. Managers are building more productive relationships between the work and the training-learning processes. Work responsibilities thus place greater demands upon employees' intelligence in planning and executing their tasks. This differs from the old notions of on-the-job training which prescribe and demonstrate the step-by-step method of performing a job followed by the worker's demonstration that he has learned the specific method. Also it is different from the casual improvisations of supervisors to explain the work to employees.

The integration of learning with worker performance is a way of organizing work objectives so that the employee learns to plan and direct his activities. This demands intelligence to find out how best to meet the requirements, including what he needs to learn. His interest in learning is increased. His training is structured to include those learning experiences he needs in order to achieve his work objectives. It may range from the study of theory and principles to seeking more practical guides, visual aids, references, and day-to-day experiences. He uses what he learns and thus assimilates it, retaining it for future use. He is encouraged by seeing his accomplishments. Feedback from his supervisor helps him know when he is making progress. He gains the satisfaction and confidence of being able to direct his work and see the productiveness of his learning.

Managers and supervisors gave many examples of this type of integration of work and learning. One manager said that he assigned projects to include new and more complex responsibilities. Several workers in that department said that they were assigned "projects that make you learn." Some workers pointed up the help that their supervisors gave them in relating their tasks to what was happening in other parts of the organization. Often the employees in areas where managers were livening productivity through demands on more creative use of intelligence remarked, "You are not required to be merely cooperative and carry out your tasks in an amiable but mediocre way. You feel you're on your own; you have to produce and learn fast." Others remarked that "competence and performance are really recognized."

One example may better illustrate this approach by supervisors who make learning productive through closer integration with the work:

> Art Sinclair is Chief of the Training and Development Branch in the Personnel Division. Jim Brown is a new employee and is being groomed to become a Training and Development officer. The supervisor thought through the tasks that Jim must be able to do in order to function independently at the journeyman level.

How did the supervisor describe and how did the employee understand the requirements for the job? They discussed the following aspects:

1. *Purpose.* A review was made of the contributions this type of work could make in terms of the organization's needs: changes that called for updating of employees, increasing complexity of technological systems, an aging work force, rigidity of procedures, conflicts of diverse interests, lack of executive and managerial interest in updating themselves and the workers.

2. *Job requirements.* An outline was made of the tasks that needed to be done: assistance to organizations in analysis of their learning needs; design and implementation of courses; individualized training plans; administration of centralized courses where necessary; information on training resources.

3. *Employee's background.* An analysis was made of Jim's past experience and training in comparison with what he must be able to do. Some preliminary plans were made for development, which gave Jim an opportunity to think about what he could do to develop himself and what help he'd need.

4. *Projects.* A review was made of projects that would provide Jim with experiential learning to help him develop competency in each of the major areas for which a training technician is responsible.

An understanding was reached that Jim would start with two or three of the less complex projects. He did well and gradually assumed increased responsibilities, the fulfillment of which would require him to learn more in the technology of learning and the dynamics of organizational life. He directed his learning, asking for help when he was unsure of what action to take. Together they frequently reviewed progress, and Art provided guidance during their analysis of the degree of success with different approaches used by Jim. Art pointed up helpful references and encouraged Jim to participate in several courses.

Jim's development was outstanding. He continued to assume greater responsibilities with persistence to succeed. His spirit of helpfulness and enthusiasm for learning was contagious. Each organization, group or individual with whom he worked responded to his efforts, and a momentum for learning replaced inertia. The depth of his understanding, his maturity of judgment in the most complex situations and his designs and implementations of training-learning experiences were unequaled by most training specialists of many years' experience.

Delegation of Work, Not Training

Often it is the way the work or project is delegated to an employee that helps the employee to learn and to grow. The manager is responsible for the performance of his people. He may, delegate a part of the training effort, but he is still responsible to see that the training is completed and to follow through on its application. Unfortunately, managers and supervisors often delegate the training responsibility, rather than the work, as the following example shows:

> Jed Harris was a supervisor of a clerical unit consisting of six junior clerk typists and four clerk typists. When a new employee reported for work for one of the junior clerk typist vacancies, Harris assigned Mrs. Elder to give her "whatever job training she needed." Mrs. Elder had been in the office for five years, knew the work thoroughly, and was one of the most productive and dependable employees. However, she had never received training in how to instruct others. Moreover, Harris neglected to make clear to Mrs. Elder and Nancy that Mrs. Elder was temporarily Nancy's supervisor during the induction period.
>
> Harris observed Mrs. Elder giving work to Nancy and was aware that she was making explanations to her as well as correcting her work. He also observed that Nancy was often not at her desk at starting time and frequently away from her work area during the day. When Harris began to look more closely at Nancy's work, he found it poor in quality. He began to take it back to Mrs. Elder, pointing out the errors. Her usual remark on these occasions was: "Oh, I've told her about this a hundred times." Several times he overheard Mrs. Elder saying to Nancy, "Don't you remember? I told you about this before."
>
> After six weeks had passed, Mrs. Elder told Harris that she was "getting nowhere" with Nancy since she continued to make many errors and either was unable to comprehend the office procedures or was exceedingly careless.

What had happened here? Harris had washed his hands

of his training responsibility, even though he may have thought he had taken care of it. In fact, assigning responsibility to train Nancy to an experienced employee, such as Mrs. Elder, could have been acceptable if Mrs. Elder had been given help in instructional methods, and if both Nancy and Mrs. Elder understood the nature and extent of the delegated authority.

Both the supervisor and the person to whom he delegates the responsibility for training need to *understand the importance of connecting what the worker is learning to what is vital in the employee's work that requires the learning*. They also need to *understand the need to keep in touch with the progress being made and to continually guide it*. Thus it is a collaborative effort between the manager and the one to whom he delegates that portion of the training responsibility. But he cannot abrogate the responsibility for developing people—it is one with his management job. Cases like this illustrate why much training fails to provide productive results. Supervisors "downgrade" the importance of learning by turning it over to someone else, without any safeguards as to its quality, and by withdrawing personal interest and influence.

Training as Part of the Manager's Task

"Supervisors do not have time to train" is a common plaint. Others point out that managers and supervisors are not qualified as experts in instruction, training, and education. Their major job is production of work. These arguments need to be examined in light of the basic issues discussed earlier. These arguments result from the old assumption that training is a simple two-way relationship, the success of which depends upon good instruction and the learner's acquisition of knowledge or skill.

But managers' and supervisors' concepts of their tasks must be redefined in light of rapid changes in organizational life and their effect on learning. Many training practices have become outmoded. Classroom instruction and on-the-job training are no longer adequate to meet today's organizational demands for whole new dimensions of learning and training. The rapidly changing technological systems demand more flexible, responsive learning in a new, lateral dimension.

The manager and supervisor are at the heart of the extension of the training-learning process throughout the organization. But they are not alone. They are the focal point since they establish the primary training-learning process. They also analyze new requirements in terms of what their people will need to learn and put their fingers on troublesome situations which they and groups of their employees can learn to solve. They reach out, when their own resources are not adequate, for external help. The variety of new arrangements for incorporating learning with work are described in Chapter 8. But the major and central task of helping workers and groups under their supervision learn productively remains that of management.

> The manager of a sales division for an industrial firm became aware that the induction of his new sales trainees was not helping them to make progress; at least it seemed to take a long time before they were able to function independently and competently. He did not know whether the trainees were reluctant, or unable, to assume full responsibility. He began to observe the initial training procedures more closely and then asked both trainees and the more experienced salesmen for their honest critiques.
>
> Their replies showed that many found the initial steps tedious. The guided tours of the plant and the reading of massive instructions and manuals, they said, were not real jobs. The continued reading of huge amounts of data on the product lines was not only

boring, but it did not relate to anything they saw as a vital requirement.

Together the manager and some of his men changed the initial induction. After a brief orientation, they assigned tasks to the trainees that required them to learn. For example, they were assigned the task of answering phone inquiries, which brought them face to face with having to find the facts they needed in order to give the correct information. By teaming the trainees with more experienced salesmen, they could go to the experts for help in order to arrive at a firm commitment and sale. By sequencing different types of work from its more simple to more complex phases and by continuing to assign the trainees responsibilities for accomplishing certain tasks, their progress and effectiveness improved dramatically.

The change of the initial learning experience for the sales trainees in the above case illustrates the importance of integrating learning with the management actions needed to build productive employees. These trainees learned by working. They wanted to do work immediately that demanded use of their intelligence. They responded to this manager who let them show what they could do. The manager, however, did not simply turn them loose. With the help of experienced salesmen, who had more recent memories of how they had learned, he designed a series of learning-by-doing experiences. He also made sure that they had guidance and information on their progress.

Arranging for Supplementary Learning Experiences

Managers in the firms where growth and development activities are providing productive results are alert to the advantage of the accessibility of real and live materials, the stuff of which learning is made. We have seen how they provide a climate that clears away disincentives that impede learning and how they integrate training with action needed to accomplish the work of their departments or units.

Managers have also done much to make learning productive by arranging for supplementary learning experiences for their people. The reason that auxiliary training resources are also productive is the manager's effort to build bridges between work objectives and the ideas that are to be learned. Managers have helped their people to see that an external course was to be more than the acquisition of information. They discussed expectations with their subordinates for the application of worthwhile ideas from the course, prior to the course. Employees expressed the motivational effects of such planning. As one said, "You are more interested when you talk with your boss about going to the course. Somehow your expectations make the learning more helpful and related to your own work. And the feeling that you're going to be able to do something and to apply whatever you get out of the course makes it worth all the study and effort." Others said they received "better insight into the plans of their boss when they talked about the reasons for going to a course, and a feeling of his support and interest in what you're trying to accomplish."

One aspect that some managers emphasized was raising the sights of their employees. As one said, "Although our agency stresses completion of courses and getting course credit in their personnel files, we must get them away from the petty notions of traditional education, like getting good marks, or gold stars." Other managers had similar thoughts on watching out for "education as a status symbol" or encouraging their subordinates to "work for the wrong things" and "just accumulate a long list of courses they'd been able to pass." The worth is in the use and application of the knowledge to the job.

Managers are finding many new ways to integrate external resources into the training-learning process within their groups. The availability of prepared programs provides new flexibilities for adaptation into productive learning. The grooming of group leaders to define, solve, and implement solutions for problems provides new learning approaches. New forms of extended instruction through modern audiovisual techniques help managers fit learning either into or close to the place of work. Many examples are discussed in Chapters 8 and 9 on new ways of initiating, maintaining, and continuing learning within an organization.

Managerial concern for their employees' interest in and their possible use of a learning experience is shown in the following example. Significant is the fact that the concern during the initiating steps for the application of learning is a determining factor in the productiveness of the experience.

> In a large government agency a series of Reading Development workshops was given. The training staff had persuaded a group of top managers to participate in the pilot course, hoping that their involvement with the first group would improve the manner of selecting their subordinates. An evaluation was made about six months later of the participation, attendance, completion of assignments, demonstrated benefits, and continuing use of what had been learned. One of the findings was that those ranking high in all factors had been counseled about taking this course by bosses who had participated in the first session. A critical factor was the supervisory-employee discussion and understanding of the program. Poor records of participation, attendance, and utilization were for the most part made by those who had been sent, either without any discussion or with little idea of what they could gain and apply from their experience.

But managerial action during the formative and planning stage of learning experiences can also be characterized by types of treatment that seek to preserve an aura of compliance, but which actually do nothing. It will be instructive to analyze such a case:

> An organization was in the process of a total survey of its training needs. One group of managers attempted to get by with the least possible effort, even though they were themselves on the brink of enormous changes in systems and technology. The survey required that managers and supervisors discuss training problems with their subordinates. Needs, as well as plans to meet them, were to be recorded.
>
> A newsletter had been distributed to all employees in the entire organization. One of the employees, wondering why no one had discussed training needs with him, went to the head of the organization. The top man looked into the matter and found that the managers in this particular department had "complied" with the requirement. They had prepared individual records for each of their 500 employees, but they had not held any discussions. The records had been rubber-stamped with the phrase "on-the-job training" to describe both the needs and the action planned.

The result of this managerial indifference to workers' needs destroyed their confidence in management and hampered their support and interest in adjusting to the flood of system changes that followed.

Participating with Subordinates in Training-Learning Efforts

Managers understand, desire, and manage the productive use of learning when they *participate with their employ-*

ees in the same learning experiences (or those that teach the same principles). Managers who develop their subordinates by learning with them and being a part of the same experiences have contributed greatly to a strategy now growing in use and strongly in line with what we know about learning theory. In this way, managers and supervisors understand the ideas that subordinates are incorporating in their work. Their support, review, and appraisal of subordinates are consistent with the ideas learned and applied.

The old notions of management development are giving way to new patterns because there has been little evidence of return on the traditional types of management development programs. There is, in fact, considerable evidence that shows business leaders often become less effective. Conclusions are that attempts at improving managerial performance through planned training programs have not produced measurable change.[2] McGregor offers the following generalization derived from his observation of the field of management development:

> There is almost no relationship between the amount of formal programming and machinery of management development and the actual achievement of the organization in this respect. I sometimes think the correlation may be negative! Programs and procedures do not *cause* management development, because it is not possible to 'produce' managers the way we produce products. We can only hope to 'grow' them. . . .[3]

What are some affirmative examples of new patterns for integrating the development of managers with their development of subordinates? Several successful examples are discussed fully in the Appendix:

1. Organizational Growth and Development, the Raymond Corporation: Organizational development labo-

ratory training sessions and continuing problem-solving teams have brought managers and subordinates together to plan for productive change (Appendix, p. 263).

2. Team Effectiveness, Western Electric Corporation: Several levels of managers and supervisors of an organizational unit participate in training which is integrated in action needed to solve a problem hindering the effectiveness of that unit (Appendix, p. 229).

3. Managerial Learning and Performance of Its Training Role, Internal Revenue Service, Western Region: Organizational development laboratory training sessions, continuing problem-solving teams and managerial contributions to a central learning resource center, have integrated managerial efforts with those of subordinates and technical experts to plan and train for productive change (Appendix, p. 279).

4. Managers play a participative role in Chase Manhattan's Manpower Development Program (Appendix, p. 249) and in White Sands Missile Range's Cooperative Education Program (Appendix, p. 293).

Unless managers are involved in learning the ideas and techniques they expect subordinates to use, they cannot truly understand and follow through on their implementation. Texas Instruments, for example, demonstrated this in experimenting with the reduction of anxiety causes in their manufacturing department.[4] They learned that reduction in anxiety did shorten training time, lower training costs, and drop absenteeism. But what was also important was that they learned that the productive results of this training stimulated managers to try other innovations.

These new learning patterns demonstrate the critical fact that instruction is being given by line managers. When different levels of managers are learning together, a common set of signals is being used. When key managers are developing their own teams of managers, they are learning too and thus being developed. This eliminates the pitfalls of the more traditional "management development" programs which attempt to produce trained managers. The process of development is more natural, because the higher level managers are helping the lower level managers to work for the same goals. Furthermore, this places higher level managers in the position of practicing what they preach from the viewpoint of the lower level managers. The common plea of lower level supervisors when they are involved in a developmental experience is "Why don't you give this to my boss?" All too often the lower levels of management see themselves as being sent to a training program the techniques and ideas of which their bosses neither understand nor support. More productive results have been achieved when key managers of higher levels are involved in the development of their lower level managers and supervisors.

Accountability for the Development of Subordinates

What brings about the interest of managers in the development of subordinates? The strategies described throughout this book show that it is not simply an attitude change on the part of the managers. It takes leadership from the top in designing not only the conditions of the organizational environment that nurture growth and development, but also the building of collaborative learning and work efforts. This was borne out in an incident described by McGregor (after failure of a "manufacturing" approach to management development which aroused passive resistance):

> Instead of concluding (as some management development staff groups have under these familiar circumstances) that the remedy was more "selling," or a training program to teach management how to use the

> formal machinery, this group decided to start again using an entirely different approach. This involved just one activity: annual meetings of the president of the company with each of his immediate subordinates individually, in which the subordinate reported in detail to the president on his activities and accomplishments in creating an environment conducive to the growth of his subordinates. Each individual reporting to him, and each individual at the second level below him, were discussed with the president in detail. The emphasis was on what the manager was doing to make it possible for his subordinates to further their own self-development. The president made it clear—not only in words but also in action—that he held his own subordinates accountable for this managerial function and that how well they fulfilled the responsibilities in these respects would make a substantial difference in their own rewards and punishments. . . . The managers themselves learned a good deal as they attempted to fulfill this new responsibility.[5]

Organizations have discovered new ways to make management development integrated with productive action and thus more effective. In many cases, managers are developing themselves through a new conception and execution of their management tasks broadened to include their development of subordinates.

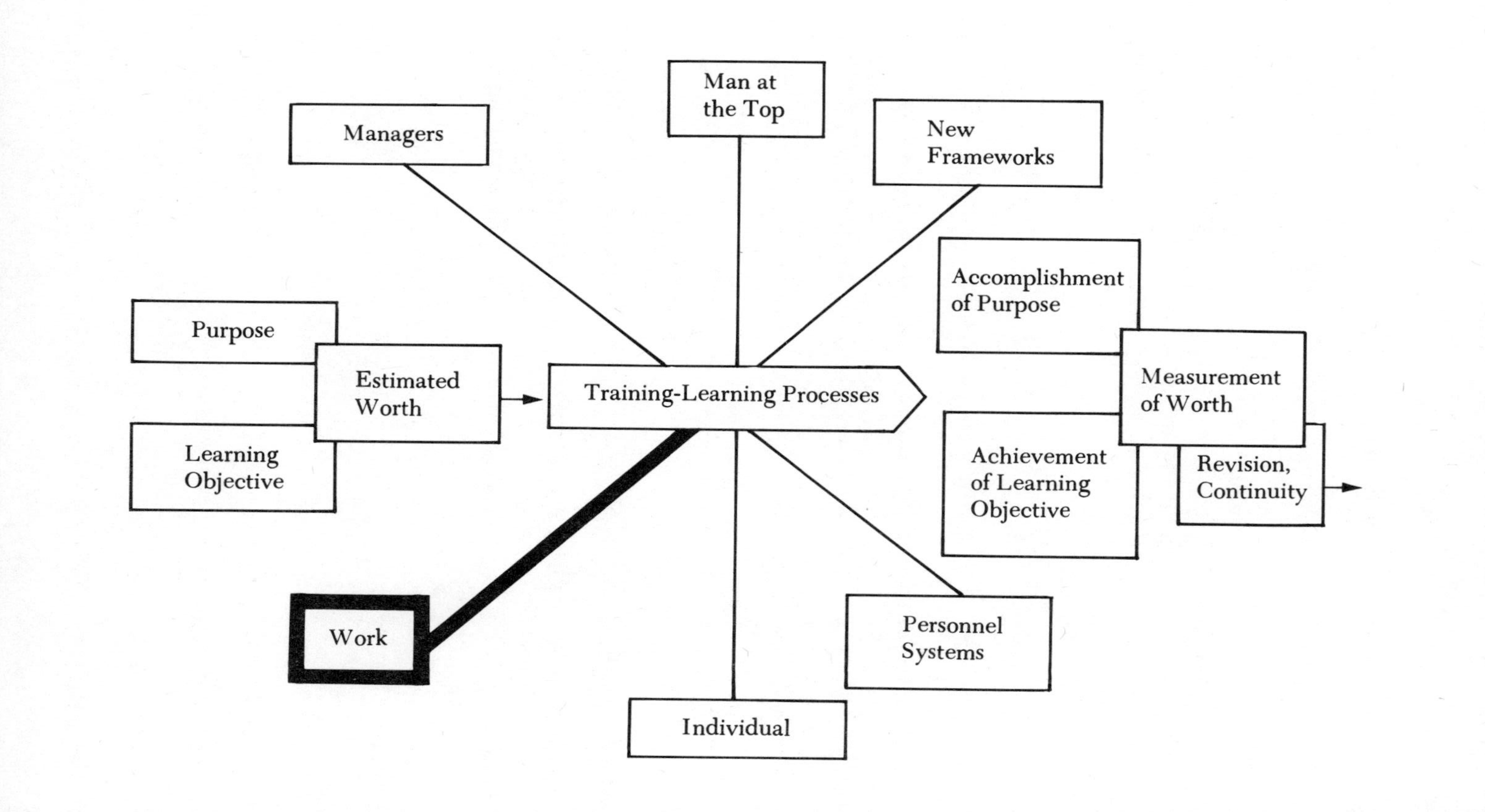
Managers
Man at the Top
New Frameworks
Purpose
Estimated Worth
Learning Objective
Training-Learning Processes
Accomplishment of Purpose
Measurement of Worth
Achievement of Learning Objective
Revision, Continuity
Work
Individual
Personnel Systems

5

Work That Sparks Learning

Evidence shows that work can stimulate or stifle learning. Organizations have found that productive training results from positive interrelationships of work and learning on the job. New ways have been discovered to assign or structure work that induce and facilitate more productive learning.

For many, work itself and the situations arising from work are the "subject" of learning. Companies are concerned with the gaps in work situations that can be helped by training. They are designing learning experiences to provide what workers need to learn, not running courses and finding out who will attend.

Many organizations are building productive training to help meet changes in work and specific jobs caused by new technologies:

1. Implementation of new systems is being accompanied by training-learning processes that provide fast and flexible transmission of know-how to those who have a need to know.

2. The changing nature of jobs is calling forth new

approaches to learning the work. Newer kinds of jobs often do not lend themselves to the industrial engineer's design of the one best method. The shift from agricultural and manufacturing jobs to service industries has been accompanied by the rise of a fourth sector, that of producers of ideas and technological innovation.[1] The newer jobs depend on the individual to plan as well as to execute the steps to accomplish the tasks.[2]

3. Elimination of jobs or certain functions of jobs causes obsolescence of workers; creation of lateral as well as vertical channels for mobility is strengthened by integrated training and work experiences, providing a hedge against obsolescence.

4. Routinization of jobs which limits workers' performance and increases deadwood, and makes the organization less productive, is being checked by integrated job and training designs.

To build productive relationships between work and the training process, organizations are discovering ways that technical changes can initiate learning, malfunctioning work systems can be corrected, obsolescent workers can learn new tasks, and training and job progression can be interrelated.

Technological Impact on Performance Requirements Sparks Learning

Technological changes modify production, distribution, accounting, processing of information systems; they also provide opportunities for ongoing efforts to update knowledge and skills of people in the organization.

Learning to live with new systems, particularly computerized processes, generates the need for adjustments. Computers and analytic techniques have become increasingly important. But they cause mixed feelings; some people are confident that these changes are in the right direction, but others are upset and apparently not willing to accept them. It is often difficult for workers to understand the implications of computer systems when they have had no experience with them, do not understand the rationale for their introduction, and do not have the assurance that they can understand and work with them. The computer systems cause changes in the work and consequently require changes in performance requirements. They also require new relationships between work groups and between people and machine systems.

Helping Employees Understand New Formats

Although the tasks of a job may not change, the specific techniques required to accomplish the job may change. An example can be seen in the impact of a centralized computer system on the formats on which data were received from or given to the data processing department in a supply firm.

> This case involved a group of inventory clerks who handled exceptions to the standard requisitioning procedure. Under a new computerized system, the processing of orders required new formats in cards and print-outs for the inventory clerks in another department in order to submit and receive information from the computer. Furthermore, the work required a much higher degree of accuracy because of the greater impact caused by an error. The nature of the new system was not easy for them to understand. The error rate mounted, feelings were strained, and the situation worsened.
>
> With the help of the training staff, the manager obtained a programmed unit on computers designed to introduce workers to the principles upon which computerized systems work and to acquaint them with the terminology. He then explained to the groups why a

high degree of accuracy was important. In order for them to gain more insight into man-machine systems, he arranged to have the course made available in the work area. Although the course on computers was not mandatory, interest and participation increased. The value of going through this programmed unit spread by word of mouth. Employees found that it helped them understand how to read the new cards and print-outs and gave them insight into automated systems.

The results were gratifying. Errors were eliminated, confidence was increased, and a general feeling of rapport with and interest in the new system were achieved. Computer-generated data were no longer the mystery they had originally been. Not only could the employees read cards and print-outs with comprehension and confidence, but they realized the waste that could result from poor communication between data processing and themselves. It showed the importance of introducing correct information into the computer. Employees frankly said that they recognized the need to stop previous practices of "sweeping errors under the rug" because of lack of help in understanding the changes.

Managers and New Management Information Systems

Managerial performance requirements are changed by the need to understand and use the new management information systems. Managers have become involved to a much greater degree in the computer and management information technology. They need to understand the significance and principles of data processing so that they can provide the programmers in the data processing departments with analyses of the output needed as well as the sources of input data. One of the major hindrances to operational progress of management information systems is the failure to define changes in performance requirements of functional managers. However, where an organization has analyzed how the new systems change the tasks of workers, and has designed a training system which incorporates the new knowledge into operations, the benefits have been great. Managerial performance requirements have been expanded to include the following: a working knowledge of techniques necessary for conducting a functional systems analysis; insight into computers that gives managers some degree of confidence and familiarity to make analyses; understanding what their clerical personnel need to know in handling input or output formats and print-outs as well as insight into the purpose of the programs. The following example amplifies these points:

> A problem faced by one regional administrative headquarters of a large government organization was how to encourage their managers to appreciate and understand the computer as a management tool. Traditionally, information on various activities such as supply, purchasing, personnel, transportation, and equipment had been received from branch offices; it was consolidated at this level and forwarded to a central headquarters. When the decision was made to convert the old manually prepared reporting methods and place progress and status information on data computerized systems, the regional headquarters realized that their managerial staff had limited knowledge and experience with management information systems.
>
> What did managers need? For one thing, they required an understanding of the implications of the broad trend in management information systems field. Also they needed to become familiar with how to approach computerized activities, recognize the capabilities of a computerized system, and have some idea of the technical considerations which influence the eco-

nomics of this method of handling information and how it can aid in decision making. They must learn how to prepare requests for the automation of their technical information.

The bases for the training-learning efforts were the new tasks to be assigned to key managers, such as making feasibility studies and the analysis and design of functional systems. Having defined these, the instructional system was developed to provide a brief introduction to computers and information systems which gave managers a knowledge of essentials in the least possible time, followed by a course in basic principles and techniques of systems analysis. Throughout both of these learning experiences, the instructors from the management information systems staff related the discussions on questions and problems to the systems currently in use. The instruction on computer systems analysis and design was also tailored to what managers needed in order to fulfill their new job requirements.

The results of this training-learning process were encouraging. Managers as well as those designated as management information systems officers for their departments responded well to the aids provided them. Managers became aware of their subordinates' needs to learn the reading of computerized information. Accordingly, they made arrangements for their orientation and training. Gradually all those involved in implementing the new systems were helped to understand how they influenced and changed their jobs. They were also equipped with techniques needed to accomplish new tasks.

The significance of this illustration lies in: (1) the recognition of the impact of new systems on performance requirements of managers and their subordinates; (2) the preparation of a training system to help people accomplish the changes in their tasks. Thus firms have been able to use technological change to their advantage when they link learning to the changing work operations and individual job requirements.

The illustration is also of interest because it used a combination of ways to learn. First, it adapted and incorporated into its total plan a programmed audio-tape course prepared by a large corporation for its executives and managers. The newer methodology helped participants to follow diagrams and undertake exercises in a manual at the direction of taped recordings. Second, it incorporated additional information from the local systems men who acted as course moderators and related the discussions to the systems' impact on the tasks of the participants. Third, the flexibility and adaptability of the materials made it possible to present sessions anywhere for any number. Accordingly, sessions were designed for small groups from different organizational units and were held in rooms adjacent to the work site. The timing of a series of short sessions was adapted nicely to the work priorities of these groups. Advantages of the new ways of learning are discussed in Chapter 8.

Corrections of Malfunctioning Work Systems Help Learning

Analysis of how information flows between components of an organization shows that faulty systems cause breakdowns on the job between people and between departments. What is commonly thought of as poor employee performance is more accurately described as errors resulting from faults in the system. Firms that have analyzed entire systems, learned the causes of breakdowns, and corrected them by a training system have benefited greatly. This is productive learning.

Porter's research and study on manpower development and the system training concept show that if the system is poorly designed training cannot improve the behavior and productiveness of the people involved.[3] Organizations thus can analyze an entire system by following through the flow of the process, the product, or the service to its end result, determining the human performance required at each step, and making sure that the system lays the basis for the performance required.

The following example describes how a new system adversely affected workers' performance and how a readjustment of the system helped the group learn new relationships with productive results:

> A large supply warehouse had computerized its requisition and order-filling system. One of the procedures scheduled each day's bin pick in such a way that the location of peak loads was unpredictable. The evening runs of the data processing department batched requisitions for material, and the computer programmed the day's pick of goods and assembly for shipment. The machine runs did not take into consideration the adequacy of the labor supply in the locations where the picks were scheduled. This forced foremen to deploy some members of their crews to areas of peak work loads. The constantly changing peak work loads placed almost impossible demands on the foremen to shift their men around.
>
> Uncertainty of work location and the lack of belonging to a stable work group, as well as the practice of assigning the weakest men to groups other than their own resulted in a drop in productivity and loss of support for the new system. Analysis showed that the productivity decline in packing and shipping rates resulted primarily from altering of the normal human relationships of the workers. Warehousemen became distrustful of their bosses and of one another. They felt in-

secure since they were unable to identify with a regular work group. They lost the feeling of work stability and orderliness. The lack of productiveness was not because the men had not learned the new codes and changes in the process. It was the result of the system's failure to take into account how the groups of warehousemen could meet the unpredictable demands for assembly of shipments.

The computer system was altered to provide for more even work loads. The foreman helped warehousemen to understand the adjustment of priorities, and a healthy relationship was established between groups and between the system's demands and the groups. Productivity went up and warehousemen assumed more interest in making the system work.

This firm recognized that direction and implementation of a system were not enough. They also recognized that training employees in new systems was not enough. What they were forced to do was to readjust the system itself. The warehousemen did not lack the understanding and know-how of the new system. Moreover, they were not unwilling to follow its procedures. It was not fear or resistance to the system. What they learned under the arbitrary picking demands of the new system was to distrust their bosses, to feel uncertain as to where they belonged, and to resent the pressures of other workers.

Learning Assists Obsolescent Workers Make Job Changes

Changes in technical systems may alter jobs partially, which requires the learning of new or changed tasks. Such technical changes may even alter entire jobs, in which case the individual needs to learn much more. Whatever the technical change, a major consequence is the demand it makes upon people to learn and upon the organization to plan assistance for them.

Some firms have successfully analyzed changes occurring in jobs because of new technical systems. Moreover, they have coordinated job redesign with the building of training efforts productive for both the individual and the organization. The dilemma occurs when technical systems outdistance social changes to help people adapt, such as the analysis of learning needs generated by technical changes.

An example of a supply and warehousing organization illustrates this point:

> This organization had completed plans for its automated system changes and was beginning to implement them, without really facing up to what these changes would do to jobs, the nature of the work, and the knowledge and skills required from its people. Although it could be said that some training efforts were being made, still they were intermittent, largely unorganized, and lacked direct relatedness to the projects under way.
>
> A joint action-research program was initiated with a local university to survey the impact of automation and technological changes on the work, jobs, the work force, and operational effectiveness, particularly to help the work force adjust to changes in their present jobs or new jobs. As the consulting group from the university helped the organization strengthen its internal efforts, it would withdraw.
>
> The survey of automation's impact was made. It showed that the nature of work as well as specific jobs had changed, causing a need to redesign jobs and to alter systems that caused breakdowns in work relationships. It recommended training be incorporated as

part of the design and improvement of systems and methods, and as part of problem-solving groups. It also recommended that the training-learning processes be supplemented by logistical supply courses and by educational upgrading to increase certain workers' abilities to learn.

Unfortunately, the action phases of the program were not continued with the university consulting group owing to gaps in organizational leadership. But the change efforts that were managed by parts of the organization did follow through on many of the recommendations. Managers were provided a wide variety of managerial and technical learning opportunities. Teams of instructors from data processing, systems and procedures, methods, and training helped managers and technicians acquire understanding and familiarity with computers and systems analysis. Managers added responsibilities to jobs which had been shorn of some tasks absorbed by the automated systems. They increased requirements for accuracy and insight into the total system. Methods engineers helped bridge the transition to changed systems by instructing groups on how to operate under changed procedures and providing them with guidance materials. Individualized training was provided for operators of computer equipment. In-house training amplified customer training provided by the manufacturer. Workers on jobs that were fast becoming obsolescent were helped through individualized training plans to move into new channels for advancement. Individual self-development was encouraged by bringing courses to the organization after working hours, so that workers were able to increase their skills and confidence, to qualify for promotional tests, and to make the transition to higher level jobs.

Jobs That Fit People

The American Telephone and Telegraph Company is trying to make work much more satisfactory for many people.[4] A plan, called STAR (System Training Application Requirements), designs jobs which take into account the human need for achievement and fulfillment of responsibilities. Job designers and training designers work together with computer programmers and analysts to make sure that the human system design parallels the machine system. Formerly the machine was the sole consideration. Now they ask: Is the new work possible to do and to teach? Will the new work be satisfying? Is the new work such that it requires new skills? Does it need special environments or working conditions? Jobs include several stages of added new tasks. Thus there is a continuing challenge in jobs because people keep on learning and growing.

A recent analysis for the U.S. Commerce Department by a group of professors at the Harvard Business School is part of a study of the effect of direct investment overseas by American companies on U.S. domestic employment. The most important conclusion of the report points up the drastic need of the U.S. worker for more job adjustment assistance. Although the U.S. has to work harder to stay ahead in business abroad, more dynamic action will be required in helping the U.S. labor force adjust to new jobs. "The most important industrial problem facing the U.S. is the adjustment of jobs."[5]

Progressive Job and Learning Experiences

Companies are finding ways to design jobs that provide progression from one level to the next. The experience gained and fulfillment of responsibility at one level demonstrates the individual's qualification to advance. Organizations are now successfully integrating learning experiences into the work projects. The objective of such developmental programs is the producing of competent workers. Productive learning experiences develop employees while at the same time they contribute to the productivity of the organization.

An example of the experience of a large government agency is cited below:

> This organization found it extremely difficult to recruit for certain jobs such as data processing programmers, operators, systems analysts, and management analysts. The solution was sought in redesigning the higher level (sometimes called journeyman) jobs into several lower level jobs, deleting certain tasks and responsibilities which called for more judgment and skill. The lower level jobs were usually an entry level and at least one interim level job. Recruitment was on the entry level job.
>
> The collaboration of the technical experts, job designers, and the training staff produced a training plan which spelled out the major work objectives at each level, or what the employee must be able to do. The employee learned by being able to fulfill his responsibilities at each level, thus qualifying himself for advancement. Different training experiences were combined in ways and at times when they were most needed by the employees to complete work projects. (A more detailed description of learning and work experiences is provided in Chapter 8. Our purpose here is to emphasize the engineering of work processes in ways that provide opportunities for employees to advance.) The managers or supervisory coaches were able to adjust projects to provide learning experiences and to help meet the priorities of work. Flexibility in the work as-

signments combined with visible production made the plans attractive to managers.

At the close of a three-year period, results were very encouraging. Most visible were 144 qualified technicians and operators who had advanced to the target jobs: data programmers, computer operators, systems analysts, and management analysts. Managers understood their own work better as the result of their efforts to organize and relate the knowledge and practical application of that knowledge to work projects assigned to their trainees. The satisfaction of the trainees in their achievements and advancement added to the morale, motivation, and increased spirit of growth in areas where they worked.

Companies and government organizations are discovering new ways and alternatives to conventional ways of training their people. One of the most productive is the arrangement that we have been describing which combines work and learning experiences. The firms that have had most productive results incorporate training in action needed to complete work projects. A diversity of learning and work arrangements is being used to meet the needs of the organizations, such as management interns, career interns, cooperative education, work-study, and many other plans. When these arrangements design work and engineer jobs in ways that spark learning, they are productive.

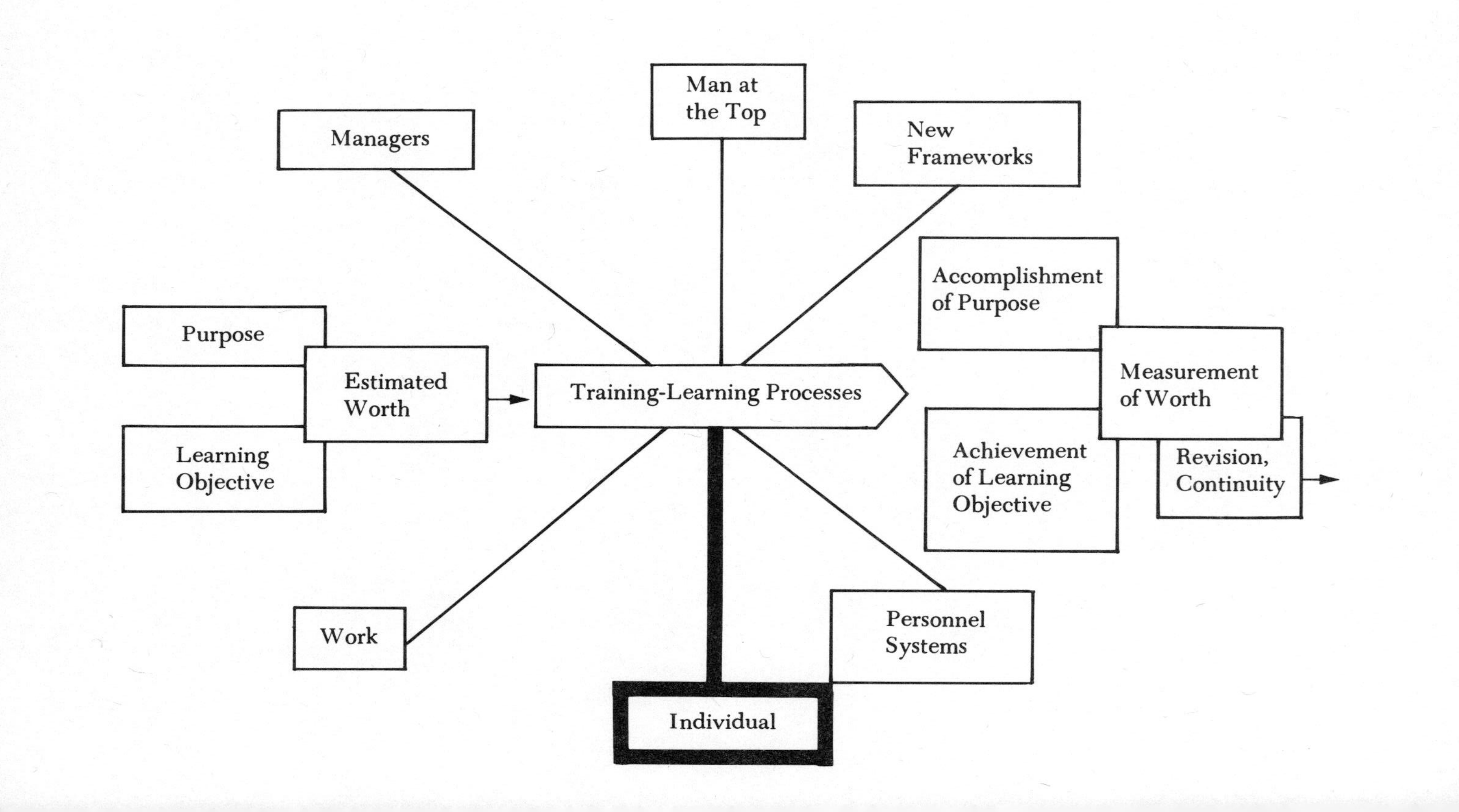
Man at the Top
Managers
New Frameworks
Purpose
Estimated Worth
Learning Objective
Training-Learning Processes
Accomplishment of Purpose
Measurement of Worth
Achievement of Learning Objective
Revision, Continuity
Work
Personnel Systems
Individual

6

The Individual: A Productive Learner

Organizations with productive learning systems have recognized that individuals have a natural desire to learn. In the last chapter we saw that work can be organized to meet people's needs as well as to achieve organizational objectives. Now we will learn that organizations recognizing that learning and development cannot be forced on their employees have designed new ways to bring about the individual's desire to learn and use that learning productively.

Organizations with productive learning systems have interrelated their means of accomplishing: (1) organizational development approaches that help individual workers learn to work together; (2) individual development processes that help workers to learn and use knowledge and skills by the systematic integration of learning experiences with work needed to achieve objectives.

Successful learning strategies balance attention given to both the organizational development process and the individual systematic learning process. Where an approach emphasizes instructional methods and programs, the ultimate productiveness of that effort is likely to be lost if the worker cannot use or is not encouraged to apply his increased knowledge. On the other hand, emphasis on collaborative team processes without sufficient attention to individual and personal development of skills will cheat an organization of the benefits of scientifically designed training processes. Complex technical systems require teachable and learnable programs that enable the human side of the organization to learn and adjust quickly, precisely, and productively.

Awareness of Need and Desire To Learn

Organizations have learned that to make the individual a productive learner the individual himself has to become aware of his need to learn. This may be accomplished through supervisory-subordinate integration of learning with work achievement, career advancement routes, and participation in learning experiences.

Helps and Hindrances

New approaches have used a variety of opportunities in the work situation to spark the individual's interest in learning. Acceptance of responsibility to achieve work objectives helps the individual realize skills and knowledge he needs if he is to successfully accomplish the job. The introduction of a new procedure, a new piece of equipment, or a new project also makes the worker aware of a need to learn.

Organizations, particularly supervisors, may use such opportunities to open up to the individual the need to relate his job to the big picture. The desire to learn is encouraged by helping the individual see how his tasks fit into larger activities and the goals of the organization.

The climate of the organization, as well as the work environment created by immediate supervisors, can let individuals know that effort in their self-development brings opportunities for better jobs. Effective career development programs that actualize these opportunities for individuals are strong stimulants to learning.

Successful new learning arrangements have recognized the hindrances that organizations can place in the path to productive training. The pressures of work priorities nag both managers and workers. In the midst of the push for production and profit, the order of the day is to get the job done. The commonly accepted belief is that there is not enough time to learn.

Higher level managers, confident that their ways have worked, may brush aside the utilization of newer techniques, particularly when they are suggested by subordinates. The work environment thus stifles the potential productiveness of workers. Older workers may fear that they will be embarrassed because the training may reveal their shortcomings; They often are afraid to run the risk of failure in a learning experience.

But organizations have designed newer training and learning approaches that eliminate these hindrances to growth and change.

Supervisory-Subordinate Relationship

Managers and supervisors must take into account their employees' awareness of need and desire to learn. The superior must be an active agent in relating any contemplated learning effort with his and the employee's mutually understood work objectives. We will discuss two incidents that illustrate this point in different ways.

> An organization found that it needed to provide some type of help to its work force, who were faced with the demands of an increasing amount and variety of reading materials. The training staff consulted with a

specialist at a nearby university. A program was designed primarily for those whose positions required a substantial amount of reading. A pilot course was conducted for a group composed of department directors, their deputies, and high level managers. Based on their recommendations five more courses were given. Members of the initial group were to discuss the nature of the course, its benefits, and requirements with those who were to participate in the ensuing courses.

Evaluations by the consultant-instructor and a further follow-up by the training staff with both participants and their superiors showed a strong correlation between those instances where the supervisor-employee discussions had clearly made the nature of the course understood—its benefits and requirements—and the productiveness of results. All who had dropped out had failed to have a discussion with their superior on the nature of the course and its expectations.

When a training and learning effort fails to take into account the individual's awareness of need or his desire to learn, the benefits are highly problematic. When a training program is mandated by top management without regard for the individual's awareness of his needs or his desire to learn, a deadlock often results as the following example shows:

A local government agency was required by its headquarters to test all its "material handlers" (warehousemen, stockmen, packers, tractor operators). The headquarters staff claimed that technological changes in equipment and systems had made the jobs of these men more complex. The required tests covered word meaning, numbers comparison, coding, arithmetic. Yet many of the jobs did not require proficiency in all of these areas. It could be argued that the trend towards more sophisticated systems would require men

> in the future with higher levels of verbal and mathematical abilities. But from the standpoint of both the material handlers and their superiors, the tests did not make sense. They saw no reason to check out these proficiencies. Actually no such tests were currently being required of new employees hired for these same jobs.
>
> The central agency, however, insisted, and the tests were given to nearly 1,000 material handlers, most of whom had never had experience in taking tests. Fearful and anxious as to the consequences, many of them literally froze. To make matters worse, the tests were administered by the employment staff, which further increased the workers' fears that a low score would lessen their chances of retention in case of a possible reduction in the work force.
>
> The local situation became more aggravated when the central office directed the local agency to "conduct" basic education classes for the 694 material handlers who scored below a cutoff point considered satisfactory by headquarters staff. What the central agency did not recognize was that neither the material handlers nor their bosses were aware that they needed to take "basic education" in order to perform their jobs. Changes in the work requirements had not been analyzed or defined. To make matters worse, the managers, in defense of their workers, pointed to a lack of correlation between test results and performance productivity. Work measurement and productivity records showed that some of the highest performers received low test scores and some of the poorest performers had high test scores.

When the need for knowledge becomes obvious because of work demands, most employees are willing to learn. But workers need to see the connection between what they must know to do their jobs and what they are being asked to learn. This places the burden on the supervisor to make the content of any learning experience relate to what he does in his job. Otherwise, if the knowledge is not connected with what's vital to employees, little learning or use of it may take place.

Routes for Advancement

Highly visible routes for advancement often make employees aware of their need to learn in order to participate in such programs. The desire to learn is prompted by the hope that it will help them to qualify for higher levels of work in chosen career channels.[1]

Companies have designed a number of ways to base employee advancement on their successful accomplishment of combined learning and work experiences. A key attribute of these organizations' plans is their stimulation of the individual's desire to learn and his awareness of need for self-development. (These were discussed in Chapter 5. See also Chase Manhattan's Manpower Development Case Study, Appendix, p. 249, and White Sands Cooperative Education Case Study, Appendix, p. 293.)

Participation in Learning

Organizations are designing and using strategies that involve the participants in various learning experiences which open up opportunities for them to use capacities they never realized they had. Take, for example, the organizational development sessions of the Raymond Corporation (see Appendix, p. 263) and the Internal Revenue Service (Appendix, p. 279). Participants become alert, through the study group exercises, of their need to learn how to contribute to the efforts of the other members of a work team. They experience the desire to learn and help others learn how to organize themselves, how to best set priorities, and how to seek out the best ideas. Their success in the discovery of strategies strengthens their desire to learn more.

Employees who tell other employees about a learning experience which they found worthwhile often spark the desire of the others to learn. The spirit of enthusiasm and zest for learning are contagious. Word gets around. Individuals value the testimony of their fellowmen. Considerable weight is given to how worthwhile other employees find the training. The following example illustrates the influence of employees upon other employees.

> A large government agency offered through its training department a home study course in supervision. Participation in supervisory courses held on duty time was restricted to those already holding supervisory positions. The course was related to everyone's work since it prescribed the fundamentals that managers and supervisors must use in directing the work of their people. In a three-year period, the number participating increased steadily: 25 had completed the course in the first year; 270 by the end of the third year. What was the reason for high acceptance of this course, particularly when it was completed on people's own time? Many said that its value had been communicated to them by those who had completed the course. Warehousemen, for example, learned that other warehousemen had been helped to pass an examination which made them eligible for promotion to higher level jobs. Others learned from their friends that "you don't have to be an executive to study the practices" and that it helps to "see both sides of the coin."

Adaptiveness to Individual Differences

An organization designing its training and learning processes faces an enormous challenge that educational institutions do not. It must accommodate to differences in age, occupational group, level, learning ability, and interest.

Older employees, instead of remaining in a single career for their lifetime because they see no alternative, are now actively seeking opportunities to enter and learn a new career. In times of rapid change, no one can complete an education. Learning, today, is always in order for the young, *and* the mature, *and* the senior, "each of whom is learning at the appropriate pace and with all the special advantages and disadvantages of experience peculiar to his own age."[2]

Firms have managed to work out a diversity of learning experiences to encourage different individuals and groups to develop in ways appropriate to each. Margaret Mead has on many occasions pointed up the benefits of the young and the senior learning together and from each other; then, as she says, "learning will come alive."

Successful approaches have integrated different individual needs with the achievement of organizational objectives. Although the individuals may have goals in common, these approaches recognize that each individual achieves his objectives in ways in which he can best learn and grow. Holt's description of ways that children learn is applicable to the individual worker-learner: "We cannot be made to grow in someone else's way, or even made to grow at all. We can only grow when and because we want to, for our own reasons, in whatever ways seem most interesting, exciting and helpful to us."[3]

Age, Occupational Group and Level

Every organization has men and women in different age groups as well as different occupational groups and levels. Successful strategies for productive learning focus on the special advantages of each of the different age and occupational groups.

Executive level. We tend to think of executives as having completed their cycles of experience and learning.

But in today's world where challenges arise from rapid advances in technology, the senior executive needs to continue learning, to remain open and receptive to change, not only for himself but to provide the leadership his managers need. Time-honored traditions about the need for bringing in new blood are being challenged. Where the older executives move through different positions without varying their managerial style, as though they can learn nothing new, they tend to select those like themselves, thus perpetuating not only their style but older techniques.[4]

Learning experiences that some organizations are providing for their senior executives activate management efforts to change the way of life in an entire organization. A development in the Federal Government illustrates this:

> The Federal Executive Institute is a part of the United States Civil Service Commission's training and development activities for its federal civil servants.[5] Its eight-week program, a "Residential Program in Executive Education," is held for approximately 60 top executives five times a year, using a topnotch interdisciplinary faculty in residence and supplemented by noteworthy public leaders as visiting instructors and lecturers.
>
> Emphasizing the concept of a learning community of federal executives, those planning and directing the Institute have succeeded in providing a learning experience which adapts to executive organizational interests and provides a climate for self-renewal. It is process-oriented and not aimed at the acquisition of more knowledge. A wide variety of educational methods is employed including seminars, workshops, lecture-discussions, films, and tapes. Emphasis is placed on the individual executive's making a choice of seminars and activities, recognizing that federal executives have different levels of educational attainment, background, ex-

periences, responsibilities, and thus different learning needs. The time-honored instructor-student two-way relationship gives way to that of a broader learning community.

Older instructional formulas have been replaced by new approaches which are based on the assumption that a growing and self-renewing individual will be the most effective leader. The uniqueness of the program lies in its methodology which allows individual programming of study, lectures, projects, and small groups. Attention is focused on the learning of national needs and goals that respond to society's changing problems, governmental systems, and managerial processes by which the organization can adapt to new demands.

The full benefits of this kind of experience for the top executive will not be measured for some time to come. Yet early indicators show that the lessons learned are being applied. After participation in the Federal Executive Institute, the Director of the Western Service Center of the Internal Revenue Service, has introduced and managed new ways of development to keep his organization live and productive (see Appendix, p. 279).

Senior and mature managers. Can an organization design a development program appropriate for both those at the top and those at mid- and lower-management levels? Yes. A case in point is that of the Raymond Corporation (see Appendix, p. 263). George Raymond, president of the firm, employed a behavioral science consultant with a broad background in management development to interview his firm's top executive group. After the group was confronted with an analysis and discussion of managerial styles, the group became convinced that it needed to plan a continuing program for all its people to create a climate conducive to creativity, high productivity, and a sincere commitment to corporate goals by all the people in the organization. These learning laboratories were continued for all 70 managers as well as non-supervisory personnel. The results in increased sales and growth in profit and the development of their human potential were enormous.

For the young. What of the young and inexperienced in an organization? Earlier we described a number of ways designed to bring the young into the organization by closely integrating learning and work progression. We also saw that the work-learning progression plan was adapted to help in facing the problem of obsolescence by moving into new lines of work.

In addition to helping the young become aware of their needs, programs are designed to recognize their achievements and, through approval, encourage them to persist. One means is the assignment of the young to bosses capable of planning and assigning productive developmental work. Another means involves progress reviews of work by the supervisor to whom the young have been assigned. The information that is given them on the results of their work, often called feedback, helps them to learn whether they are doing the work correctly. Still another means is that of reinforcement, which is the strengthening of action provided by some reward that follows that action. Supervisors can reinforce their subordinates in a number of ways, such as approval, recognition, rewards, or verbal praise. It provides support to the employee in continuing to achieve his goals. Knowledge of results provides awareness of progress.

Organizations are helping senior managers perform the generative task of bringing along the next generation. This helps senior men to meet their need for sharing in the growth and success of younger members of an organization, rather than feel threatened by them. Dalton and Thompson suggest the possibility of using older engineers to develop younger engineers. This, they say, requires defining the older engineers' tasks and getting them to think about their careers in new ways.[6] In Japanese industry, a similar use is made of older and highly respected men passed over for top jobs, as coaches for the young.[7]

Both Chase Manhattan's Manpower Development and White Sands' Cooperative Education (see Appendix, pp. 249 and 293) are excellent illustrations of training processes that provide encouragement and recognition to the development of the young.

Old and Young Learn Together

When the older and the younger learn together, learning comes alive. The older tend to teach the past unless they are confronted with the new ideas of the young. The younger can temper their untried ideas with the experience of the older. Just as the educational system suffers from teaching the past, so in organizations the tendency is to teach the systems that have always been followed. But the need is to unlearn as well as to learn things. Include the people who are learning with those who are teaching, then the education system will come alive. Then communication will be restored between generations.[8]

Learning Abilities

Many organizations have taken advantage of recent strides in educational technology which make it possible to accommodate training to the individual's capacity to learn. The following incident illustrates this point:

> In an effort to help supervisors in instructional skills, a training staff used an audiovisual slide-tape program which presented basic principles of how to prepare and present training. Participants saw, read,

> and responded to the lessons. Later they prepared a demonstration of how they would teach their employees in a particular operation of their work. One participant confessed that she was having difficulty comprehending the written instructions on the slides. She was able to complete the programmed part of the training because the coordinator discussed the concepts with her. Later, in a group session, participants presented what they had been able to prepare as an instructional unit based on what they had learned from the programmed material. This particular supervisor was acknowledged to be an excellent instructor. She had thoroughly grasped the principles, demonstrated her ability to teach, and particularly shown her commitment to helping her employees learn.

Enormous improvement in educational technology makes it possible for people of different abilities to acquire and apply knowledge at their own speed and in ways best suited to them, without anxiety. Individuals avoid a learning experience that might prove embarrassing, or in which they might fail, as the following example shows:

> An organization with a large number of blue collar workers wanted to help them learn basic mathematics. The use of a local junior college facility with its standardized classroom approach was not satisfactory, owing to the wide range of abilities of the participants, and their varying amounts of mathematical knowledge. Some found it difficult to keep up with the class; others considered it repetitive and boring. The use of these outside facilities also presented problems of release time from work.
>
> The training staff initiated a programmed type of mathematics course which was made available on a con-

tinuing basis in the organization. Flexibility in scheduling the course made it possible to adjust learning times to the convenience of the supervisor, the employees, and their work. Even more significant was the supportiveness of the design and the methodology which made individualized learning possible. A participant started at the point where he most needed help, e.g., decimals, fractions, or whole numbers. By taking a pre-test, the participant found the point where he lacked the necessary understanding of math, and thus was not forced to repeat those principles he understood. The participants were able to restudy concepts when they found their answers were incorrect. Before they returned to the concept which had not been clear to them, the program explained why their thinking, which had caused them to select the wrong answer, was faulty. The program used errors or failure to get the correct answer as a learning process. By freeing the employees from the fear of making mistakes, the program helped employees recognize the importance of learning from errors.

Of special interest here was the fact that the program adjusted to the differences in the individual's learning capacities. It was designed that all would learn what they needed to know with confidence gained by being successful learners. This organization learned that the use of an individualized and programmed teaching approach which adapted to a wide range of differences in worker needs and learning abilities resulted in effective learning and its application to work.

Supervisory Approval and Individual Worker Persistence

The most critical factor in helping individual workers to persist in being productive learners is the supervisory-subordinate relationship. Supervisory approval and encouragement are absolutely essential in making learning productive. Unless employees receive feedback on their performance from their supervisors that lets them know how the results of their work are evaluated, the employee lacks positive reinforcement of his work. Positive reinforcement is the strengthening of his work by approval in the form of praise, recognition, or reward. Progress reviews by supervisors inform employees about the results of their work and whether it is being done correctly.

In addition to the internal supervisory influences, training strategies use external programs as supplements to the major developmental influences on the job. A supervisor's concept of his training task in these instances is more than turning his employee over to someone else for training. The supervisor, together with his subordinate, determines what participation in an external course is expected to accomplish. The supervisor and his subordinate also will follow up on ways of applying what has been learned.

An example will illustrate the need for a process whereby supervisors guide individuals in participation in external training courses as a part of the major developmental influences on the job towards productive achievement:

> An organization set up a central Education Selection Board representing all components of that organization. Its purpose was to monitor the investment of the organization in outside training recommended by managers for their employees. The board required that the initiators of the recommendation show what they expected to accomplish, confirm the high quality of the resource to be used, and assure the board that the individual who was to receive the training had manifested efforts to direct his own development. The outside

training thus would supplement internal development. Through the board's encouragement of more careful thinking and planning in the use of outside resources, individual employees and their superiors became more selective. They also appeared before the board to report on what was learned and what they were able to use from this learning.

As a result, during the two years that this board guided the use of outside training resources, the organization built up a series of outstanding investments in quality training in new techniques, new knowledges, and new equipment that were of great help to this organization in its productiveness and in its effort to adapt to change.

When a program of external training for employees is too casual in conception or too mechanical in administration, it can result in firms or government organizations spending much time and money without productive return either for the organization or the individual. Productive learning, on the other hand, is learning that brings the individual and the organization together in attaining a common goal.

Individuals Who Lack the Desire To Learn or Develop

Can organizational designs for learning overcome the complacency and inertia of some individuals? Most people have a natural desire and ability to learn, but some do not. Some people have a tendency to become slaves to formats or procedures, pieces of equipment, and cling to the ways that things have always been done. Complacency blocks receptiveness to change and the initiative to entertain new thoughts and increase conscious adaptation to change. Individuals often point to external barriers as reasons for not changing, but many times these are excuses to defer action. Organizations cannot afford to leave to chance the persistence of individuals to learn and achieve. Designs of ongoing efforts must involve workers both as individuals and as groups in learning experiences. Thoughtful engineering of the work environment and the learning processes will provide the challenge and approval and help workers learn productively for themselves and their organizations.

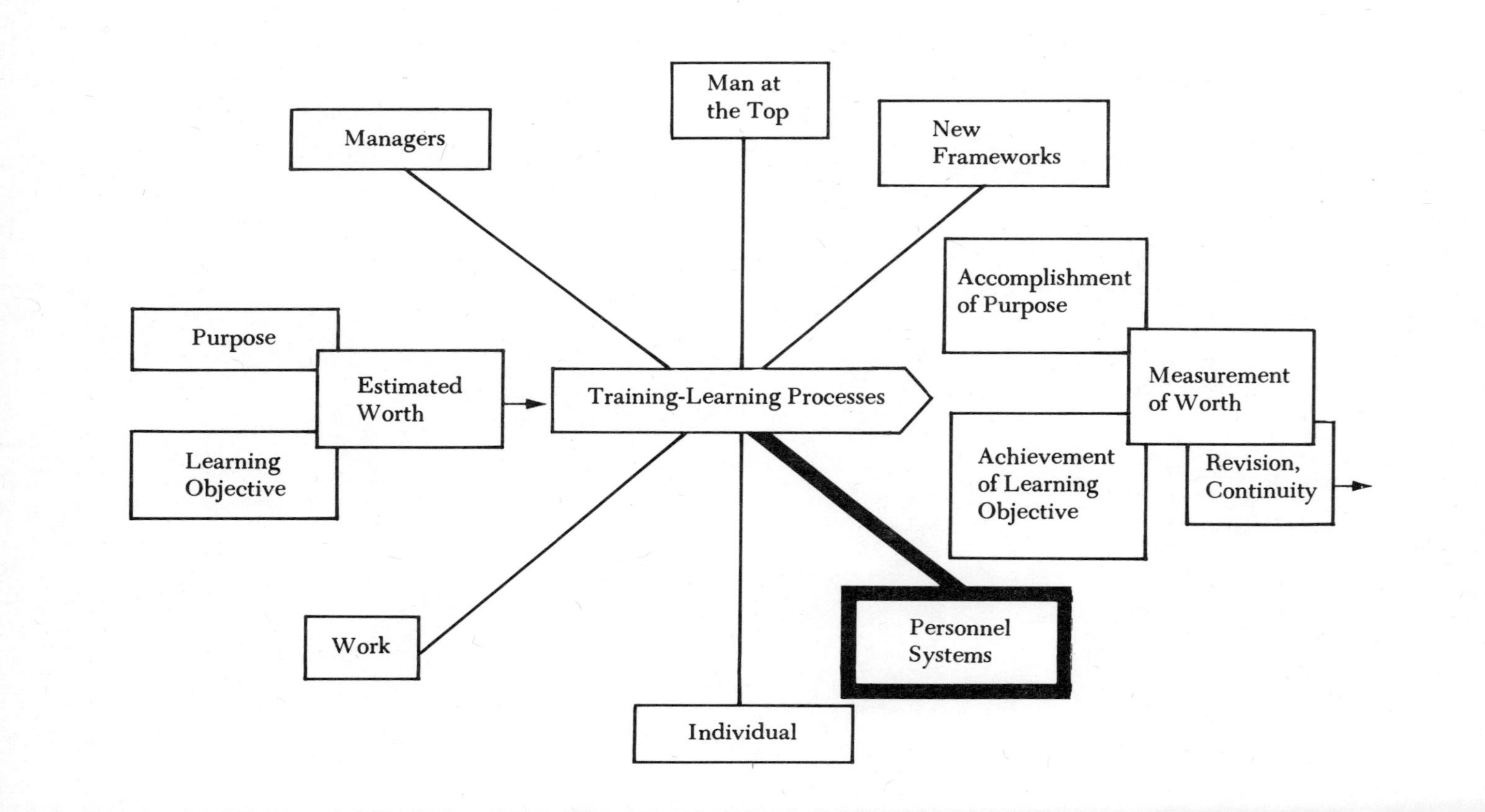

Managers
Man at the Top
New Frameworks
Purpose
Estimated Worth
Learning Objective
Training-Learning Processes
Accomplishment of Purpose
Measurement of Worth
Achievement of Learning Objective
Revision, Continuity
Work
Individual
Personnel Systems

7

Personnel Systems: New Links with Learning

The function of all personnel processes is to build and develop a competent work force. Yet personnel practices are often not evaluated as to their impact on learning and development of employees. Some personnel programs may be expedient and relatively easy to administer, but they are too narrowly conceived and too inflexible to contribute to the development of competent performers.

The management of personnel is divided between the staff functions of the personnel manager and the personnel functions of the line managers and supervisors. We pointed out in Chapter 4 that the development of subordinates is one with the whole task of managers. Here we will look at staff personnel processes and how links between them and training processes can make a significant difference in the productiveness of the learner-worker.

Essentially the staff personnel job is getting management to examine the principles and practices it uses in managing people. Hopefully this assistance and guidance will bring about improved managerial practices, including the way in which employees are helped to learn and adapt to change. This educational and developmental process must be shared by all members of the personnel office. It is not just a matter for training staff, nor is it just a matter of providing standardized forms and procedures for managers to use in the administration of personnel matters.

Personnel systems and practices must be evaluated with respect to their influence on employee growth. For example, how does the staffing and recruitment function of the personnel staff make it possible for the more capable to be identified and given assignments for growth necessary for positions of more responsibility? How do personnel specialists in the position design function make it possible for managers and supervisors to be flexible in the assignment of tasks and delegation of responsibility? How do those charged with staff assistance in performance appraisal bring about the relatedness of supervisory work performance reviews to specific achievements of employees at the time when the information can help the employee learn?

Staffing and Manpower Development

Organizations have found that, by linking their designs for the recruitment and placement of personnel with training processes, learning activities have had more productive results. Personnel seek employment with organizations that offer growth opportunities. A foundation is laid for individual growth and development when the recruitment process is linked with a tangible developmental plan.

Selection Process Is a Learnable Time

The selection process, whether it is the initial assignment of an employee to a job or the transfer, reassignment or promotion of an employee, provides the teachable moment. An employee about to take on new duties has a high degree of interest in learning how to fulfill his new responsibilities. Hence, from a psychological standpoint the indoctrination period is the time when the readiness of workers to learn is high. They are eager to make good and want to learn. The selection and placement process, including the first months of work, provides a foundation on which to build and develop competent and productive personnel. Determination of new employees' learning needs can be profitably made a part of the initial recruitment process. The induction of new employees can then be appropriately adapted to what they need to know to perform their work. An incident illustrates benefits gained from training provided at the time of initial employment:

> A procurement department had hired twelve new clerks in order to carry out a newly added purchasing function. During the interviews, the manager of the purchasing division realized that these new hires needed to learn various forms and procedures required in processing purchases. After conferring with the training staff, he decided that a week's training off the job should be provided before the new employees were placed in operations, since the department had no ongoing program, nor did its supervisors have the capability of training twelve new clerks all at once.
>
> The training staff helped two experienced purchasing technicians plan group instruction alternated with periods in which the new clerks could practice the preparation of each type of document. The senior purchasing technicians in charge of the instruction inspected the work of their trainees and let them know how well they were doing. They provided them plenty of opportunities to get help and have their questions answered. The supervisors of the newly trained clerks

> came to the class to get acquainted with them. Despite the crash nature of the training, the high morale and enthusiasm of both instructors and clerks resulted in the rapid assimilation of materials. The trainees said they had "a chance to learn without pressure or fear that their initial mistakes would be costly to the company." Freedom from anxiety as to errors that "would be held against me" gave impetus to the learning. The learning process was strengthened by the lessening of fear and the quality of guidance from instructors who "knew their business." The new clerks made a smooth transition to their work in the purchasing operations. According to the manager and his supervisors, a follow-up of their progress during the first several months of actual work showed very productive results.

The critical factor in this case was the timing of instruction—the result of the coordinated action of the manager and his supervisors together with the employment and training staff of the personnel office. Although the training was hastily devised and not a designed "course" in the usual sense of the word, it came at the time when the new clerks needed and wanted the help.

Selection Based on Genuine Evidence of Accomplishment

The basis on which selection for reassignment, transfer and promotion is made influences the learning and growth processes. Individuals find learning worth the effort when it is related to what is vital to them. When their effort to learn has resulted in the successful fulfillment of their responsibilities, the selection process must be capable of identifying and transferring them into different and more complex assignments, eventually providing promotion to higher level and more responsible positions. Otherwise, employees receive no practical recognition of their demonstrated efforts.

And they are not encouraged and tend not to see the worth of persisting in efforts to learn and apply their learning productively.

Selection processes that overemphasize educational achievement may hamper genuine development and growth. Some systems for identifying those who are to be promoted may be linked—or so the personnel staff believes—to the crediting of training and educational achievement. But often these systems focus on the acquisition of course completion records and the accumulation of credits or hours in certain subject matter areas. Such systems are not genuinely linked with the developmental process, for they may fail to identify the more outstanding performers. The system needs to recognize the actual demonstration of the workers' ability to integrate learning with productive work. The criteria are not how many degrees, courses, units, credits and the like, but rather: *Did the added skills and knowledge contribute to better performance?* Courses are not ends in themselves, but supplement the developmental influence on the job. An actual situation is cited here:

> A government agency set up a procedure for ranking candidates for promotion. As part of this system it included the ranking of employees under four levels of educational achievement: A—bachelor's degree; B—relatively thorough or recent pattern of self-development through formal education above high school; C—high school graduation; D—less than high school graduation.
>
> The B level became highly controversial. Employees anxious to be put in that category scrounged to find every scrap of evidence that they thought could be counted. Fruitless hours, too, were required of those "evaluating" these claims which could be interpreted in many ways. Employees became disgruntled if their ef-

forts to "prove" their claims did not succeed in giving them the competitive edge in promotion they desired.

The result of this ranking procedure, even when the records were finally straightened out, was certainly not the goal which the training and development staff had been trying to achieve: the facilitation of individual self-development as a means of incorporating and strengthening the worker's performance.

Opening Up Routes for Advancement

When firms have designed processes which incorporate training with systematic job progression and advancement, the results are productive for both the organization and the individual. The traditional notion of long years of experience providing the best qualification for advancement is now being questioned. Jennings says that the "old formulas practiced during the first half of the century" are being questioned both by "men who wanted faster routes to the top" and by "corporations needing a systematic speedup in the development of highly talented executives."[1] The most critical process to organizations today is the integration of knowledge with work operations. This places a premium both on successful ways of applying knowledge to work and on systems that link advancement with learning progression.

A healthy interest in learning is stimulated when people in an organization *know they are able to move ahead, with the full support and encouragement of their own bosses.* The example of people moving into more responsible jobs is much more stimulating and real to employees than policy statements that speak to equal opportunities for members of an organization to compete for promotion. In one firm, for example, supervisors repeatedly helped their employees develop so that they might be reassigned or promoted to more responsible positions. Employees in that firm said, "The effort to learn is really worth it." And in another organization where supervisors encouraged employees to apply for promotional opportunities and readily made them available through willingness to release them, the employees said, "You know they'll give you a chance for the openings when you show you're serious about learning and using what you know." In another organization, where there was a lack of clear promotion policies or practices, one employee echoed the feelings of many when he said, "Why not let people know what you get promoted for? If it's not clear how you get promoted then you begin to wonder why learn the job."

Personnel systems not only fail to clarify routes for advancement, they also fail to recognize those who have made the effort. The following incident illustrates this point:

> A suggestion had been adopted by a personnel office which recommended that medical terminology training be provided for clerk-secretaries to enable them to be promoted to medical secretary jobs which not only paid better salaries but also led to further advancement. The training officer secured a qualified instructor and arranged for the staffing specialist of the personnel office to outline the knowledge and skill requirements of the entry level medical-secretarial job. The instructor designed the course to provide the required qualifications.
>
> The course was outstanding, and participants demonstrated high achievement throughout the year. Later several of the course graduates applied for vacancies in medical-secretarial jobs. Although hospital managers were interested in the newly trained applicants, the staffing specialist ruled that these applicants lacked the actual experience required. This, of course, represented a change in policy of the personnel office from the previous year, and came as a blow to the secretaries

who had understood that by completion of this course they could establish their eligibility for advancement to the medical secretary jobs. Neither the training officer nor the instructor were able to persuade the staffing branch of the personnel office that these graduates were competent to perform the jobs. The secretaries who had spent a year of considerable after-hours training and study in the medical terminology field were frustrated. Training technicians were discouraged in their efforts to provide upward mobility for clerk-secretaries with demonstrated performance records and the addition of the technical training in the medical terminology field.

Incorporating Training Progression with Personnel Mobility

Some firms are now linking their designs for job progression with training progression. When the employee demonstrates his competence by successful application of what he has learned through the training process, he does move progressively to new tasks which in turn demand learning and its application. When Chase Manhattan sought to improve its career development and training efforts, it designed a system which enabled employees to advance to a new job when and if they demonstrated they had learned, and effectively applied what they had learned to their current job. Advancement was contingent upon demonstrated learning progression. (See Appendix, p. 249).

The work-learning progression plans of an organization were discussed in Chapter 5, p. 77; these plans linked job design, training-learning process design, and qualifications for personnel advancement with the accomplishment of work. The redesign of jobs provided the routes for advancement from the less complex to jobs requiring more responsibility and judgment. The actual advancement of the employee requires evidence of demonstrated competence in both learning and making practical application of knowledge and skill to the job. This strengthens the function of training and the contribution it can make to a productive work force. Research has shown that taking on help merely to meet immediate vacancies weakens the function of training.[2]

Career Development

Career development programs in government and industry that seek more systematic advancement for executives, managers, career interns, minorities and women stress the importance of job mobility. But mobility can be of benefit to the organization and to the employee only when it is based on the employee having demonstrated competence to move and ability to apply what he has learned to operations. Such career development plans must be incorporated with other personnel processes, as well as that of staffing.

Job Design and Position Descriptions

The personnel staff function of job design and preparation of position descriptions is to assist managers in their assignment and delegation of work responsibilities. This function then is to help clarify to employees what their responsibilities are and also to provide a basis for the equitable payment of salaries and wages for different levels and kinds of work.

We have already learned that the way a manager assigns and delegates work to his subordinates can be a powerful element in his development of subordinates. But the question persists as to whether the procedures for the preparation of position descriptions truly contribute to the goal of productive behavior of employees. Some position description systems seem designed more to fit the criteria of administrative convenience and control purposes. Although job descriptions may give management the feeling that everyone knows what he is supposed to do, this may be a false assumption. The system probably did provide a sort of systematic way to standardize on paper the classification of jobs as well as provide the basis for standardization of job methods. But under rapidly changing conditions that demand continual adaptation, job descriptions can become straitjackets and can have a negative influence on the development of people. The situation described below reveals how the rigidity of the job structure system immobilized development:

> The Comptroller Division of a small organization had six jobs: the comptroller, a deputy comptroller, a budget analyst, and three clerical positions. All work required of the comptroller division was divided between these jobs according to their level of responsibility and complexity. When one of the lower level clerk jobs became vacant, a young, capable student was selected, a recent graduate from a business college. Although she had done no budget work, she showed potential as well as a definite interest in this field. The comptroller, whose attention had been called to her ability and interest, asked for help from the training staff to prepare a training plan. The training representative, aware of previous negative decisions from position analysts on similar proposals for internal development, suggested a meeting of the comptroller, the staffing specialist, the position analyst, and himself.
>
> Neither the staffing specialist nor the position analyst would agree to a developmental plan for training the new hire to do higher level budget work. She could not qualify for the higher level job unless she were assigned the higher level duties. For this purpose

she would have to be relieved of her clerical duties. They argued that this would be impossible since they had no authorization to set up another clerical job to handle the duties she was now performing. And if she were assigned higher level duties they could not recognize her promotion by establishing a higher level job for her unless they took duties away from the higher level positions already established. It seemed there was a fixed amount of work at fixed levels; there was no flexibility, no place for her to go, and nothing for which she could be trained. The plan for helping the individual to learn and advance in the budget field was abandoned.

We saw, however, in Chapter 5 that firms have found alternative ways of designing jobs in more flexible structures. The rigidity of job descriptions has been replaced by incorporating expansion links between more simple and more complex tasks and between less and more responsible jobs. These innovations have fostered the growth and development of employees.

Performance Appraisals

Organizations have found that performance appraisals correctly used in timely ways can positively influence the employee's desire to learn and his persistence to achieve. But its success as a positive influence depends upon its being linked with the achievement of work goals. Organizations have learned that supervisory feedback to employees on their work progress is a learning experience both for the supervisor and the employee. The supervisor is required to look at his own objectives in order to make reviews of work progress with his subordinate. He also learns where he stands with respect to accomplishment of his own work priorities. The feedback he provides his employee helps that employee learn what he is doing correctly and strengthens his interest in continued achievement.

An illustration of the productive results of supervisory feedback (i.e., information supplied by the supervisor to the employee concerning performance of work) is contained in the following incidents:

> A computer systems analyst, working on a combined work/learning progression plan, commented that "the worthwhile elements were putting the training to actual use on the job, using the know-how from the lesson sessions, and learning from my supervisor the ways that I could improve. In fact, I think my most productive learning came from understanding his appraisals of my progress and his continual effort to point out what was happening, and what I needed to do to perfect my part of the projects."

Where there was a lack of feedback on performance, the employee felt it to be a constraint on his productivity:

> A junior management analyst found that, although he was being given added and more difficult responsibilities, he had more need for review of his work by his supervisor. "I find myself at a loss for critical insight into what I am doing. I feel that I could learn better if I were given some concrete information on what either my supervisor or management thinks of the quality of the surveys I've completed. I'm sure there must be ways that they could be improved and have a greater impact. But I feel I'm coasting along and not making progress."

Performance appraisals, when used to give encouragement and approval to ongoing work of subordinates, are a part of the basic developmental and training process. Workers learn most by seeing the progress they are making. McGregor said some time ago: "People do learn and change as a result of feedback. In fact, it is the only way they learn."[3] It requires the personnel system to design links between the training and performance appraisal processes. We have discussed the example of Chase Manhattan Bank's Manpower Development in which the performance appraisal process was closely linked with the training, application of learning to the job, and advancement to the next phase of the career. The integrated use of periodic performance feedback to trainees as part of the work-learning job progression plan is described in Chapter 8.

Performance appraisals in their more traditional forms and processes do little to encourage growth and development; in fact, research shows the opposite to be the case.[4] Appraisals tend to fall into the rut of administrative processes, and it is not unusual, even where the procedure requires discussion between supervisor and subordinate, to find that communication breaks down in the area of feedback information on performance.

The negative effects of performance evaluation systems were noted recently in a survey by Professors Dalton and Thompson. The rigidity of performance appraisal systems is shown to be contributing to the obsolescence of engineers occurring at an increasingly early age in technology-based companies.[5] Expedient for the firms, they have negative effects on older engineers who are at the lower level of the performance ratings. This does not strengthen the confidence of the older engineer or his ability to learn. It may indicate the need for giving interesting and challenging new assignments to the older men, according to Professors Dalton and Thompson. New kinds of personnel appraisals are being suggested that would place more responsibility on management to use a man well, to be aware of the direction of his contributions, and when or if the contributions are declining. To help him counter this decline in contributions, management can assist the older engineer to do what is best for his own growth.[6] Part of this problem may be caused by a situation which forces an employee to remain with the firm in order to receive his pension from it.

Seniority, Pensions, Retirement

There are other parts of the personnel systems that have definite impacts on the learning and development of personnel such as various types of security afforded through retirement, pensions, and seniority for job retention. Workers are often reluctant to take steps that could upset or threaten their "investment" in pension rights, grade or rank even when they recognize the worth of opportunities for updating themselves.

Obsolescence

The problem of obsolescence of workers is partially solved by providing continuing learning opportunities such as training as an integral part of work, formal company training, or sabbaticals off the job. The problem, however, has more complex relationships, such as performance systems, technological obsolescence, and age. The recent survey by Dalton and Thompson found that certain factors contributing to the accelerating obsolescence of engineers were: the increasing rate of technological change; psychological changes resulting from dull assignments; being passed over for promotion, and a "what the heck" attitude; pessimism as to the results, even if they did an outstanding job; the failure of evaluation systems to reflect the individual's actual contributions; and the relative immobility of older engineers.[7]

These authors found a number of answers to the problem of accelerated obsolescence that are pertinent to our discussion of the need for personnel practices that are positive influences on productive learning:

1. Continuing education, provided that it is not

limited to the taking of courses. Evidence showed that engineers over forty years of age, taking company-sponsored courses, were the ones whose ratings declined. Creative new ways of integrating the updating into integral parts of the work are needed; it is not enough to say "get some refresher courses."

2. Better management practices, such as job assignments that require older men to use new technology.

3. Better performance evaluation systems that give positive reinforcement.

4. Portable pensions that make it possible for older engineers who are discouraged in their present positions to move to other jobs and not lose their pension benefits. This would also lessen the company's reluctance to take on older engineers because of the cost of their pensions.

5. Redefinition of roles for older workers. It is suggested that both individuals and organizations need to assess periodically the growth and productivity of an individual worker in his field. The counseling aid of an organization can provide thinking about careers in new ways, and provide developmental tasks for older people. The assignment of older experienced men as coaches and sponsors for younger men provides a generative role. Others have advocated this role which allows senior men to meet developmental and participative needs through coaching and helping younger people, but not necessarily supervising them.[8]

Retraining and Seniority

The problem of training workers to move into new lines of work when their jobs are becoming obsolescent is influenced by many factors. An analysis of a Xerox Retraining Program found that the major constraint was employee concern about the impact of a move on their seniority and pay.[9]

Xerox designed and carried out a retraining program to meet the needs of workers made obsolescent by the company's increased production of copying machines and decreased paper manufactures. The critical factor was the lack of clarification and understanding of seniority and pay, which should have been provided during the orientation phase. The disappointment and frustration of those who had chosen to enter the retraining and replacement program was enormous when they found they had lost their seniority and that their wages were considerably lower. They had been told that if they did not go into retraining their security would be affected. Yet they found that those who had done nothing simply remained in their old jobs and retained their seniority and their wages.

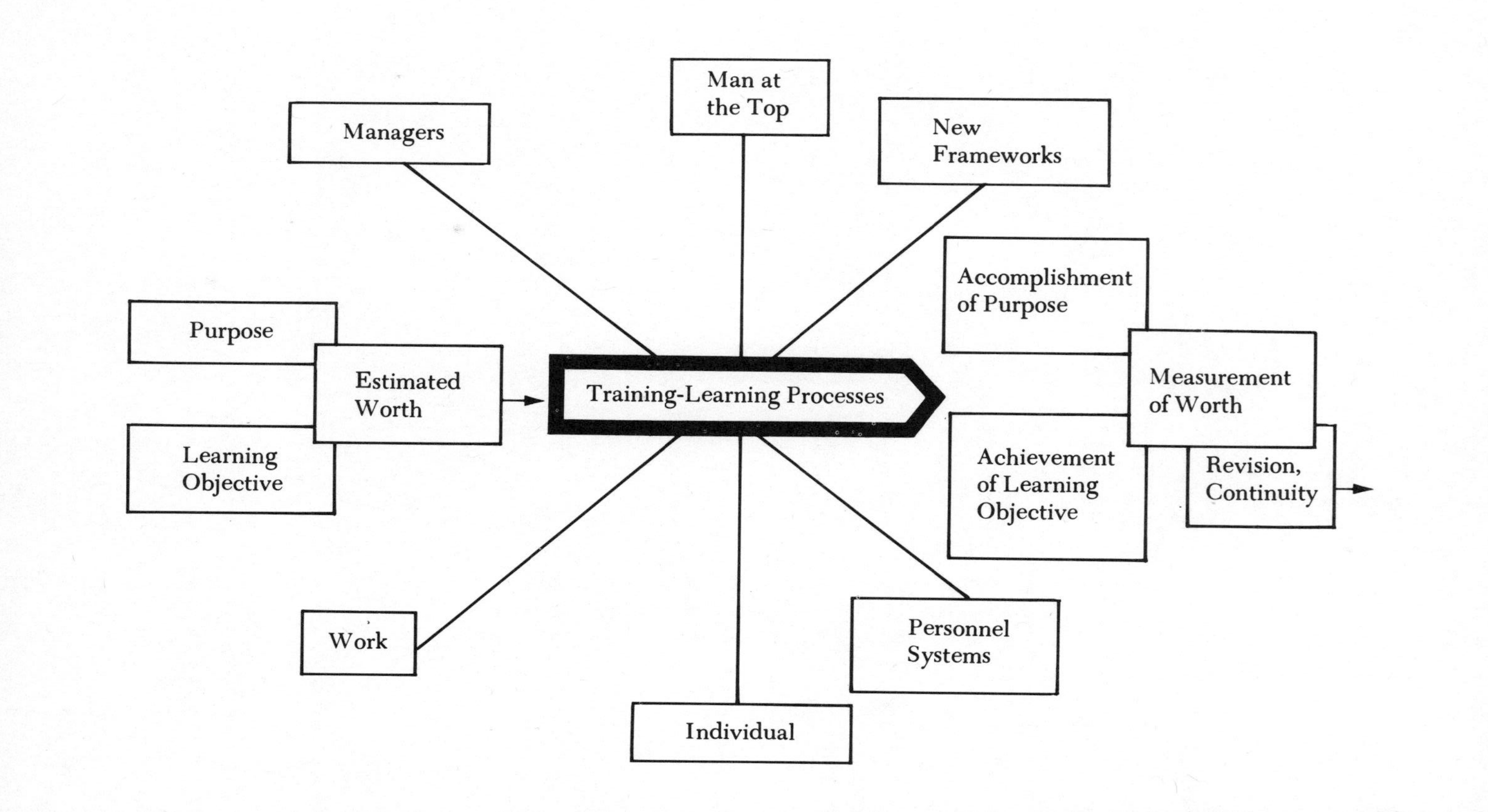
Managers
Man at the Top
New Frameworks
Purpose
Estimated Worth
Learning Objective
Training-Learning Processes
Accomplishment of Purpose
Measurement of Worth
Achievement of Learning Objective
Revision, Continuity
Work
Individual
Personnel Systems

8

New Patterns for Learning

The learning processes which have brought productive results constitute a whole new approach to training within organizational life. The approach is structured enough to make sure that workers learn what is needed in order to effectively accomplish their work goals. Yet it is sufficiently flexible and individualized that workers can direct and control their own learning in ways and at a pace they can best learn and use what they've learned. Concrete learning interrelated with real work operations is a means to an end. Learning functions naturally as a part of the whole action.

The focus of previous chapters has been the forces of the organization's *environment* that enhance or block learning. We will turn here to the training-learning *process* itself and look closely at four patterns that have been an enormous help to organizations and their people in achieving fuller use of their capacities.

Attributes of Training Processes

What are the qualities of these new patterns of learning which organizations have found are successful in meeting their needs?

1. These training processes are structured in ways that *utilize man's ability to learn by linking it with action,* and at the same time lifting the quality of learning. The focus is not on acquiring more information but in gaining *greater depth of understanding* through the *utilization of knowledge* to handle new situations and find solutions to different problems.
2. The training processes are based on the fact that *development cannot be forced on the individual.* It must come from the individual's desire to learn and his persistence to achieve.
3. These training processes *function in order to achieve the purpose for which they were established.* The basis for selecting the curriculum, methods, materials and instructors is how effective they will be in accomplishing the objective for which the learning experience was established.
4. The process *integrates training and learning with action* needed to achieve the solution of a problem *critical* to the organization and its work force.

As a result, the training processes provide learning experiences different from traditional approaches. They have proven themselves more effective in bringing about the utilization of new ideas and new concepts of the work. The four patterns of the training-learning process to be discussed here are: individualized work learning progression plans, group problem solving, collaborative instruction, and day-to-day development on the job. These are not mutually exclusive and in fact enhance each other.

The way the newer training and learning processes are structured makes a difference in the spirit with which managers and employees enter into the work and learning efforts, devote energy and thought to them and make them productive. The major characteristics they hold in common are:

1. *Objective.* There is a feeling of real purpose in these processes because they are geared to the attainment of an objective. The objective itself is part of a critical need, such as action to solve a problem, implement a new system, build a cadre of trained manpower. This means that the work objective must be translated into learning objectives: what employees and the organization need to learn in order to accomplish the objective.

2. *Curriculum.* The content of these processes is adapted to the function they serve. Since the process grows out of needs, its content must help the individual learn what he needs to know. Thus, what employees are learning is vital to them and closely related to their work.

3. *Instructional procedures.* Instead of a single course, these learning processes make use of a combination of techniques, methods, and instruments. These are selected for their appropriateness to achieve the objective, for the ease and adaptability with which they can be incorporated with work, and for their learning effectiveness. The emphasis is on learning by doing, accompanied by feedback to the learner on his progress.

4. *Sequence.* The sequence and timing of the learning experiences are flexible and adapt to the worker-learner's direction of the learning process to what he needs to learn at the time he most needs it.

5. *Instructors.* In all of these processes, the responsibility for instruction is shared by members of the organization such as supervisors, coaches, managers, technical ex-

perts, instructors, training specialists and the employees themselves. It is more a matter of what instructors do *for* the worker-learners than what they teach *to* them. The tasks of instruction include analysis of needs, translation of needs into learning and work objectives, design and preparation of learning and training experiences, presentation of courses, guidance, evaluation and feedback to the learner-workers. The major concern is guidance to help employees learn so that they may accomplish their responsibilities.

Individualized Work-Learning Progression

Work-learning progression plans provide workers with *both* the training that qualifies them for advancement to higher level jobs *and* definite advancement steps to higher level jobs. The purpose of such plans is usually to provide better trained personnel, to meet the organization's needs for certain skills, to open up channels of internal advancement to employees, or to cut down on turnover of personnel. The two most significant features of such plans are: (1) advancement is dependent upon having successfully applied the learning in competent performance, and (2) employees contribute to production while they are learning the work.

The training plan covers progression from an entry level to a target job, with varying number of interim jobs. We will use the term "trainee" although it could mean an intern, a cooperative student worker, a worker-trainee, or any number of work-study students or employees. In essence, the "trainee" learns in order to demonstrate that he is able to fulfill responsibilities, and he is eligible to be advanced to the next level when he successfully demonstrates that he meets the qualifications of the next higher job level.

Individualized Work-Learning Progression

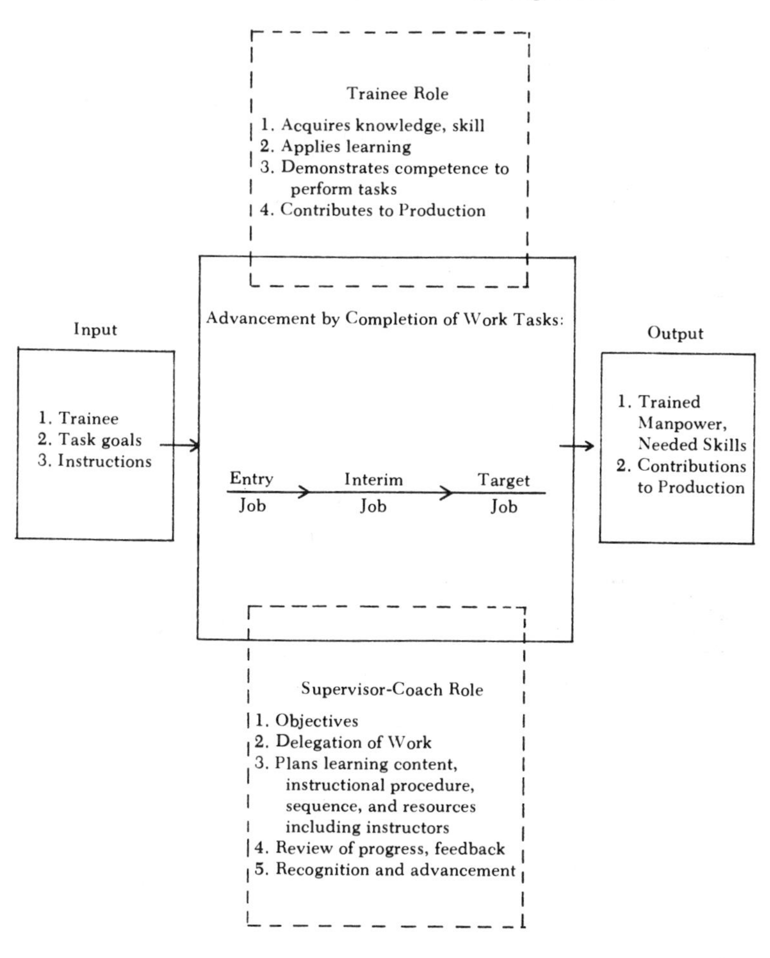

We use the word "supervisor" broadly here, for there are different levels of supervision involved, and the term covers the role of managers, coaches, key trainers and others. The supervisor with the help of organization, personnel, and training staff prepares a plan for work learning progression. To do this, he needs to understand and be able to:

1. analyze job requirements and translate these into behavior objectives which assist the trainee in seeing what he will be doing when he is performing the job satisfactorily;
2. delegate responsibility to the trainee for achievement of the work tasks;
3. organize the work and instructions on the work in learnable units, specifying the curriculum, instructional procedures, sequence, instructors, supplementary resources such as reading, guidance materials, courses;
4. control the input of work and instructions as to type and amount;
5. observe the output, correct, provide feedback, help trainee maintain confidence;
6. recommend trainee for advancement when performance shows he is qualified for the next higher level job.

Work-learning progression plans bring meaning to the trainee, quicken and strengthen the learning, as well as utilizing it in productive activities on the job.

Objectives

The starting point for this training process is a statement of behavioral objectives. When objectives are clearly stated and understood, trainees see what is required for advancement to a higher level and direct efforts to acquire the necessary skills and knowledge, demonstrating their application in acceptable performance.[1]

The objectives require that the trainee demonstrate that he can use and apply knowledge. Take, for example, the behavioral objective of an intern in the Computer Systems Analyst field. One of the objectives for which he had to demonstrate capability to perform in order to advance to the next higher grade was to be able to design an ADP system:

1. to write preliminary systems;
2. design document test procedures and operating philosophy;
3. establish system data standards;
4. create design specifications for systems;
5. prepare systems test plans;
6. prepare preliminary systems design document;
7. develop functional test requirements.

The clarity with which the objectives are described and the independence allowed the trainee to direct his own work and study encourage trainee progress. As one trainee remarked, "I've been able to work with more confidence and less supervision because I've been given the opportunity to program my own work toward the objectives of this training." Sometimes trainees are not given the benefit of clear explanations of their objectives and are at a loss to know how best to direct their efforts. According to one trainee, "The training objectives could have been more clearly and completely defined before the training began. By the time I realized what the objectives were, I had wasted a lot of time and effort."

When organizations—particularly the managers in charge of trainees—neglect to outline specific objectives, they fail to give the trainee a clear picture of what he must learn and be able to do. Schein found this failure a crucial point in his appraisal of why college grads leave their first jobs.[2] His study followed college graduates from M.I.T.'s Alfred P. Sloan School of Management into their early career years. He found employers and the college intern do not understand each other's needs and consequently fail to establish mutually agreed upon objectives. The college graduate, he says, enters the organization with the understanding that he is being counted on to bring fresh points of view and new management techniques into the organization. He usually finds, however, that he is expected to put his "concepts into deep freeze and develop the sort of ad hoc wisdom which he was taught to avoid at school."

Curriculum

The subject matter to be studied is not content in the conventional sense of the word but rather studying the task or project to be accomplished. However, the process requires the trainee to do—rather than passively to read about—the task. There are normally instructions, such as written and oral presentations of the task, and background materials, such as organizational and functional charts, policies and procedures related to accomplishment of the task, and guidance materials. Since this content is vital and usable, the trainee is interested and learns well.

The supervisor amplifies the relationships of tasks to the total job by discussions, explanations, and examples. The trainee is helped to grasp general principles and to see the smaller task in the context of the total job. This stimulates learning, encourages understanding and insight, and helps retention. One trainee said that the review by his supervisor of the plan gave him an "excellent idea of what my job will consist. Since I have a detailed guide on the skills I need to acquire, I look forward with confidence to the coming training and work."

In this process, the "content" of what is being learned extends to and includes application of learning. The trainee fits learning into productive action. "Content" in this sense both stimulates and reinforces the worker. One trainee said,

"Being able to apply the knowledge I've acquired on programming was the challenge. This was the most difficult and most valuable way of learning." And another felt that his rate of actual achievement on the job was in direct relation to the early opportunity for applied programming: "It reinforced my feeling of progress."

Instructional Procedures

The training process in work-learning progression plans uses many methods and media, but the primary method is learning by doing, accompanied by feedback information from the supervisor or coach. Work tasks are delegated by the superior to the trainee, who thus has the opportunity to demonstrate what he can learn to do.

One trainee found that learning and work interact with beneficial consequences to both. He said, "I find that as I acquire new skills I am able to learn faster, and understand more completely. Hence a momentun is gathering which allows me to assume duties of increasing responsibility. This in turn makes my work more interesting and challenging." And another remarked, "Actual participation in the full budget cycle, from the receipt of dollar guidance to final programming, provides an understanding of the fiscal process not readily available elsewhere." Still another trainee said that "the experience which helped me become competent in doing the work helped me to understand the function." A further comment was: "What I actually did with the knowledge was what helped me to understand how it all fit together."

How did the trainees learn? The primary ways were: (1) delegation of work projects—the challenge; and (2) feedback and review of progress—reinforcement and approval. One trainee found that "the projects for which I've been given responsibility are what help me find out what I'm really able to do. My supervisor helps me and so do other people in the branch. I knew pretty well what I had to read and then I asked lots of questions, and my supervisor let me know when I was getting off the track. Two courses that I took were a help, primarily in figuring some of the things out that I was doing and also because they came before a more difficult assignment."

Feedback lets the trainee know whether he is performing his projects correctly and is the most important way of learning. The trainee may receive information on the results of his work in any one of several ways—oral progress review, written evaluation, testing; it may be the acceptance and approval of a completed piece of work that helps him to know and see the progress he is making. As one trainee said, "It made all the difference in the world when I saw the position analysis I had done, approved by my supervisor and signed by myself." The trainee in this process also learns when his work is incorrect, why it is incorrect, and is encouraged to continue by applying the correct concept. The process uses failures as a way of learning.

Some trainees indicated the value of *testing themselves* on what they had learned. One said that on weekends he was placed in charge of the computer runs and found that he could test his abilities through this responsibility and self-reliance. But not all supervisors really delegated projects that helped trainees find out their capabilities. Some on-the-job training consisted merely of small "bits of work." Although the bits were part of the larger activity, the trainee was unable to see how they fit into the total job.

Where the training process provides trainee control of learning experience, the trainee learns more effectively and faster. This bears out Mager's finding on learner-controlled instruction with a group of newly hired engineers for the Tube Division of an electronics firm.[3] Six months had been required to bridge the gap between college training and meeting the job requirements. The first experimental group were given control over their curriculum and completed their training in three months. The second experimental group were given detailed behavioral objectives in addition to curriculum control and completed the course in seven and a half weeks.

Flexibility of Sequence

Sequence of learning experiences and their timing are adaptable to the task at hand, the trainee's needs, and the time demands of the job. Training is provided at the time when—from a psychological standpoint—the trainee is ready for it. This avoids forcing a trainee to attempt to learn what he cannot yet grasp. As one trainee commented, "I took the procurement course and did very well. The timing of that course was excellent. Earlier I would not have known enough to gain full benefit from it." Trainees said that "where there was planned use soon after a course was completed, there was continued growth and learning on the job."

When plans were rigidly adhered to without consideration of trainees' need for additional time on a project, a feeling of frustration resulted. As one said, "Too tight a control left me without sufficient time in each unit to which I was rotated. I needed to feel that at least I had completed a few tasks or projects." Also, delayed participation in a related learning experience was found boring and repetitious. As one said, "Making me take the recommended course at this late date was really a waste of time. There was very little new that I had not already learned by experience on the job."

Instructors

Instruction—in this process—is a team effort, which combines the talents of managers, supervisors, coaches, trainers, and technicians. The trainee is the learner and the instructional team provides guidance and support. The supervisor is a manager of the process and a manager of resources: he analyzes job requirements and translates these into behavioral objectives, delegates responsibility for fulfillment of the tasks, structures the work and learning experiences, discusses work targets with the trainee, makes progress reviews, and analyzes performance and recognizes trainee progress. The training staff helps the supervisor understand the principles of design and activation of this kind of learning process, suggests ways of providing reinforcement and feedback, and helps in locating and providing resources such as courses, programmed instruction, audiovisual materials, and guides.

Qualities of the instructors are as much of the heart as of the intellect, appealing to the workers' feelings as well as their minds. The ability to relate learning to concrete things and to operations brings warmth, appeal, and vitality to the experiences. This stirs the spirit of the workers, making them feel the spark of the instructors' and coaches' interest and enthusiasm.

The ability of the supervisor-coach and his willingness to assist the trainee make a great difference in the success of this process. One trainee said, "Mr. ——'s interest in my work, his encouragement of learning and discussing ways we can use these ideas really motivates me to work for him. He makes me feel a definite part of the organization." Another trainee put it this way, "My supervisor opens up new vistas of what I can accomplish, shows me how I can be a part of new situations—and thus I progress." Another trainee said that when his supervisor asked him to report on any ideas from his course that could be incorporated in the work in their office, he found himself making an effort to think in terms of converting ideas into his job practices.

Those involved in instructional activities learned to prepare and present learning experiences; they also updated their own knowledge. They were helped to break away from ways in which they had been taught and were stimulated to embark on experimental ways. Learners were included with instructors. The older had to unlearn as well as learn many things in order to help others learn. This spirit of concern for the development of others makes learning come alive.

Productive Payoff

These work-learning progression plans were productive in many ways. In one trainee program, 144 men and women learned the jobs of computer programmer, computer operator, systems analyst, methods engineer, management analyst, and inventory technician. At the same time that they learned these target jobs, they contributed to the productivity of the organization. Over 80 percent of the cooperative students completing the program at White Sands were employed as scientists and engineers. This contribution to the manpower needs of that organization is in addition to the productive work contributed by the yearly number of cooperative students (ranging from 88 to 200 a year). Chase Manhattan Bank lowered its turnover rates and increased its development rates, with an average of 174 trainees completing their programs in the first few years and over 100 more in the process of being trained.

Higher levels of competence were reached in less training time. Managerial practices were strengthened. Communications were opened up laterally and vertically in areas where these plans operated.

Group Problem Solving

Essential to organizational development is the training process which makes it possible for people to learn to work together in groups. Although we tend to think of workers as individuals, yet organizations accomplish work targets through work teams. Beckhard describes teams as being

Group Problem Solving

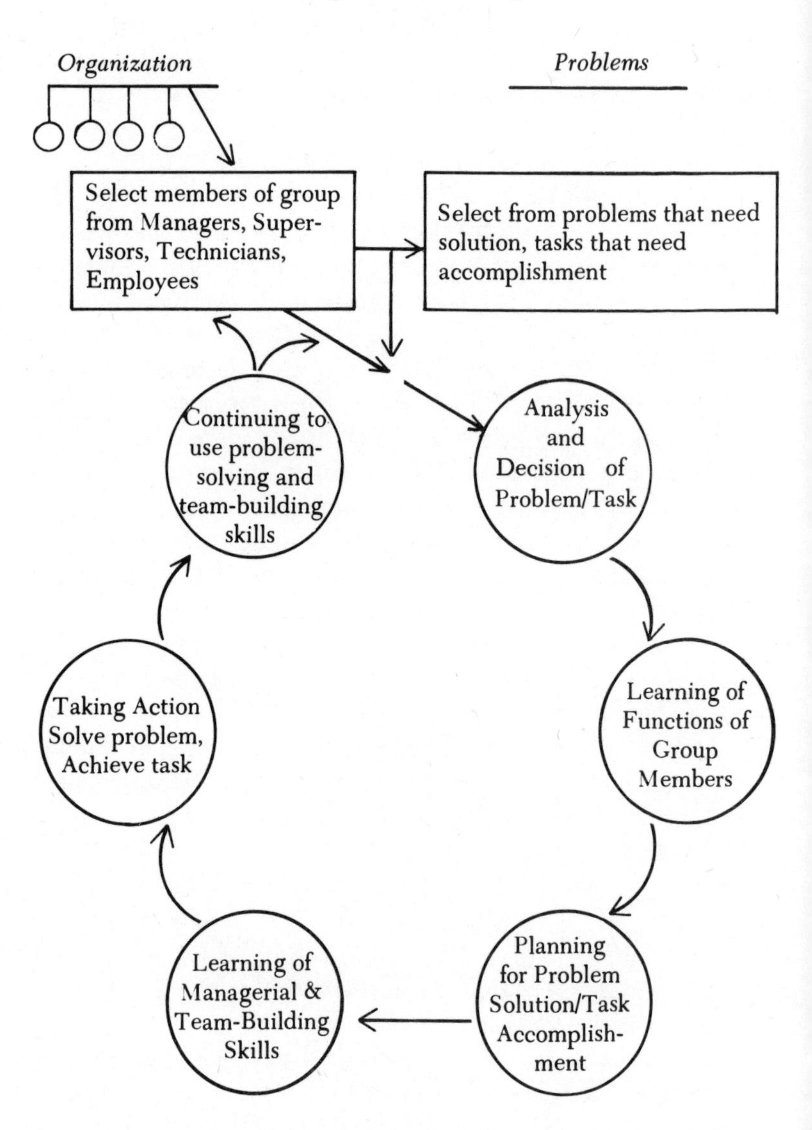

"family" teams—the boss and his subordinates—or project teams with members from a variety of functions brought together for a specific objective, or colleagues such as division directors of an agency, or technical teams such as quality control groups.[4] Often there are start-up teams in new enterprises, and from another perspective there is the top management team.

Such groups, not individuals, are the basic units of change. In an effort to bring about change, the training process is basic when the objective is to help groups learn to work together more effectively through: (1) improving working relationships and team techniques; and (2) accomplishing a task, such as the solution of a problem. Such processes integrate training with the necessary action to solve a problem critical to the organization.

We discuss several variations of this kind of training process in the Appendix. Although these examples differ in detail, we will generalize the steps in the training process from their main features.

Objectives

The objectives of this process are to:

1. Give workers the opportunity to learn by actual experience the problems of management.
2. Solve a specific problem or situation that impedes the effectiveness of the organization.
3. Make fuller use of the know-how and resources of group members.
4. Open channels upward and downward as well as horizontally between parts of the organization.
5. Encourage learning by doing and risk-taking.

Curriculum

Emphasis in this training process is placed on the action-research efforts to accomplish the group's task or solve its problem, and to learn specific skills, abilities, and knowledge needed for organizational development efforts. Thus the content includes: problem-solving knowledge and skills, awareness of self, ability to manage conflict; a knowledge of managerial styles and their consequences, organizational diagnosis and goal-setting; improvement of own team effectiveness, individual styles of members and effects of these on the team's functioning; identification of present conditions of organization and gaps between these and the desired effectiveness.

Groups are highly interested in learning the processes and techniques they need to accomplish their task. The processes practiced and learned by groups are experienced firsthand as the group pursues the achievement of its task, seeks the information it needs to plan its effort to solve a problem, and to place the solution into effect. Examples of the immediacy and usefulness of learning through participation in groups are discussed in the following cases: Team Effectiveness, Western Electric (Appendix, p. 229), The Raymond Corporation (Appendix, p. 263), and Internal Revenue Service, Western Region (Appendix, p. 279).

Instructional Procedures

The group learns to solve problems by solving a problem. The methods combine exploratory, acquisitional, and experiential learning. The group explores all obstacles that stand in the way of its effectiveness and discovers what is to it the most important problem needing to be solved. Through listening to presentations of its trainers, reading articles and book references on group processes, the group absorbs theories and concepts. Through watching, listening and thinking about what happens in the group in relation to what is expected, the group experiences by participating in group exercises and in action taken to solve the problem. Members of the group learn through feedback: seeing themselves on video-tape, listening to comments of group members and from the trainer. The group learns by experiencing the frustrations of not being able to organize themselves, not getting the best ideas from its members, or from failing to arrive at a decision. On the positive side, each member learns that he can make a contribution to the group and sees its value in helping the group bring about a change.

With the help of feedback from trainers and self-critiques, the members analyze how to improve the way they work together as a group. They then apply these skills in the solution of a problem. Because of the opportunity to integrate their learning with action, the method of learning is highly effective from the individual standpoint, and also makes a productive contribution to the group and the organization.

Flexibility of Sequence

This process is structured to provide for the group's direction of its learning and its task completion activities. This heightens the interest of the group members as well as helping them to focus on that which they need to know in order to accomplish their objective. The sequence is not entirely unstructured since the agenda are planned to introduce concepts in managerial and interpersonal relation skills, and practice and application of the techniques.

Instructors

The group members learn with the help of a team of instructors. They draw upon the know-how of their own members, and learn from their own experiences as they proceed with their work. Managers from the organization and trainers provide guidance and feedback on the group's progress. The group may call in technical experts. Managers may act as instructors, moderators, consultants, or observers. Using managers as instructors sets an example which increases the participants' desire to learn. It also opens up communication between upper and lower level employees, strengthening the abilities of both groups. Managers' insecurity and fear of competition from younger trainees is replaced with confidence.

Productive Results

The results of group problem solving are impressive. The following are some of the benefits resulting from this training process: increased product changes, increased sales, increased rate of profit growth, beneficial use of new organizational structures, coactive teams accomplishing better coordination between company divisions, increased capacities of personnel, improvement in coordinated production efforts, reduced cost on production of transistors, correction of large backlogs and errors, motivation and commitment of employees through coordinated change of placement, wage increase system, and performance appraisal.

Collaborative Instruction

Collaborative instruction is a training process by which members of a large organization contribute the following to a center for instructional resources:

1. Technical and managerial know-how from which to create instructional experiences.
2. Personnel to develop and present instructional experiences.
3. Information on training requirements.

The center thus is an instrument of the organization and makes it possible to share in the development and transmission of needed knowledge and techniques throughout the organization. It enables an organization and its parts to learn through systematic analysis of what it needs and to prepare resources that help it meet its objectives. By sharing in the

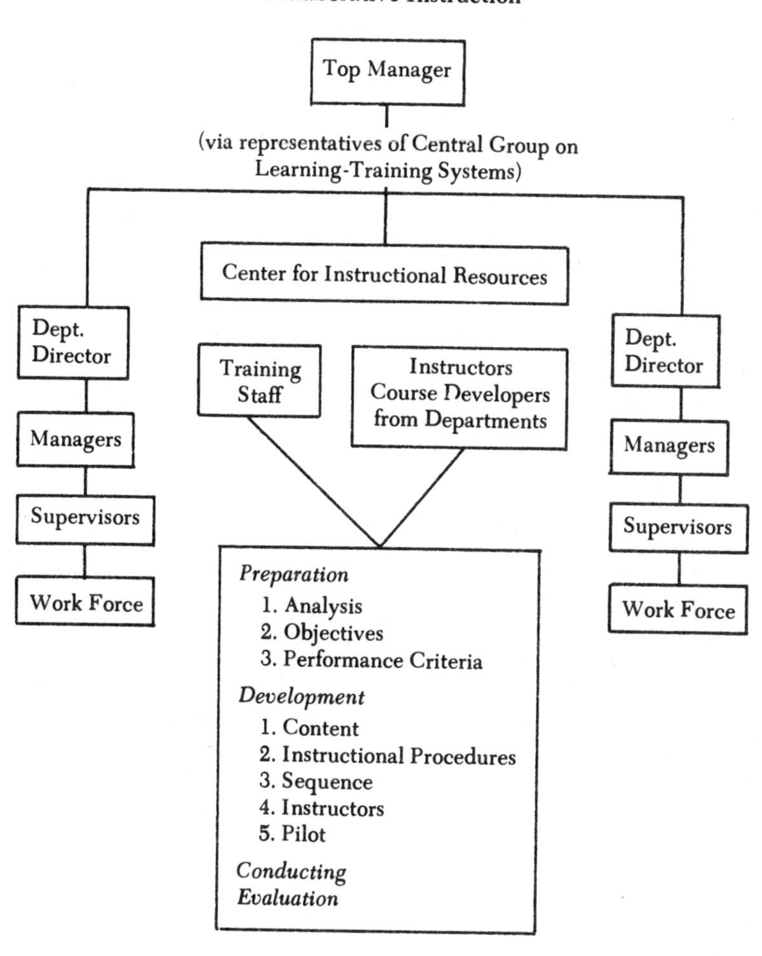
Collaborative Instruction
Top Manager
(via representatives of Central Group on Learning-Training Systems)
Center for Instructional Resources
Dept. Director
Managers
Supervisors
Work Force
Training Staff
Instructors Course Developers from Departments
Dept. Director
Managers
Supervisors
Work Force
Preparation
1. Analysis
2. Objectives
3. Performance Criteria
Development
1. Content
2. Instructional Procedures
3. Sequence
4. Instructors
5. Pilot
Conducting
Evaluation

creation as well as the utilization of the instructional resources, the organization regenerates its abilities and adapts to change.

The steps in this training process have been generalized from examples discussed in the book and in the Appendix. In Chapter 3, we discussed a special task force approach to implement the conversion of an organization to automated procedures. Incorporated in this was a center for the planning, designing, and monitoring of instructional experiences needed to make the conversion a success.

The collaborative training process sets up instructional resource sharing. It provides a way that large organizations can help individual units learn and help each other adapt to changing technological systems. Individual departments alone do not have the technical knowledge of organization-wide systems; nor do they have the understanding and ability in instructional processes. Centers for instructional resources are integral parts of the organization. They are not central schools giving courses in the formats they elect and to which the parts of the organization must adapt. It is the other way around. They design instructional formats to fit the functional and operational needs of the managers and the employees of the organization.

Objectives

The objectives of the centers of instructional resources are:

1. To learn the training needs of the organization and its work force.
2. To develop instructional resources that can be shared with the parts of the organization needing them.
3. To strengthen instructional know-how and skills of managers and technicians of the organization.

4. To support managers' and supervisors' development of their subordinates.

Curriculum

What goes to make up the content of the instructional resources developed by the center is primarily what the work force needs to know in order to perform their job and prepare for advancement. Instructional experiences have high relatedness to work since they are designed to fit the function they serve. Thus they are highly useful to participants, and the consequent interest improves the quality as well as the rate of learning. More important, this quality of high relatedness makes easier the carry-over of the ideas learned to the job.

The collaborative training process provides for updating instructional materials and thus content is fresh and new. This stimulates workers to learn and keep themselves updated in their work.

Instructional materials are provided through internal development or external selection.[5] Where excellent programs already exist and do fit the objectives of the organization, there is no need to recreate such programs. But the need still exists to incorporate what is learned in work operations.

Instructional Procedures

A variety of instructional procedures is available for presenting information and transmitting skills. The centers educate the members of the organization on how to select the most appropriate instructional procedures for the objectives to be accomplished. Today, as a result of advances in educational technology, the range of available procedures is enormous. And many of the older methods and media are effective when used appropriately: lectures, case studies, role playing, open- and closed-circuit television, video tapes, cassettes, films, slides, transparencies, filmstrips, on-the-job instruction, guided experiences and coaching, planned reading, correspondence courses, tours, field trips, incident process, seminars, games and simulation.

The wide range in instructional methods and media allows for adaptation to individual differences in employees' learning abilities. This increases the effectiveness with which people learn.

Flexibility of Sequencing

Traditional time requirements and established sequences of subject matter are replaced in these centers with training processes that adapt the format to the function. The size of groups varies from individualized programmed courses to large lecture and seminar groups. The sequence of instructional experiences is determined on the basis of the need. Scheduling of courses can be expanded to meet increased demands in kind, number, and geographical location. Whether the center is developing its materials internally or adapting them from outside resources, the content is adjustable and can be readily rearranged or updated to adapt to organizational changes in operations and systems.

Instructors

A small permanent staff who are qualified in instructional technology is augmented by personnel assigned from parts of the organization. The team concept of instructors centers on what the instructors do for the learner-workers. Primarily instructors function as managers of learning resources rather than being the source of knowledge. Their interest in the development of people is matched by their faithfulness in selecting and developing instructional materials.

The team of instructors functions to (1) find ways to better incorporate training in work operations; (2) help supervisors develop their subordinates; (3) research newer and more effective instructional procedures; (4) develop courses and present them; and (5) help personnel learn how to develop and present instructional materials.

This concept solves the dilemma of organizations: how to maintain an instructional staff and develop courses with which to keep the organization updated while its mission, procedures, systems and structures are constantly changing. The size and identity of the organization's personnel also change. With a permanent staff augmented by temporary additions, the centers can increase their instructors and yet not be forced to retain them permanently in an instructional capacity.

Experienced managers and technicians are knowledgeable in how things are done in the organization and thus make learning experiences more related and understandable to participants. The capacities of the instructors are strengthened when they learn to teach others because they develop an appreciation of how to work with people. Managers develop a greater concern for training their people as their understanding of instruction grows.

An Experimental Center for Collaborative Instructional Resources

An illustration of how instructional resources can be developed internally and incorporated with external materials for the benefit of the entire organization is shown in the case of a small training center that established a programmed learning laboratory to supplement more traditional courses. The training staff developed internal instructional materials and selected outside programmed materials which supplemented each other to meet learning objectives in supervisory, managerial, clerical, administrative, and computer information technology fields. It helped supervisors and their employees establish individualized training plans, selecting those instructional experiences from the center which met their needs and which could be supplemented by additional outside courses.

Some examples of its activities were:

1. The amplification and enrichment of a traditional classroom course, mandated by higher headquarters, with effective audiovisual materials. When the training staff needed to update the contents of the supervisory program with newer techniques and ideas, they researched a variety of programmed materials in the management field, selected the most appropriate program, tested it in several pilot programs for a one-year period, and then made available an expanded, flexible series of supervisory and managerial learning experiences. Participants were started in programmed units without delay and were later scheduled for group seminars. In cases where shift work, or geographical distance, made it impossible for participation at the center, cassette and workbook versions of the supervisory program were sent to participants.

2. A programmed unit on writing improvement was placed in a department to provide easy access for personnel in need of this help.

3. An organization—implementing a management information systems program—was helped to orient its top directors and managers through the use of audio tapes and work manuals on computer information technology. This instructional unit, instead of demanding time away from the office, actually penetrated the board room and work places, bringing to busy executives the basic knowledge of computers they needed.

4. A communications department whose personnel

worked around the clock was able to provide new opportunities for learning for its night shift personnel through the decentralization of several programs on computers, executive practices, and supervision.

5. A secretarial skills program using workbooks and cassette instruction needed information on the requirements of the local organization's clerical procedures. The training staff, in a do-it-yourself approach, prepared tapes and slides with a guide on the required procedures. This simple program provided a helpful introduction to the procedures the secretaries needed to know and gave them a handy reference guide for future use.

This center provided workable, satisfying, and personalized programs for a wide variety of needs. The increased interest of participating personnel was contagious and the enrollment increased steadily. As one top manager said, "Somehow it overcame the complacency that affects many of us about the use of better managerial techniques and started us thinking in new directions."

Day-to-Day Development on the Job

We turn now to the most fundamental of training processes: day-to-day development on the job. It is the basis for the other training processes, because it is the primary channel between the supervisor's and the subordinate's efforts in the utilization of learning-in-work achievements. A typical instance is its interdependency with a collaborative center for instructional experiences, such as the one we have just described. Unless supervisors have a mutual understanding with their employees as to what can be productively utilized from their learning, the training experiences made available by such a center may have little benefit to either the employee or the organization.

Day-to-Day Development on the Job

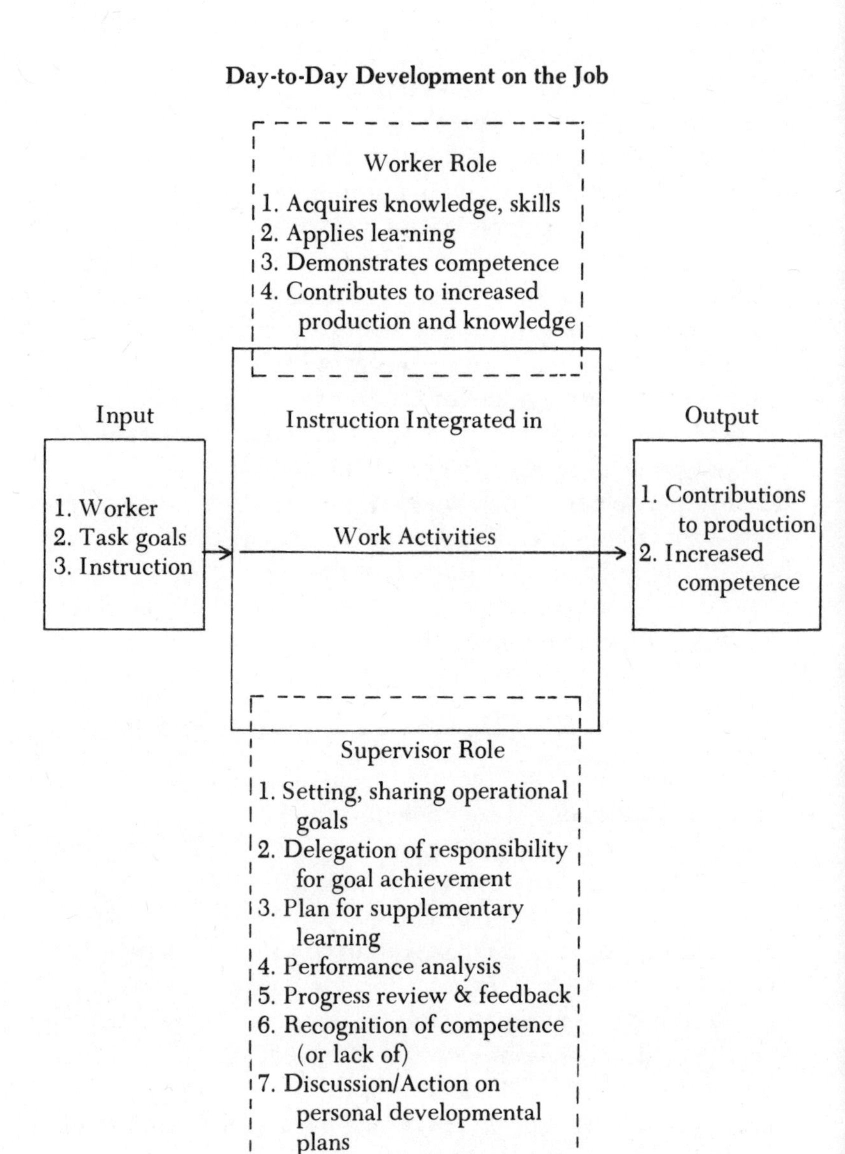

Earlier we said that development cannot be forced on the individual and that it must come from the person's desire to grow. Thus, the most critical task of any manager is helping his subordinates become aware of their need to learn and to develop their interest. Intelligent delegation of work responsibilities that will use all the strengths of an employee and require him to grow is the heart of the training process on the job. The supervisor sets goals, assigns work, reviews progress with his employees, and sees that internal influences are conducive to the employees' development.

It is in the way the supervisor ties learning with the planning, delegating, and follow-up of work that integrates instruction on the job. He incorporates training with work when he mutually establishes work goals with his subordinates; when he plans with them on how, when, and the manner in which work will be accomplished; when he delegates the responsibility to his subordinates for accomplishment; and when he makes progress reviews and provides feedback to his subordinates on their progress in accomplishing the work.

The day-to-day tasks of supervisors contain the most critical parts of the training process. When a supervisor gives a new assignment to an employee, he is discussing with him why that assignment needs to be done and what is involved in completing it, sharing with the employee what its objective should be. When a supervisor indoctrinates a new employee and makes explanations on the work, he is helping him to learn the job, and setting up various resources that will continue to provide help to the new employee. When a supervisor holds meetings, he is helping his employees learn.

In handling his responsibility for the development of his subordinates a supervisor must analyze performance problems. Robert Mager and Peter Pipe have written an excellent guide for supervisors to help them determine the cause of performance discrepancies.[6] Action to improve performance depends upon analysis of the cause. Performance discrepancy results from skill deficiencies, failure of supervisors to utilize skills, unwillingness of employees to apply know-how, and work conditions which negatively influence performance.

Objectives

The objective of the training process is to help employees learn and continue to adjust to any changes in their job. Is the employee able to perform his job? If he is not, what is the reason? Does he lack the knowledge and skill? Or does he have the knowledge and skill, but is not performing for other reasons?

Curriculum

The focus of this training process is helping the employee gain and use those skills he needs to accomplish his responsibilities. The content of learning experiences which the supervisor arranges for his employee is about the work, whether it be the subject, the functions, the regulations, the methods, or the equipment; the principal quality is that the form of the content fit as closely as possible the function.

Instructional Procedures

Much of the instructional procedure is integrated with doing the work; the setting of goals, the planning of how the work will be done, the delegation of responsibility to do the work, and the review of progress. Part of the supervisor's planning of work with his subordinate is the analysis of what the employee needs to learn in order to do his job. The supervisor structures a series of experiences that achieve both learning and work objectives. This means that such tools as textbooks, programmed instruction, demonstrations, case studies, seminars, and on-the-job instruction are arrayed so that the employee can experience the theory and practice of the skill that he needs for his work.

Important to both supervisor and employee is information on results: feedback that is *immediate* and lets the employee know how he stands in relation to his goals; feedback that is *positive* which tells him what he is doing well.

Flexibility of Sequence

The supervisor's awareness of his employee's progress triggers the use of learning resources when they are needed to strengthen employee competence. The supervisor thus fits the learning experience in at the most appropriate time, whether it is discussion, demonstration, reading, the study of guides, participation in a course, or whatever.

Instructors

The supervisor is the crux of the instructional team in this training process. The supervisor delegates part of his training task to others to help him instruct his people in what they need to know: employees, managers, technicians, programmed instruction units, instructors of external courses. Arrangements for an employee to attend a course may not seem to require much planning; but if the learning is to be productive, the supervisor's analysis of how it will be utilized is critical. How will the skills and know-how from the learning experience contribute to better job performance in the most economic and effective way? This is the question he faces. Any external training is an extension of the internal development process on the job. It must be managed so that it contributes to the strength of the individual and to the effectiveness of the organization.

Interrelationships of the Training Process

The four training processes described in this chapter

are mutually interdependent. The basic one is the day-to-day development on the job. The healthy functioning of this process is the foundation for the others. For example, a center for instructional resources depends upon the way the individual is selected for participation, whether as instructor, course developer, or participant. An administrative procedure for selection that lacks the human understanding needed to relate the learning experience and its use to the individual's accomplishment of work goals weakens the eventual productiveness of the center's activities.

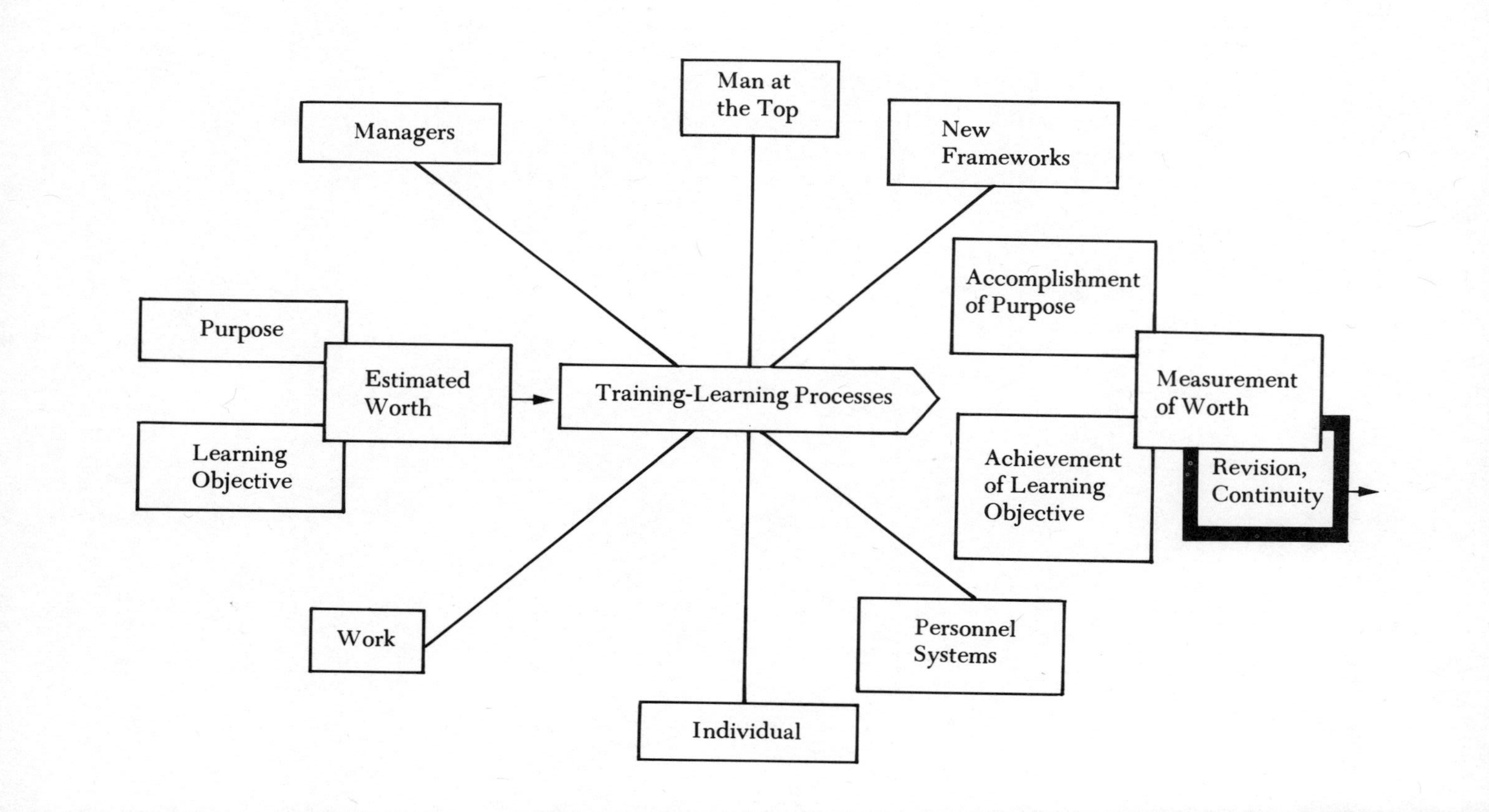

Managers
Man at the Top
New Frameworks
Purpose
Estimated Worth
Learning Objective
Training-Learning Processes
Accomplishment of Purpose
Measurement of Worth
Achievement of Learning Objective
Revision, Continuity
Work
Individual
Personnel Systems

9

Continuity and Renewal of Learning

Correctly designed, learning processes check the aging of organizations and individuals and provide for their continuous renewal. Learning is not for the moment but must serve the organization and its employees in the future.

Successful training-learning programs within organizations are characterized by continuing measurement of their worth, revision, and improvement. A training program designed yesterday needs to be continually measured not only as to its success in accomplishing what it was meant to, but there also needs to be a "re-look" at the initial objectives. Continuity of organizational training efforts is an important way to provide for continuous renewal. John Gardner says, "That human institutions require periodic redesign, if only because of their tendency to decay, is not a minor fact about them, nor easily overlooked. Taking the whole span of history, there is no more important lesson to be learned."[1]

The end product of learning for an individual is more learning. Thus learning not only takes the learner somewhere but allows him later to go farther more easily.[2] An article by Jacques-Yves Cousteau was captioned "Each Year

He Dives Deeper, and Learns More." Learning requires people to continue learning from their experience, experiments, and discoveries. Continuous learning means helping the work force adapt to change. Rapid technological changes require systematic provision to provide learning options for the senior and mature, as well as the young.

Continuity of learning means improving its quality by critical appraisal of the learning experience itself. This appraisal is focused on the extent to which performance is better able to accomplish its objectives through utilizing what has been learned. Learning requires more than "putting over" a training program, for the danger is that it does not stay "put." Short-run training efforts may arouse interest, but this is not the same as a steady effort to keep them closely integrated with the organization's and the individual's accomplishment of their goals. Training that provides entertainment and attention-getting devices merely arouses the short-lived interest of the passive spectator.

Continuity in organizational learning-training processes correlates with employee acquisition of the habit of continuing to learn. As Gardner suggests, the ultimate goal is "to shift to the individual the burden of pursuing his own education."[3] It must be understood why continuity is a productive element in successful learning efforts, what causes the precariousness of training, and how designs build continuity into learning.

The Precarious Aspects of Training

Many training efforts are not much more than the offering of courses. They are often disconnected efforts, separate from the work situation, and fail to carry over into the productive processes of work. Bosses always have work priorities at the front of their timetables. The common plaint is, "We don't have time to train!" Managers learn that rewards are received for efforts with more visible and immediate results than training. Managers often send subordinates to training courses which they themselves do not understand the need for, nor do they want their subordinates to utilize the newer concepts. Under such conditions, training courses are precarious; their content is unable to gain a foothold in work operations. This results in a lack of continuity in learning and growth.

Underlying the precariousness of training is a lack of understanding of the function of learning within an organization. As a result, those who initiate training-learning processes fail to clearly articulate the purpose, to analyze what needs to be learned, and to design learning experiences that can achieve the objectives. Thus training efforts fail to produce results and do not contribute to continuous learning.

Evaluation and Continuity of Learning

In the examples of productive learning discussed in this book, the measurement of worth is part of a continuing training-learning process. *We cannot speak of evaluation of learning efforts without also speaking of the initial purpose for the training.* When management evaluates training efforts, it positively influences both the continuity and the productivity of that training, particularly when action is taken to redirect efforts to better achieve the original purpose. The following is an example of the positive benefits of evaluation where managers measured the worth of a program against its initial purpose.

> In preparation for the conversion of many systems to automatic data processing, the Data Processing Department received much training. But this was not

true for managers and staff people in other departments whose work was affected by these changes and who felt handicapped in performing work connected with the data processing systems because of lack of understanding and familiarity with them. Many who felt at a loss to relate to the new systems expressed the desire to gain some understanding and confidence in dealing with the new processes.

At first, arrangements were made for managers and technicians to attend the nearby education center of a data processing manufacturer. Evaluations showed that the courses were high in quality, but it was difficult to apply the principles learned to the corporation's systems. The training staff arranged for the manufacturer's representative to present a course at the organization's location and attempted some discussions of the firm's systems. Participants, however, said they were still unable to carry over this information to help them understand how the corporation's systems worked.

A top manager of the Data Processing Department and the Training Officer collaborated in the design of a course based on what the managers needed to know about the systems. A work group was formed of representatives from the data processing departments, the principal department users of the systems, and the training staff. Together they designed and developed a new course called "Computers for Managers." The learning experience was worthwhile to the participants because they found its content highly related to their problems. The practical examples used in the course sparked helpful discussions. The instructors knew the systems and could relate their experiences to the participants' questions; their answers had credibility as well as worth.

When the group in charge of the course viewed the results as well as the participants' reactions, they found built-in advantages. First, Data Processing Technicians, through their instructional work, had recognized "soft spots" in the system, which they remedied. Second, managers adjusted their internal operations to accommodate systems they now understood. As one said, "It helped me schedule our input into the computer." Another found that he had "a better understanding of computer operations which will preclude the requesting of operations too costly or too difficult to program." Third, attitudes toward the new systems changed. One participant said, "Many local matters were brought to my attention for the first time, which has motivated me to get more knowledge of our data processing systems." Others expressed "new insights into problems of the data processing people."

The course "Computers for Managers" was continued for the managers and technicians of the corporation who wanted and needed the help it could provide them. It also sparked other more specialized sessions designed to help lower level workers obtain more facts which would enable them to understand their phases of the work. The helpfulness of these continuing sessions is illustrated by remarks of participants. "Light has been shed," one worker commented; "I've learned how and where to find the procedures I need." Another found he had "learned how to recognize and live within the limitations of the current situation until things get smoothed out." An interesting observation was made by another who said, "By giving us a picture of the interrelationships we will be able, even though we do not yet have adequate knowledge of the new systems, to project what effect trial and error transactions will have on disk files." Still more encouraging was the evidence of results: fewer errors, faster processing, and a spirit of interest in and cooperation with the new systems. Not only were the technicians transmitting their knowledge of the new systems but in essence they were helping to create new knowledge.

Why was the program of this organization eventually productive? It was the continuity of effort to evaluate and revise the program until it provided the help the managers and their subordinates needed. The continuity was made possible by a team effort of different organizational units which had the technical knowledge. It could not have been accomplished if managers had not been leaders of the group. They evaluated the earlier efforts and found them wanting; they made further efforts because they recognized this as a part of their job. Organizations learn by feedback just as individual workers do. The way in which the evaluations were made, what was evaluated, who made the evaluations, and what action was taken as a result constituted the continuity of the learning effort. Not only *did the training take them somewhere,* but it *enabled them to go farther* by *revising and strengthening* the program until there was a high degree of relatedness and usefulness. Continuity enabled them to test out different programs and use constructively the lessons they learned from their experience. Continuity also provided time in which to develop the instructors from within the organization who would be capable of helping participants incorporate their learning in their daily work.

Another case illustrates what happens when the managers do not participate; where they do not face up to their task of measuring the worth of an effort, particularly the degree to which the training-learning process achieves its purpose.

For several years the rapid changes in supply

systems had caused the managers of a large government agency to become seriously out of date and out of touch with the realities of its supply systems and procedures. Action to meet the need had been recommended by a consultant's survey, but it was not until the national agency required its local activities to develop a series of supply courses that action started. A central training committee under the leadership of its chairman undertook the development of a supply management course.

The task of determining the content of the course was assigned to a subgroup of the committee. The chairman of the group felt that this task was rightfully the responsibility of the training staff. But, as the chairman of the training committee had recognized, the training staff lacked the technical expertise in supply systems and procedures. The training staff suggested that, in order to articulate clearly the objectives of this program, the needs and expectations of different managerial groups be identified. However, the subgroup felt this was unnecessary and outlined the topics it thought should be included. Department managers and key technicians agreed to present sessions when asked to do so by the training committee chairman. Individual preparation of talks by these instructors proceeded without interrelating their content or preventing overlaps.

The course was presented the first time as a pilot seminar. At its close, participants were asked to prepare a written critique. A consolidation of these critiques showed the course to be of benefit and that it should be continued; however, it needed considerable revision. Some felt it had been "foisted" on the organization by the training committee and would not actually help managers. The weaknesses that needed correction were:

its lack of continuity and integration of material; overlapping and duplication between sessions; too large a number of instructors; and lack of professional instruction.

A report of the above findings was made to the top manager. It recommended that a qualified supply logistics technician be assigned to work with a member of the training staff to reshape the course for continuation. The top manager referred the recommendations to the national agency with a request for technical support, but it was returned without action; and the national agency indicated that there was similar training available at the national agency's schools. However, the local organization's training staff had earlier made an exhaustive search for either a course already prepared or materials that could be borrowed for this local effort. None of the national schools had been able to contribute anything. Even if there had been a central course that did fit the needs of the local agency, the cost of travel to the east coast and daily subsistence would have been prohibitive. As a result the course was shelved. Copies of sessions and tapes were loaned to other agencies, and some of the local managers who participated were able to present portions of them to their employees.

What went wrong in this case? There was no analysis of managers' needs. The program, as it was developed, became a series of talks about different aspects of supply. It presented a mass of information about changes in supply systems; but it did not meet either the criteria of a well-constructed course, nor did it furnish the answers to the problems and questions of managers. Most serious was the lack of management involvement in helping to direct the content of the program and to evaluate the worth of the course. If there had been managerial involvement such as that in the previous example—Computers for Managers—and an effort made to fit the training to the learning needs, the results would have been more productive.

This effort lacked: (1) the collaboration of the technical experts and the training staff; (2) managerial assumption of responsibility—the reluctance of the subgroup's chairman to get managers involved in the specific analysis of their needs; and communication—making it impossible to articulate clearly what it was that the supervisors and technicians needed to know. Even after the pilot course had been presented and evaluated, the subgroup could have given leadership to the effort. The situation was far from hopeless. Much worthwhile material had been collected even if it had not been organized in learnable units. The participants were unanimous that the course had value if it were revised and better constructed. Despite a thorough, accurate, and honest appraisal of the program, no part of management took hold of the action needed, and the program was discontinued.

How Training-Learning Processes Measure Worth

Continuity as a productive quality means evaluation of how well the training-learning process achieves the objectives for which it was designed. In this sense, evaluation can be made the basis for continuing a learning effort that is worthwhile.

Evaluations are made, however, in a number of ways, not all of which are dependable. Participants are often asked to give their reactions to a course. Or the instructors of a course may query the supervisors of the participants, asking to what extent there has been improvement in the employee's performance. Evaluations of this kind do very little to integrate the learning with the work operations, primarily because the questions are asked too late. As we will discuss in Chapter 11, it is at the outset of the process that the purpose of the training-learning process should be determined.

Other kinds of evaluations are provided by instructors who may rate the degree or proficiency with which the participant learned the materials in the course. A group or a committee may evaluate a program by holding a sort of postmortem to review the course, interview participants, and relate it to previous criteria. Or it could be an informal evaluation, where some part of the organization makes a decision largely on the basis of self-interest; e.g., the course "takes too much time" or it "costs too much" and therefore "it is inefficient."

But such evaluations have little to do with comparing achievement with the intended purpose and comparing its benefits—some of which may be unexpected—with the cost. The important factor in continuing a training effort is the basis on which the worth is evaluated: the achievement of benefits minus the cost. The evaluation looks at the way in which learning experiences are successfully integrated with action to achieve a piece of work or solve a problem. Evaluation also looks at the way the learning experiences grow out of the needs rather than prescribing subject matter. In Chapter 8 we looked at four training-learning processes, used successfully by organizations in their training and development programs. Each of these had built-in ways of providing feedback to participants to show how well they were doing, with information on which to base improvements.

Individualized Work-Learning Progression

In this process, the primary method of learning is doing, accompanied by feedback information from the supervisor or coach on the results of the trainee's work, with reinforcement and recognition of correct performance. The trainee advances to the next higher position on the basis of an evaluation that shows he has demonstrated his competence in fulfilling responsibilities. The trainee continues to improve his performance through evaluation and correction of it until he advances to the next job.

Group Problem Solving

In this process, instructional procedures emphasize learning to work together. Feedback is provided to the members of the group on how well they are learning the group process. Self-critiques as well as evaluations by other members of the group make participants aware of their progress. The learning process is strengthened and quickened by making it a group activity. Feedback is what makes the difference between group conferences that merely provide the opportunity for individuals to exchange ideas and experiences, and group problem-solving processes where a major part of the agenda is devoted to looking critically at how well the group is making progress in the achievement of its task. Critiques are fed back to both individuals and the group on how they help or block advancement, how they contribute to the group in reaching a decision, how they help in organizing and executing their task. Groups both as individuals and as members of teams continue to use team skills learned in this training.

Collaborative Instruction

The process whereby an organization uses a center of instructional resources for the joint development and transmission of knowledge depends upon the feedback from parts of the organization on the extent to which these resources meet their needs. This provides a means to update the learning experiences available to the members of the work force. In addition, those who take part in the development and presentation of instructional materials are given the benefits of feedback on their performance.

This process maintains the vitality of a work force through helping them remain receptive to change, updating knowledge needed for current performance, and gaining knowledge and skill in fields other than that of their specialty. Drucker describes the Japanese concept of "continuous" training and why it may be the secret to employee willingness to accept continuing changes:

> Every employee, very often up to and including top managers, keeps on training as a regular part of his job until he retires. This is in sharp contrast to our usual Western practice of training a man only when he has to acquire a new skill or move to a new position. Our training is promotion-focused, the Japanese training is performance-focused.
>
> Second, the Japanese employee is, for the most part, trained not only in his job but in all the jobs at his job level, however low or high that level is. To illustrate:
>
> The man working as an electrician will automatically attend training sessions in every single area in the plant. And so will the man who pushes a broom. Both of them may stay in their respective jobs until they die or retire. Their pay is independent, in large measure, of the job they are doing, and is geared primarily to the length of service, so that the highly skilled electrician may well get far less money than the floor sweeper. But both are expected to be reasonably proficient in every job in the plant, that is generally speaking, at the same level as their own job.
>
> An accountant is expected to be trained—or to train himself through a multitude of correspondence courses, seminars, or continuation schools available in every big city—in every single one of the professional jobs needed in his company, such as personnel, training, and purchasing.[4]

Drucker also points out certain built-in advantages of the continuous training practice:

1. The emphasis is to condition workers to ask, "What have we learned so we can do the job better?" Work improvement is built into their operations; new products, equipment, processes, are introduced through training sessions.

2. Training is not limited to helping a man achieve an acceptable standard of work productivity. Work standards of the Japanese may be lower, but training is continued and eventually their work productivity exceeds the standards.

3. Their traditional attitude and custom is to keep in continuous training so that skill never lessens. Their industrial engineers, Drucker says, set up foundations and the worker builds "his own edifice." One learns how to improve his own productivity.

4. The idea of continuous training prevents the extreme specialization that characterizes American production. The Japanese are specialists, but they are also generalists in that they keep on learning until they know the work of all other functions. The special skill is *the foundation for, not the end of learning.*

Day-to-Day Development on the Job

Where individual worker development is integrated with the work, the training process provides for feedback and evaluation to the employee by the supervisor. Thus the feedback helps the worker redirect his efforts and continue to develop. Although the fundamental developmental process is on the job, the supervisor may incorporate an outside instructional resource to supplement the learning on the job. The supervisor's evaluation, together with that of the employee, looks at how the skills and know-how from the learning experience did contribute to better job performance.

The premature selection of external courses, without first having determined how they will meet the workers' or managers' needs, results in nonproductive training. For example, organizations have spent considerable time and money in sending managers and executives to university and commercially sponsored programs. Evaluation of such programs is of increasing concern, as was mentioned in Chapter 4, because little improvement is seen as a result. But the concern for the evaluation *after* the programs are completed leads to a measurement of the wrong things. The experience may be producing very significant benefits, which may not be visible in the way the organization is attempting to evaluate. Unless the purpose has been mutually agreed upon prior to the educational experience, the evaluation may miss the kind of benefit that the experience provides. McGregor has well described certain types of generalized university exposures whose purpose

> is not, and should not be direct practical application of the learning to the job. Their purpose is not to provide answers to problems, formulas, or tricks of the trade. It is to broaden the manager's understanding of his job, to challenge some of his preconceptions, to make him better able to learn from experience when he gets back home because he will have acquired a more realistic understanding of the causes and effects with which he must deal. To the extent that this kind of education is successful, it will not reveal itself in immediate or obvious changes in his behavior back home. The learning which takes place will more probably be reflected in fairly subtle ways of which he himself may often be unaware. Nevertheless, these changes in perception do affect behavior, sometimes profoundly. It is certainly rea-

> sonable that management should want to evaluate the achievements of university programs in management development, but it is important that we understand the purposes of these programs so that we evaluate the right things.[5]

The element of continuity in learning is a strong influence on the efforts to renew the strength of organizations. For continuity in learning to be successful in this respect, it requires continuing evaluation of how well the training-learning processes of the organization are meeting the objectives for which they were established. Where the training effort falls short of attaining the objectives, management must redirect its efforts in the development of its work force.

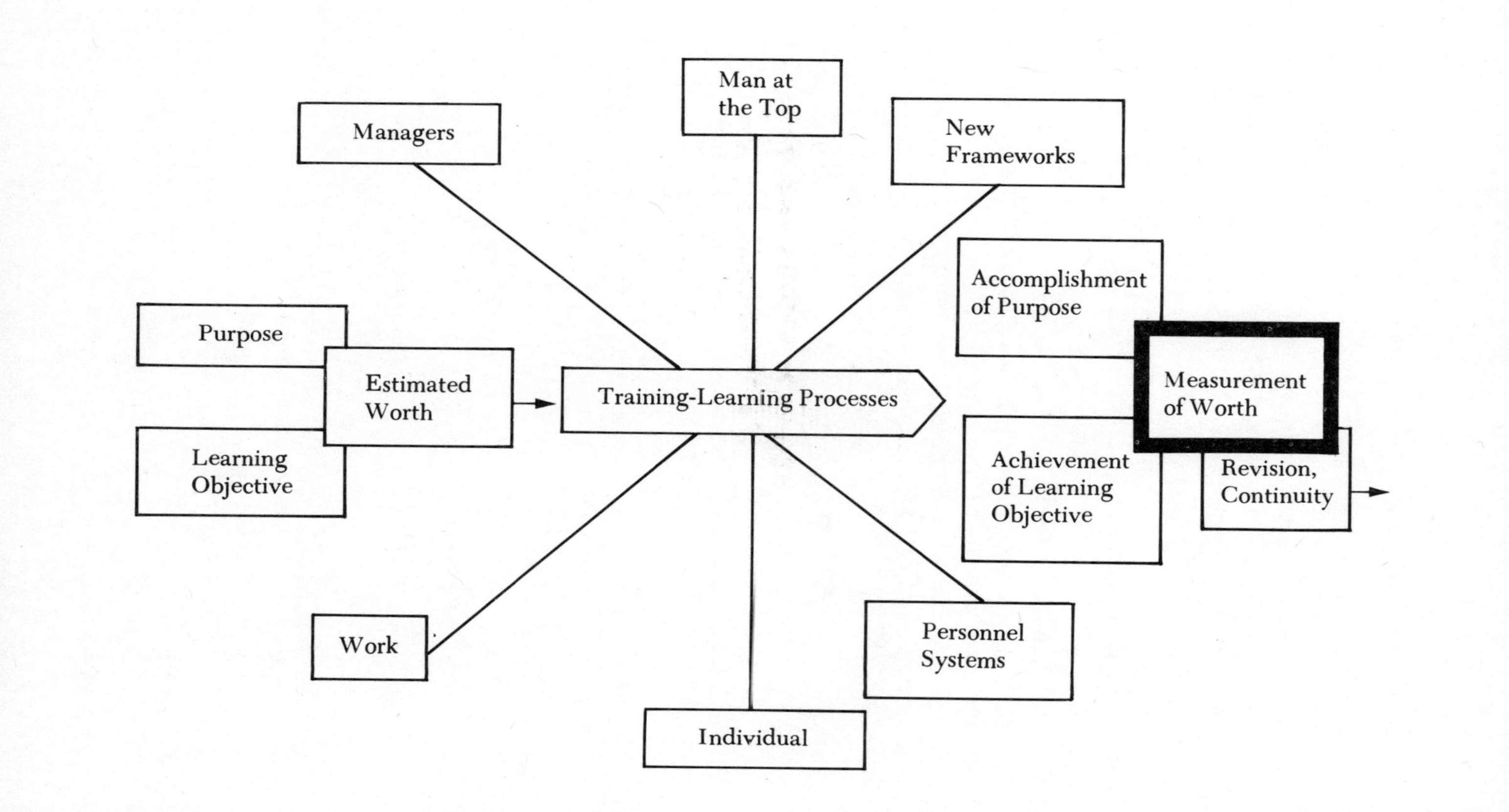
Man at the Top
Managers
New Frameworks
Purpose
Estimated Worth
Learning Objective
Training-Learning Processes
Accomplishment of Purpose
Measurement of Worth
Achievement of Learning Objective
Revision, Continuity
Work
Individual
Personnel Systems

10

What Makes Training Worthwhile

Training and learning are worthwhile to organizations when they help people solve problems critical to the organization and improve the way the organization gets its work done. They are worthwhile when they help people assimilate the learning which they can use to increase their competence. We often hear the phrase "It was really worth the effort." What makes training and learning worthwhile are the calculations made by managers or employees that the benefits were worth the cost.

Practical Payoffs

A consolidation of productive results from the cases and examples discussed throughout this book show tangible and practical payoffs as well as improvement in the quality of working life:

1. Increased productivity, such as profitable product changes, increased sales, growth of profit rates, improved processing of orders and shipments, better services.
2. Improved performance, broader scope as well as

higher levels of competence achieved; successful passage into supervisory and managerial positions; more effective induction of new employees; increased utilization of knowledge in work.

3. New approaches that link career patterns, work, and training to provide qualified manpower for present and future needs.

4. More effective development of managers through their helping their subordinates to know and apply their learning.

5. Reduction of cost-incurring items, such as the elimination of confusion, the correction of malfunctioning systems, elimination of errors, the lessening of backlogs, the solution of problems critical to the organization's effectiveness, correcting the dysfunctions of organizations, such as rigid adherence to outworn practices, and preventing dissipation of new knowledge and skills gained from learning efforts.

6. Counteracting fragmentation and specialization of work by providing workers with insight into the functions of other parts of the organization.

7. Facilitation of the introduction and acceptance of new systems and new equipment.

8. Transferring to individuals the responsibility for self-direction in learning and its utilization; continuing the process of self-renewal and building hedges against obsolescence.

9. Creating as well as consuming knowledge through learning from experience, the discovery of new ideas and ways of working together; learning to solve conflict through the integration of interests in the concern for all.

10. Raising the sights of the entire organization and its people through growth and satisfaction in accomplishment; the gaining of confidence to succeed.

Individual Measures of Worth

To understand why managers or employees find training worthwhile it is necessary to look more closely at how they measure worth. *For if their measures are faulty, their evaluation is incorrect.* The measures are often at fault because the initial conception of the training was at fault. If managers do nothing more than give consent to their people going to classes, without relating that learning to how it will be incorporated in work and for what purpose, it comes as no surprise that not much benefit is received.

Managers' Estimate of Worth

Managers differ in the ways they regard the worth of training. Their estimates are often cues as to the pressures and influences of the organizational climate on them as well as individual social and psychological needs.

Relationship to work. Many managers look at training and development efforts as competing with work rather than as a part of work. Some managers say they "wish the time and money had been put on something else." Yet others find that a training effort such as a problem-solving group is very worthwhile: "Although four hours a week seemed a sacrifice and we all had to rearrange our activities in order to participate, I think we made up for lost time. Of course you have to select a problem that everyone is convinced needs attention and one that is actually within our capabilities to do something about." Time is apparently the great stumbling block to most executives, managers, and supervisors. One top executive remarked that "when a manager says that it takes too much time, this is an excuse. What he is saying is that he does not want to develop his people." In organizations with productive training programs, operations are effective because of managerial concern for the development of people.

Accountability. Accountability for dollar results makes training in the manager's mind a competitor for productive manhours and a burden to their dollar costs. One concerned with the shortage of funds asks, "How do I know I get the training dollar back?" And those who feel the pressure of work deadlines ask, "Who minds the store while employees are in training courses?" One government accounting system caused managers to shy away from training efforts because the system classified training hours as "nonproductive time." As one manager in that organization said, "Training only puts us further in the red." But in organizations that have designed and implemented worthwhile programs we found that managers are recognized for developing their people.

Compliance. Some managers feel that they must go along with training programs that require their compliance. Measuring worth in this manner shows little interest, understanding, or commitment. For example, one manager said that his people "expect to get to a course every now and then. And I'm supposed to go along with this. It's part of the program, even though I don't see much in the way of results." Some felt required to ask for quotas for courses when inventories of training needs were made. Others said that they had to use course quotas at times when they did not need them.

Trained manpower. Often managers want trained people, that is, if the supply comes through the efforts of someone besides themselves. "I don't want training programs. Just give me experienced people" is a common expression of managers. They turn to the recruitment to find workers for them who are already trained, or they expect a training staff to do the entire job of turning out completely trained employees. Others say they help new employees learn their jobs by turning novices over to an experienced employee. "Let them work with someone who knows and they'll catch on." Some managers have a limited concept of their training task, such as sending people to courses and reviewing the number of hours and courses completed.

Threats to security. The question in the minds of many managers is: "Will this training put my position in jeopardy?" Responsibility must be delegated to employees if they are to grow. They must have room to fail in order to demonstrate that they can succeed. Managers, however, are often reluctant to place complete trust and confidence in subordinates.

A manager's security is highly important to him. If he has spent many years accumulating experience, he often is not willing to share it with a subordinate. There is always the threat that the subordinate may become more capable than his superior. The manager is apprehensive about training when it is incorporated in action needed to solve a problem critical to the effectiveness of the organization. For if the training program were successful in locating the causes of a problem it might mean that weaknesses in the manager's practices would be exposed.

Managers are often concerned as to how well they will do when they participate in training activities. A common question is: "How will I look to others in the course?" Another type of anxiety arises when the learning experience requires too long an absence from the job. Then the worry becomes, "Will they miss me?" The fear is that operations will proceed smoothly and the manager may be found not necessary to the organization.

Apathy and selfishness. Many managers feel that it is easier to stay with what they've been doing than to change. Such inertia is reflected in their lack of self-development as well as in their failure to help their subordinates. As one executive said, "If it's too much effort, they find a reason to be somewhere else." Some managers, however, welcome periodic opportunities for learning and renewal of their mental abilities. The satisfaction with things as they are often deters a manager from supporting learning activities. As one manager put it, "Part of us will resist change whether it's because of laziness, inertia, or the uncertainty of the unknown and untried." Another put it this way, "There's a tendency to be a slave to equipment or to a format or a process."

Training credit, or actual competence? Some managers regard the completion of certain courses as a good thing to have on their record. Certain training experiences take on a prestige value. Other managers prize the worth of the training to gain confidence, self-assurance, and an opportunity to convert techniques learned into effective managerial skills. Their plans and expectations include the hope of improving their decisions and judgment.

Employee Estimate of Worth

Employees look at the benefits from training in many ways. And the difference in the ways they estimate benefits and costs provides us with cues as to what causes those measures of worth.

Work facilitation. Employees often discuss the worth of training in terms of how it helped them in their work: learning new skills, understanding new procedures, moving into a new position, gaining insight into the tasks of a supervisor, preparing for a new step in one's career. These descriptions sometimes emphasize training as "making the work easier" or providing "deeper insight" or "greater confidence."

But not all see training as facilitating their work. For example, one employee said that "it makes a lot of difference in what you're actually able to do with the ideas you've gained. Unfortunately I don't get very far with mine." Other employees echoed this comment, adding in some cases that they were not encouraged or allowed to apply new ideas.

Some employees felt their participation in training was hampered by their inability to concentrate on the learning when they felt that "things might be going wrong" in the office. Others amplified that thought by commenting on the failure of the supervisor to redistribute work in the employee's absence due to a training course. On the other hand, there were those employees for whom the training did not seem a punishment because their bosses reassigned work during their absence. Others felt that having to make up work as a result of attendance in training courses wasn't a problem. As one said, "Everyone knows that you can catch up on your work if you want to."

Quality and relatedness. Employees know that sometimes it has not been possible to use the training they have experienced because it could not be assimilated for later application. The quality of the instruction may be poor or the content of the learning experience may be impossible to convert to work practices. Often no one takes the responsibility. One employee said that "helping you learn on the job is sort of a myth. It's never very clear who has the responsibility." Another employee was informed that one of the girls would train him. "But she was leaving and not very interested, nor was she good at showing me the work."

Achievement and satisfaction. Many employees' measure of the worth of their learning experiences is the degree to which it provides an opportunity to take on greater responsibility. Of special value were those learning experiences that included tangible plans for moves to higher level positions. Others appreciate the help given them to continue to learn. As one said, "I'm happy with the motivation provided me to keep on learning and not stagnate." Many employees are concerned about getting out of date and appreciate the stimulus provided by participation in the group. As one said, it helps the "will to continue."

Insight into relationships. Many people find that the understanding of functions in the organization other than their own helps them in their work. Employees indicate they get much from training that provides for insight into a larger picture of the organization and its goals. Workers also find that when they participate in certain learning experiences they have a chance to meet other employees and establish valuable contacts. One employee expressed the wish that there were some way that courses could show them the importance of their work and how other people depended upon them for accuracy and timeliness of information. "But," he said, "I don't suppose it could be taught in a course." Some employees mentioned the help they received when their supervisors pointed out the significance of their tasks to the total organizational effort. One said his boss not only "showed me the beginning, but the end of the process." Another said that most employees who complain about the lack of challenge in their assignments "never get a chance to see the objective. That's why the work seems menial."

Actions set an example. Regardless of policy statements, employees know whether an organization makes learning a mainstream activity. This influences the importance a worker places on training. What fellow workers say about learning experiences is a very strong factor. And top leadership provides an example that means more than words. Where managers are concerned about learning and its utilization, their employees tend to be concerned. The way employees are selected for participation in training makes a difference in the worth they attach to training. Often when employees are told to attend a training course, they are unaware of why they are being sent, or of their need for it, and how it is related to their responsibilities. One employee asked why he had not been sent, but others in similar jobs were being sent. "I was told," he said, "that there was no particular reason, which was probably true. They really didn't know why some went and others did not. But as an employee I'd like to know. If I'm poor in my work, they should have told me." Employees find themselves at time in training that is not appropriate and which they cannot apply. As one said, "A decision was made that every supervisor should take a course on Conference Leadership. But most of our supervisors are running labor gangs. Most of them don't speak English and cannot understand the training, let alone use it."

Timing. The measure of learning worth often depends upon the timing for an employee. "The course wasn't really worth the effort because it came too late," said one. "I guess my supervisor just didn't keep track." One employee made the interesting comment that having the training when you needed it was probably more important than the quality of the training itself.

Personal interests. Participation in some educational and training activities may require too much of a sacrifice of an individual's own time. This is true in organizations which pay for training and education but make them a matter of evening and weekend activity. Where employees have been provided the opportunity to fit in learning experiences before and after working hours at the place of work, their estimate of the cost in terms of requirements on personal time lessens, and worth increases. As many expressed, it is difficult to go home after work and then go out to school.

Some employees find that it seems to make little difference to their supervisors or the organization whether they participate in training activities or not. Consequently, training doesn't seem worth the time and effort. We discussed earlier the example of engineers whose ratings declined despite their continuance in evening training activities (see Chapter 7, pp. 124-125). This illustrates the questionable worth of a training program supposed to prevent the employees' obsolescence. Other factors, such as internal negative influences of poor job assignments and unfair ranking in the performance appraisal system, contributed to their obsolescence.

Credits or application of learning. Some employees look to credits, degrees, and certificates as valuable for their records, particularly where companies stress the value of having more education. The worth of participating in learning experiences is measured accordingly. Others' motives are different. Some, for example, may want to attend more generalized management courses to gain the benefits of insight into organizational theory and practice, a broadened understanding of their job, and increased ability to learn from experience upon return to the job. In other cases, participation in courses may provide updating in management sciences, decision making, management information systems, behavioral science, or computer simulation techniques which can be directly applied to work.

Employees who know what they plan to do with the new knowledge, and how they plan to use it, generally estimate the learning experience as valuable and profitable. This is particularly true where expectations are mutually shared by supervisors and employees. The generous and well-meant support of educational activities may appear worthwhile, but unless the learning experience is linked with its assimilation in work processes the full measure of worth is not being achieved.

Why Measures of Training Worth Differ

Managers and employees, as we have seen, look quite differently at the worth of their learning experiences. Some managers bemoaned the lack of time for training; but others were active and involved in their development programs for their subordinates either as individuals or groups.

Some managers restricted their efforts to compliance with surveys of training requirements and sending their employees to courses. But others built productive learning experiences into the day-to-day job assignments.

We saw that employees, mindful of organizational policies stressing acquisition of a certain number of courses or hours of training, focused their estimate of worth on the accumulation of credits and records of course completion. In other cases, however, we found employees who realized their greatest benefit came from their assimilation and successful use of what they had learned.

Why do learning experiences vary in the benefits they provide to managers and employees? The reason is the presence or absence of an organized design to integrate training with action vital to both the organization and the individual. Genuinely productive learning is not a matter of chance, nor is it solely due to good instruction, or conscientious learners. It results from understanding what it takes in an organizational situation to make learning work productively. The elements of a favorable work environment and systematic instructional design have been described throughout each of the chapters of this work. It is these elements that must be engineered so that training functions to achieve an intended purpose, whether it be action to solve a problem critical to the organization, development of competent personnel, or the achievement of a project.

It becomes evident that high appraisals of worth *result from* and *do not determine* productive learning. Productive learning in the context of organizational life requires *the design of environmental conditions and systematic training that enhance each other*. It is through managerial and employee participation in the productive experiences that their worth is known. It is difficult to appreciate what one doesn't know and hasn't experienced.

A Training System That Was Worth Its Salt

The measure of training worth depends upon no single element. To demonstrate how an organization successfully engineered a training system as an integral part of a total work environment, we review here and amplify an example discussed in Chapters 2 and 3: that of an organization's conversion of old procedures for orders, inventory, and stock maintenance to new automated systems required by its headquarters. *Our purpose here is to see the interrelationships of the elements that were built into the design and the interdependency of the various parts of its framework.* Thus we can see that this was not just another training program but a design for learning that was worth its salt. The training plan was an integral part of the total conversion effort both from the standpoint of the special organizational structure and the technical systems.

Special Organizational Framework

The group assigned responsibility for the design and preparation of the training system was a part of the total organizational framework set up for the accomplishment of the entire conversion (see Chart 15, opposite page). This training task force was a part of and directed by the governing board to which it made recommendations for the training system and from which it received its authority and resources. Twelve supply technicians were selected from the line to become the key trainers in the training task force. They were linked with the training staff, the procedure writing groups, and the automated systems analysts.

The Training System

The purpose of the training system was to produce workers competent to use the new procedures. The develop-

An Organizational Framework for the Learning System for Conversion To ADP Procedures

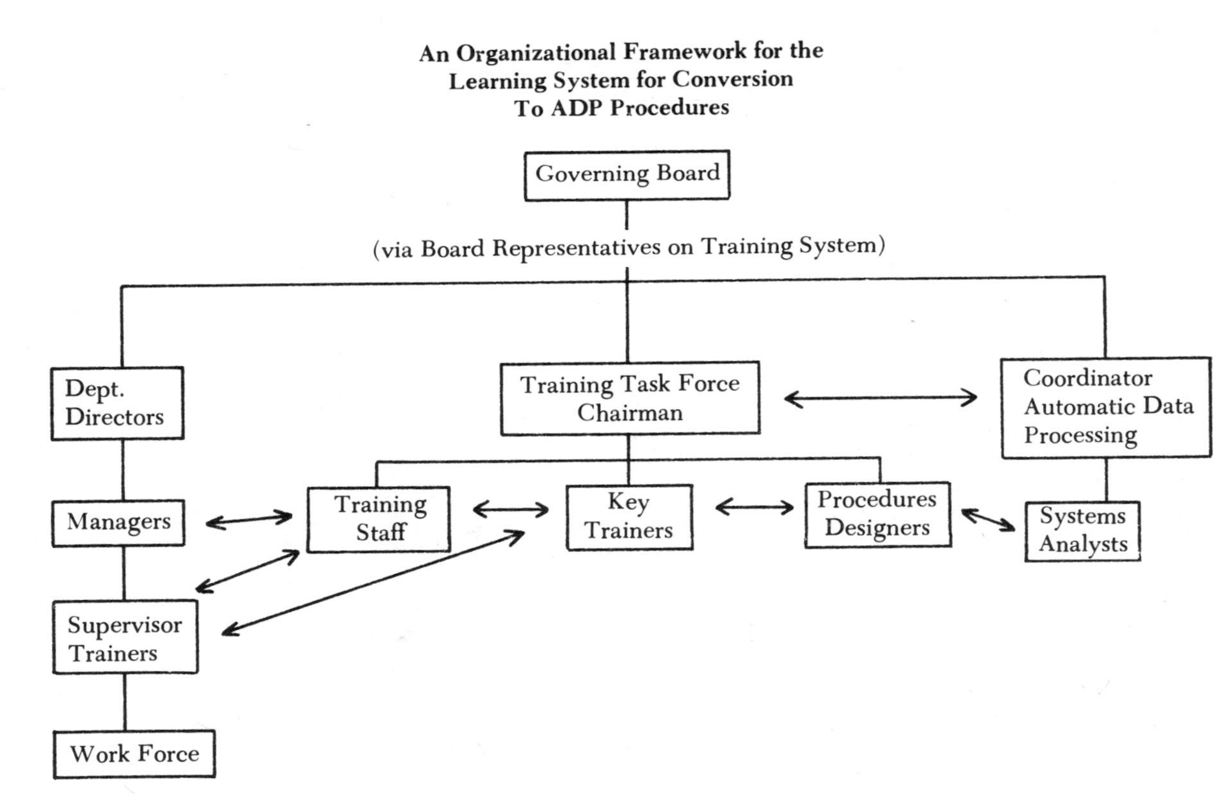

Steps in Training System for Conversion To ADP Procedures

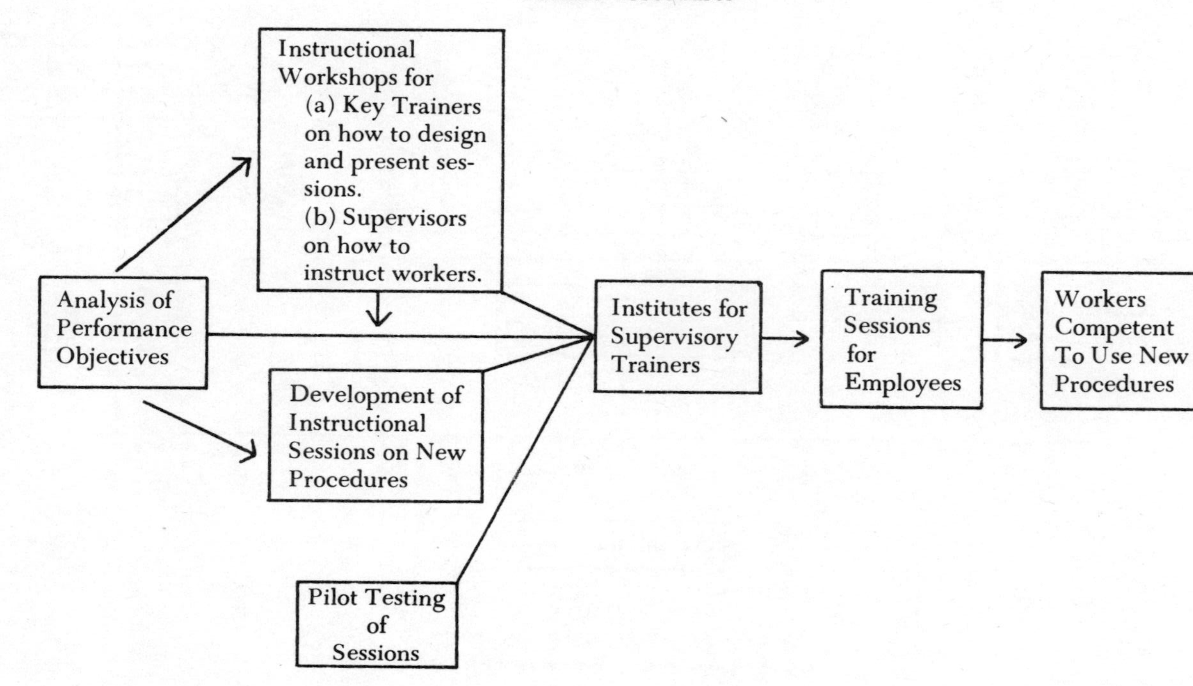

ment and implementation of the plan included (see Chart 16, opposite page):

1. *Analysis of performance objectives* by the training staff and the systems analysts who considered how the individual job requirements of people in different departments and units were changed as a result of the procedures, what employees would have to learn in order to perform under the changed procedures.

2. *Instructional workshops* that: (a) trained the key trainers in how to design and present sessions; and (b) trained supervisors in how to instruct their workers.

3. *Development of instructional sessions* on the new procedures by the key trainers coached by training staff.

4. *Pilot testing of sessions* presented by key trainers with critiques for accuracy of technical content by procedure writers and for effectiveness of training techniques by training staff.

5. *Institutes for supervisory trainers* given by key trainers on each of the new procedures.

6. *Training sessions for employees* on new procedures as structured by supervisors to include those modules pertaining to those procedures that must be applied by their employees.

The worth of the training system. The top manager acknowledged that the training system had helped workers to learn and use successfully the new procedures and that it was a significant contribution to making the new operation work. Managers recognized that their investment of the time of the key trainers was more than repaid by their being able to receive the help of prepared teachable units on the procedures created by the central training task force. They also found that the grooming of their supervisors to instruct their subordinates had an excellent payoff. Supervisors said that they had been helped to make the transition to the new systems, that they had gained a better understanding of their own jobs, and that they had gained confidence from their instructional tasks. Employees found the learning experiences effective and interesting. The units were tailored to employees' needs, and this precision eliminated unnecessary learning and focused specifically on changes they had to make. Demonstration was accompanied by an opportunity for practice, test, and feedback which gave confidence to workers prior to the system's implementation.

Systems and procedure writers learned to prepare less complicated and more understandable procedures. Cooperation with the training designers clarified the processes so that they were both teachable and workable. Key trainers found the instructional work personally rewarding. Working with other specialists they gained greater insight into the total operation. The training staff was strengthened by operating as part of the total framework, and it, too, gained greater insight particularly in functioning to achieve a critical organizational goal.

What made this training system for the conversion to automated systems measure up to the demands of the managers and the employees? Many elements entered into its final productiveness. To outward appearances, the training sessions were deceptively simple: (1) the objective of the session showed participants the specific changes they would make and why; (2) a demonstration was given of how the changes were to be made; and (3) participants practiced the operation and checked their results with the instructor.

But behind the smooth instruction and the guided learning were orderly steps in well thought-out preparation. The seventy supervisors could not have provided effective learning experiences for their employees *if* the key trainers of the training task force had not prepared the materials in ways that made them learnable; *if* the training staff had not coached them in how to instruct; *if* the Governing Board had not resisted attempts of department heads to withdraw some of their personnel serving on the task force. *If* procedure writers had not been linked with the key trainers, the content of the sessions could not have had such a high degree of relatedness; and *if* automated systems analysts had not been linked with the training staff, the design of the total training system could not have so precisely geared the training to specific applications of the procedures to different organizational units and their workers.

The transfer of the knowledge on how to apply the new procedures was not guaranteed by analysis of the learning needs, by the design and preparation of the learning units, by the grooming of the instructors, or even by the learning experiences in the training sessions themselves. The new knowledge had to be assimilated by the minds and the hearts of the men who wanted to make the new system work. No one organizational unit could have accomplished a task of this proportion. It took the training task force as a part of the framework of the Governing Board. The training group designed, tested, and made the learning available to those who could, if they wanted, get it into the mainstream of operations. But it took the Governing Board directing the managers and supervisors to make it run.

We learn how to make a training program productive by applying and using it. The same elements that make training productive to the organization are the ones that make the learning worthwhile to managers and employees. Training systems measure up when their purpose and use are known before they are initiated. Their objectives become their measures of worth. Once you have decided upon your purpose and objectives, you know what your measures are. They are the basis for evaluation.

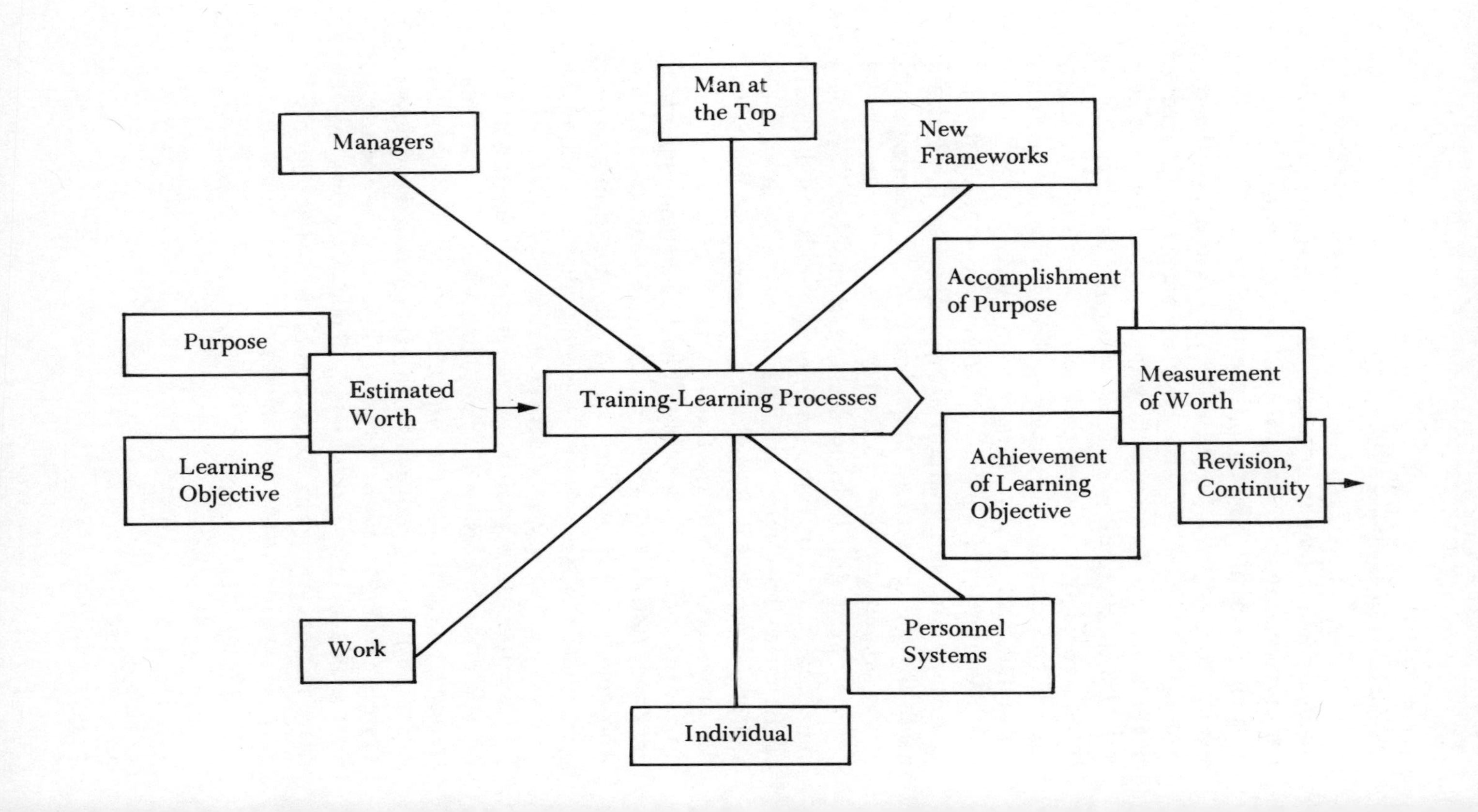
Man at the Top
Managers
New Frameworks
Purpose
Learning Objective
Estimated Worth
Training-Learning Processes
Accomplishment of Purpose
Measurement of Worth
Achievement of Learning Objective
Revision, Continuity
Work
Individual
Personnel Systems

11

Engineering the Training System

If learning is to function in helping an organization and its people acquire knowledge and use it to achieve productive results, the training-learning process and the elements of the environment that influence the application of learning must be engineered so that the desired results are achieved. What makes the difference between productive and nonproductive learning is the presence of an orderly design —understood and wanted by both management and people— integrated with action to achieve a purpose vital to the organization and individuals.

In this chapter we are bringing together all the elements discussed in previous chapters, that of engineering a training-learning system, putting ourselves in the position of initiating, planning, and maintaining the training and development efforts. This approach is generalized from the examples which have been reviewed in this book. It includes:

1. Recognition of a problem or situation which may require training and learning.
2. Analysis of the causes, ascertaining whether

11-1

ENGINEERING OF TRAINING—LEARNING SYSTEMS

Recognition of: Situations, Problems	Analysis	Planning	Action	Measurement of Worth
Productivity uncertain Introduction of new projects, changes in systems Manpower staffing needs not met Training-learning processes ineffective Workers becoming obsolescent	Determine extent to which cause lies in lack of knowledge, skill Determine feasibility of utilization of learning Estimate worth (benefits minus cost) Determine how critical the task, situation, or problem	*Criteria:* Is the objective clear? a) What needs to be learned? b) How will this learning be productively used? Is it worthwhile? Can learning be integrated with action needed to accomplish task or solve problem?	*Distribution of responsibilities between:* Top executive Department managers Supervisors-coaches Technical experts Personnel staff Training staff Planning staff Employees Center for Instructional Resources	*Achievement of:* a) purpose b) learning objectives Measurement/evaluation against purpose Modification and revision Improvement Continuity

Rapid technological changes outdistance human systems Impact of continuous personnel changes Work flow characterized by backlogs, excessive error, waste, breakdowns Decline of motivation	Determine organizational and work environment influences	Do attributes of training-learning process help to achieve objective? Are methods such that they establish climate and conditions that spark desire to learn? *Training-learning systems:* selection of most appropriate process to achieve objective and integrate with action needed to accomplish purpose plan for environmental conditions that will provide organizational readiness and utilization: a) man at top b) framework for collaboration c) managers d) work systems e) individuals f) personnel systems g) evaluation, revision, continuity	*For the following activities:* Establish priority for learning Help in understanding the meaning of learning-training within an organization Advise and help managers to diagnose, plan, and execute training Diagnose, plan, and execute training-learning systems Review of subordinates' development of employees and recognition Contribute personnel, technical expertise to collaborative instruction Develop instructional skills Prepare learning-training materials Select supplementary, external programs Feedback on progress in accomplishment of results	

training-learning processes can achieve objectives or can help solve the problem.

3. Planning: decision of objectives, comparison with criteria, and making the plan.

4. Action: making the plan work.

5. Measurement of the worth of the results, modification, continuity.

Implicit in all of the steps is the gaining of acceptance by everyone involved. An elaboration of these five steps is presented in the chart 11-1.

These steps in the engineering of the training-learning system are used in the case analyses in the Appendix. In actual practice, these steps are not always rigidly followed in the sequence here outlined. Learning is a dynamic process, as is the utilization of new concepts in work operations. Thus it will continuously open up new things to be learned and used. A group may be implementing certain training-learning processes while it continues to diagnose and plan for other actions.

When we look at the successful engineering of learning experiences within an organization, we see the function of learning as a *whole*: the interrelationships of the organizational influences and the training-learning processes. One cannot be diagnosed, planned for, or activated without consideration of the other. The positive functioning of environmental forces must be planned in the early stages. To get the results desired we need to design more than an effective learning process, more than the integration of learning with needed action; we must also design a positive organizational environment—one ready to absorb and utilize fresh concepts.

For example, unless an endeavor is made to see that learning is recognized as a mainstream activity wherever the training-learning process is being initiated, the amount and quality of management effort in the development of the employees will be negligible. If the training-learning experience itself lacks the qualities that provide productive results, the uselessness of the effort will deter future willingness to participate and support such programs. But where the benefits of training-learning efforts are visible and where employees are helped in their work to achieve and contribute productively, both managers and employees are interested and willing to participate.

The Situation: The Need for Learning

There are many signs that indicate organizations and individuals may be in need of learning: pressing organizational problems, warning signals of trouble ahead, systems breakdowns, conflicts or lack of communication between self-contained parts of the organization, challenges caused by technological changes in work methods. The question is: What knowledge and skills are needed in order to take appropriate action to handle the situation or solve the problem?

Organizations with successful productive training efforts have focused attention on ways of recognizing as well as examining the relation of their instructional learning processes to operational and behavior problems. The responsibility for recognizing and detecting situations which require attention is basically that of executives, managers, and supervisors. The responsibilities inherent in their managerial jobs are at times supplemented by staff training and by a temporary or permanent collaborative framework, both responsible to the top executive and making possible the co-diagnosis, co-planning and co-action of components and expertise.

What are situations, needs, or problems that suggest a need for instruction and learning in an organization? From examples in this book, we find indicators such as the following which led to diagnosis, planning, and action:

1. Productivity of an organization is uncertain: forces impede the utilization of people's abilities; breakdowns in communication between self-contained departments and failure to achieve organizational goals; future growth uncertain; organization lacking vitality.

2. Corporate planning calls for introduction of new projects: changes in systems and procedures, additions of new functions, reorganizations. An appropriate question of high priority is, "What skills and knowledges does this planning require of our employees that they do not now have?"

3. Manpower staffing needs are not being met: increasing turnover, low rates of internal development, poor quality of personnel available on the labor market; young college graduates often leave jobs, or become apathetic about work.

4. Training-learning processes are ineffective: methods are not productive; there is overemphasis on acquisition of information; or there is failure to carry over principles and techniques to work operations.

5. Workers become partly or entirely obsolescent: lack of assistance in job change; aging work force; tendency to be rooted in one place; apathetic toward change.

6. Rapid technological changes outdistance human systems for adjustment to changes: jobs, or parts of jobs, become obsolescent; job requirements continually change.

7. Continuing personnel changes require assistance: induction and helping new workers to adjust; assistance to reassigned and promoted workers; aid in transition to supervisory and managerial roles.

8. Work and work flow is characterized by backlogs, excessive error, waste, breakdowns.

9. Performance problems indicate the decline of motivation: results fall short of standards of time, quantity, and quality.

Initiating Training without Diagnosis

The organizations successful in getting to the root of their problems shy away from the quick leap from surface indicators of performance deficiencies to a decision to conduct training. What happens when a decision is made by one person in authority that training will be given to improve performance? Let's consider what happened in such a case:

> A top manager decided that the key secretaries in his organization should have some training. He felt they needed it to improve their communication and correspondence techniques. His judgment was based on his contacts with the department secretaries and with correspondence sent to him for review and signature. The mandatory start-up of the secretarial course, however, caused problems. The secretaries' bosses, who were responsible for their performance, had been bypassed. And the secretaries were ordered to take courses for which they saw no reason: to them their performance was satisfactory.
>
> Due to the pressure to get the course under way, a consultant-instructor was engaged. At times interest in the sessions was high, due to the cleverness of the instructor. Undoubtedly, as one secretary said, they "learned some things." But when attempts were made to measure the amount of change in the performance of the secretaries, there was little evidence of productive results. From the standpoint of carrying over the new concepts, neither the bosses nor the secretaries had any awareness of a need to change, nor did they desire to. The consultant-instructor could not bridge that gap.

Analysis of Need and Feasibility of Training

The decision as to who will make the analysis is exceedingly important. In many of the successful approaches to productive learning, an essential ingredient is that those involved in the diagnosis are also involved in the planning and execution of the training-learning processes. For example, the departmental work team that was appointed in the warehousing and supply company (Chapter 3, p. 40) to locate and correct causes of excessive backlogs and error rate, analyzed the trouble sources, planned and carried out the corrections, and integrated the instructional and learning processes with action.

Purpose

The purpose of diagnosing the symptoms and situations that present problems to the organization is threefold:

1. to determine to what extent the cause lies in the lack of knowledge and skill, or the failure to use the knowledge or skill. Symptoms and indicators may be incomplete, misleading, or erroneous.
2. to stimulate correct planning and implementation of learning experiences.
3. to lay the basis for learning experiences productive to both the organization and the individual.

The diagnosis must get at the root of the situation so that the proposed plans for solutions will be successful. And the diagnosis must make certain that training is necessary, and that it can be functional in helping to achieve an objective critical to the organization.

Who makes the analysis of the situation, its symptoms, the problem needing solution, or the task that must be accomplished? Essentially this step can be regarded as helping the manager to define his problem. For it is management which needs to learn how to integrate development of people as part of its overall job, helping its employees to learn and adjust to changes. As Mahler points out, accurate diagnosis of data with respect to determining what training and learning are needed enables the manager to see the needs for change.[1] It also helps him to identify an appropriate solution as he sees it, and provides a basis for his measurement of results, enabling him to take an experimental attitude toward his own efforts at change.

The process of problem diagnosis, planning the solution, and taking the necessary action is itself a learning experience. It helps individuals and groups learn. They learn through discovering the cause(s) of a problem, and they also learn through experience how to solve a problem or accomplish a task. Whether the solution of the problem or accomplishment of the task actually requires that training be provided, the diagnosis and planning process itself brings about learning.

Crucial to the development of productive learning is the initial determination as to whether learning is critical to the solving of the problem or accomplishment of the task. When it is found that certain employees must learn to do things they do not presently do in order that the task be achieved, learning takes on a sense of direction and vitality—it has meaning from the outset and is important. The learning objectives are seen in relation to making possible the accomplishment of the task. And this makes possible the development of the kind of training and learning experiences that function effectively.

Take, for example, a case where management has recognized failures in meeting manpower staffing needs. Managers complain of poor quality of performance, and the internal development of personnel is declining. Managers claim that the decline in the quality of the work is due to the poor quality of the new workers hired. A staff personnel group finds, however, that data do not entirely support this claim. Therefore, additional data are secured. A diagnostic survey is made of factors that affect positively and negatively the skills, abilities, and willingness of workers to accomplish their jobs. Discussions are held with other staff groups and interviews are conducted with managers, supervisors, and workers. The staff personnel and training group conduct a pilot program that demonstrates that new employees can learn effectively provided an appropriate learning process is designed and used. The staff also finds that certain changes in the environment are needed:

1. Managers and supervisors must recognize and fulfill their obligations for the development of their people.
2. Achievement in training is not accompanied by job progression, nor are there clear lines for personnel advancement.
3. The work itself lacks substantive opportunity to learn and demonstrate one's ability for advancement.

The completeness of this diagnosis laid the foundation for the development of a workable and productive manpower staffing program. The diagnosis had looked squarely at both the training and learning processes that would have to be developed and also at the supportive elements in the work environment that would need to exist in order to make the plan work. Furthermore, the diagnosis involved managers, supervisors, employees, and other staff groups, such as organization and planning, who had responsibility for work distribution and systems.

Value of Diagnosing the Need for Learning

Correct diagnosis of the symptoms that point to the need for training avoids costly, unnecessary, or erroneous solutions. For example, a food store manager requested the training department to train the checkers because of increased customer complaints of errors in amounts charged, and the careless packing of bags. But a test showed that the checkers knew the proper charges for items and the proper way to pack bags. Apparently it was a case of not using their knowledge. Interviews with the supervisors showed that they were lax in supervising the checkers. It was found that when checkers handled an unusually large number of customers, supervisors failed to recognize what was truly commendable performance. In fact, the supervisors were unconcerned about the performance of the checkers. The real problem was getting the checkers to use the proper procedures and to apply their knowledge of prices. It was decided that those most in need of training were the supervisors of the checkers, and that they should be given help in how to review, recognize, and reinforce the correct checking procedures. Mager and Pipe have written an excellent guide for analysis of performance problems.[2]

In another case, a group of dock workers were required to change codes used on their shipping documents, as part of a new nation-wide system. There was considerable apprehension as to whether the dock workers would understand and participate successfully in the training sessions being prepared in connection with the changes. A training consultant met with the key managers of the group and suggested that the dock workers might not need to participate in training sessions. What, he asked, would the workers actually be doing that was different from what they were doing now? As the managers indicated these changes, the consultant listed the categories and classifications of items being handled on the docks, circling those that were being changed. The consultant then asked for the new codes that would be used for the items circled, and wrote them next to the items being changed. He then suggested that—unless there was something else required of the dockmen—a card could be printed which the workers could keep in their pockets, listing those items which were being changed, and providing the new codes. There was no need of a course, nor of memorizing the changes. All that was needed was to make available the changed codes and the necessary encouragement to the workers to use the guidance information printed on the card. There are many forms of performance assistance, such as guides, samples, manuals, that provide reference and guidance material which help the employee learn to use the correct codes, formats, or whatever. When the analysis is correctly made of what needs to be learned and how it will be used, it may be found that a training course in its traditional sense is not needed.

Unproductive learning experiences result from mandating a course without having diagnosed how training will function to achieve the productive results desired. It is not uncommon for a top executive or the training staff to present a course because it has been successful elsewhere and it "seems like a good idea." In such cases, the executives rarely learn and understand the concepts and techniques being taught to subordinates. Effort is still being made to provide a homogeneous grouping in courses such as first-level supervisors or middle managers or executives. But by focusing attention on subject matter rather than on functions and problems with which they are all concerned each level is deprived of learning how the other levels function on problems that are the concern of the entire group. Furthermore, this traditional approach to training blocks the integration of learning with action since the higher levels are handicapped in following through in the application of the new concepts.

An executive accepted the offer from a higher headquarters to present a three-day management seminar at his local activity. He directed that quotas be assigned each department, and gave the list of nominees to the training director who was told to coordinate the seminar. It was a good course, and critiques were favorable. But the critiques represented only the offhand reactions of the participants to the course itself. Six months later when the training staff followed through to determine the program's impact on managerial practices, it found that little benefit had been realized. Participants expressed appreciation for "opportunities to meet with other managers" and for "insights into broader principles," but no one had done any thinking about his own managerial practices, nor how they might be improved. In fact, it was difficult for some to recall the experience, and some openly said they could not see why they had been nominated to attend.

Why didn't this management seminar have more productive results? For one thing, managerial abilities are not developed by an occasional one-time "shot in the arm." In this case, the unilateral decision of one executive was made without diagnosis of managerial and organizational needs and problems and without planning for how such a program could be used on the job. In fact, no one had specific information on what the program actually contained. Motivation was low and therefore learning and the desire to initiate any changes were almost nonexistent.

A marked contrast is provided in the approach of another top executive. He was aware of his organization's need for revitalization. Managerial practices were failing to mobilize the efforts of workers toward the achievement of desired goals. Productivity was precarious and future growth uncertain. In this case, the top executive worked with his top managerial group to diagnose what stifled the abilities of his people. The top managerial group participated in a problem-solving learning experience during which they discovered how the lack of open communication between them prevented their facing the real issues that held back organizational growth. For example, the top executive learned that the top managers, when he had consulted them for their ideas, had reported back what they thought he wanted to hear, since they knew that he had already reached a decision. The top managers were convinced, by their own experience, of the benefits of this instructional procedure and together decided that the group problem-solving session should be continued throughout the organization.

In this case, the top managerial group that diagnosed the situation also made the decision to extend the program to their entire organization. Members of this top group also continued to participate as consultants, trainers, observers, and instructors in the continuing groups. As a result the training was enormously productive.

Diagnosis of Organizational Environment[3]

The cases of productive learning have shown how important it is to have organizational readiness to put to use the ideas and concepts learned. Diagnosis therefore must look at environmental conditions: in the case of a problem needing solution, the influences and factors acting as obstacles to the utilization and incorporation of learning; and in the case of task accomplishment, an analysis of factors in the environment which will be needed to make the learning productive.

Elements in the organization that should be looked at in their relation to training and development of personnel are:

1. The extent to which top management makes learning a mainstream activity and the priority given the development of subordinates.

2. The need for a special organizational framework over and above the established structure; the need for coplanning, and coaction between separate components;

the condition of interdepartmental relationships; the need for combining different knowledges and skills to provide a broader scope of development opportunities shared by all members of the work force.

3. The part played by managers and supervisors—to what extent does accomplishment of the task or solution of the problem depend upon their handling of training tasks; the degree of their understanding of the training function; their willingness to help their people to learn, and to utilize their learning.

4. The extent to which work itself sparks or stifles learning; the degree of integration of technological changes with the work requirements.

5. The extent to which methods are used that enable individuals to become aware of need for learning and personal development and that encourage their desire and persistence to apply their learning.

6. The extent to which personnel systems enhance the worth of learning—advancement assured by demonstration of performance competence resulting from training; flexibility in job descriptions providing for development of productive performance; provision for updating of knowledge and skills at time of personnel changes.

Planning for Training-Learning Systems

In firms with productive learning efforts, analysis of data pertaining to problems, situations, and symptoms that suggest the need for learning has enabled managers with the help of staff personnel to define their problems and compare the benefits of alternative solutions.

Criteria

The following criteria have been generalized from successful training models discussed in this book. They have enabled organizations to decide between alternative actions:

Is the objective clear? What needs to be learned and how will this learning be productively used to accomplish the work task or solve the problem?

Is it worthwhile? Are the expected benefits greater than the cost? How critical is this task or problem to the effectiveness of individuals and the organization?

Can the training-learning process function to incorporate learning with the action needed to accomplish the task or solve the problem?

Do the attributes of the training-learning process—content, instructional procedures, flexibility of sequence, the instructors—have the qualities that will achieve the objective? Will they help people to learn and utilize their learning to accomplish the task or to do whatever is required to solve the problem?

Are the methods such that they will make things happen, not by forcing development on employees but by establishing the climate and conditions that spark the desire to learn and the persistence to achieve?

Who Does the Planning?

Organizations with productive learning systems have most often used a group collaborative process to develop the plan for their training system. Rather than turning over the planning to a training staff, these firms have used the training staff as part of the group. Recognition is given to the critical difference between designing a training-learning process and engineering a total training-learning system.

Generally, managers who have been involved in the diagnosis of problems and analysis of tasks to be accomplished see more clearly what the problem is; they see the need for change and willingly work out appropriate solutions. The staff training man is a possible source of help to managers in setting up training plans (provided the diagnosis indicates the need and strong potential utilization). But the staff trainer will not be seen as a source of help if his approach is to impose what he thinks should be done. Even where training staff are excited over the potential worth to managers of their own notions of a valuable training and learning experience, they must be ready and prepared to help managers solve their problems in ways acceptable to the managers. In other words, fundamentally the staff trainer must literally create a situation in which managers can learn rather than one in which they are taught. Managers must learn to acquire their own insights, discover for themselves (with the trainer's or consultant's aid) why their behavior has not produced results in solving the problem, discover their best answers, and take the responsibility for achieving the task, and making their solutions work. Thus the plan represents the managers' integration of training with their total managerial task. The skill of training technologists is used to design detailed materials, provide content, suggest instructional procedures, and groom managers and supervisors in their training and instructional roles. The knowledge of managers is needed to plan for the smooth functioning of environmental elements, and the lessening of potential obstructive forces.

Planning for the Training System

The training-learning processes. The training-learning process selected is that most appropriate to achieving both the learning and work objectives: what employees must know and be able to do. Where the need is for training experiences to solve a problem, to build teams to achieve a common cause, to open channels of communication between self-contained units within the organization, a group problem-solving process is appropriate. (See Chapter 8, pp. 141-146.) Where the objective is to train employees not only for their present jobs but to qualify them with competence to assume higher level responsibilities, to open up channels for advancement, a work-learning progression process is appropriate. (See Chapter 8, pp. 132-141.) Also, there would be a need for a collaborative instructional process. The supervisor's development of his subordinates would depend on his being provided help with specially designed and prepared instructional materials closely related to and amplifying the trainee's learning on the job. This requires a center for instructional resources which helps supervisors gain techniques for setting work goals, making progress reviews and providing feedback on work accomplishment, and recognizing good performance.

Implicit in the building of a training-learning process is the use of newer ways of structuring learning experiences within organizational life that provide those qualities needed for productive learning. (See Chapter 8, pp. 130-132 ff.) Most successful have been patterns that incorporate learning as an integral part of the work operations; a curriculum that helps employees learn what is truly vital to them and has job immediacy; instructional procedures which make use of a combination of techniques and methods selected for appropriateness to achieve objectives and for maximum facilitation of integrating learning with work through opportunities for application and feedback; flexibility of sequence that provides for a worker's self-direction of learning which provides him with what he needs to know at the time he most needs it as well as its being of advantage to the work at hand; instructors who are selected because of the appropriateness of their contribution to the training-learning process whether it be the manager, supervisor, special coach, technical expert, instructor, training specialist, or employees themselves.

Environmental design. In productive learning and

training efforts that we have examined the diagnosis shows that organizational elements were engineered so that productive use was made of the learning. Even the simplest plans using the most fundamental of the training-learning processes—that of day-to-day development on the job—require a work environment with the distinctive quality of managers and supervisors being expected to develop subordinates and being recognized for their efforts. This requires planning that the top executive participate in the plan particularly in his follow-up with his subordinates as to what they have accomplished.

Where the system requires a central apparatus for merging the expertise of technical staff, line experts, and training technologists to produce from local materials the kinds of training experiences that are highly useful, related, and in learnable patterns, then the top man must get departmental managers to agree to share their resources.

Where the training process provides for job progression dependent upon the trainee's demonstration of his learned competence, the personnel systems will need to provide paths for mobility as well as links between the evaluations of progress and the promotion actions. The training will be productive—in the sense that this is a manpower development process—only where there is both the trainee's satisfaction in his having achieved the learning and task accomplishment and the personnel system that in coordination actually advances the trainee upon evidence that he has demonstrated his competence.

External Courses as Part of the Training-Learning System

The selection of employees for participation in external courses is a part of a total training-learning process and should be treated as supplementary to the basic developmental process on the job. Take, for example, the individualized work-learning progression plan where the major focus is on the internal developmental process, not the external. The selection of an external resource is supplementary and it should amplify, strengthen, and add further insight into the basic task(s) which the trainee is learning and which he is demonstrating that he has the competence to perform. When the internal conditions favorable to growth and development on the job are neglected, there is the tendency to focus on external resources.

But the use of external training can be productive only when: (1) there is an understanding of how the learning will function to achieve the behavioral and work objectives; (2) both the employee and his superior see the training as a vital help to the employee in learning that which is needed to accomplish the desired results; (3) the work conditions make it possible to apply and incorporate the learning in work operations.

Unless both the individual and the managers understand the purpose for the training, incorrect assumptions may be made, as several illustrations show. One manager recalls a "shattering experience." His boss told him he was going to send him to school. Unaware of the frame of reference for his going, the manager thought management was "recognizing his ability." He worked "like the devil" and tried to gain much from the course. Later he discovered that his boss had had to get him out of the job temporarily because of a slack work period. Quota systems often force participation, and as a result management sends those they can "afford to spare."

One interesting study of how executives are selected for participation in management development showed that whether the executive is *sent* or *seeks to attend* is likely to have significant consequences.[4] The type of needs, the kinds of experiences sought, and the degree of involvement in the process of learning and development were found to be different depending on how the executive got to go. When an executive is sent, he tends to respond in terms of what he perceives as management's motives for sending him. In cases where the executive seeks to go, he tends to desire the experience, to be aware of the need for learning and to see opportunities for the utilization of the knowledge. "The fact that social and psychological needs can provide the motivation and also set a limit to both learning and development is of central importance to programs of management development."[5]

When shortcuts are taken, and not enough attention is given to laying the groundwork for external training courses, observations show that erroneous assumptions limit the effectiveness of the training. Individuals may get the notion that participation in a course is a fringe benefit, or a reward (not getting to go is a punishment), or a status symbol. Where career development programs list certain courses as recommended or mandatory, an individual may regard them as necessary to have on his record in order to be considered for promotion. All these "reasons" fall short of the essential one—that of providing a learning experience that functions toward a broader purpose, whether that is increased competence of an individual, the solution of a problem, or better productivity.

Shortcuts to Implementing New Systems

Some managers do not believe that diagnosis and planning need to precede actual training. An example illustrates this point:

> A large warehousing operation automated its supply procedures. The industrial engineering staff prepared warehousemen's guides which diagrammed

> and explained the changed procedures, and showed the impact of the new systems on warehousemen's jobs. Not all warehousemen were required to know all of the changes. In fact, the guides recommended that plans be made for adapting training to the specific situations.
>
> However, the manager, avoiding any analysis and planning, took a shortcut and decided there would be one standardized series of classes which all warehousemen would attend. He told each of seven foremen to prepare a presentation. Each one was assigned a different section of the guide.
>
> The results were disappointing. Judging from the comments, the warehousemen found the new process "just another one of management's ideas to make the job more difficult." And many reflected that "we are continually forced to make changes." The foremen—who acted as instructors—were hard pressed to attract the interest of the warehousemen. The group was much too large, and the foremen had not received any help in the organization of their material. Some, in fact, were told of their assignments as late as the day before the session. All warehousemen had to attend all sessions. Yet much of what they were forced to listen to did not apply to their particular job.

In this case, the manager skipped the most important part of the training-learning process—that of designing it so that productive results were assured. What was needed was a functional approach to what each warehouseman needed to learn to do that was different from his previous methods.

Action: Making the Training System Work

The test of a successfully engineered training system is in making it run and produce the benefits it was designed to contribute. In the execution of a total training system, those responsible for each phase or part of the whole system must review progress critically, provide feedback to those participating, and make needed adjustments in the functioning of the training-learning processes. If elements in the organizational environment are found to be roadblocks, these negative influences must be brought to the attention of responsible managers so that smooth functioning is assured.

As a guide to the implementation of action, a responsibility distribution chart helps the effective functioning of each part of the whole training-learning system (see Chart 11-2, p. 218).

The action taken to make training systems work requires continued attention to see that the interrelationships of the training-learning processes and the elements of the work environment mesh harmoniously to achieve the desired result. We refer back to an example discussed in Chapter 10, "A training system that was worth its salt" (pp. 188-193). In that case we saw different parts of the organization collaborate and share responsibility for part of the action to produce workers competent to use new automated supply systems. It was noted that the worth of the training system was recognized by the top executive, the department managers, subordinate managers and supervisors, as well as employees, all of whom were helped by the training system to make the conversion to new automated procedures a success. Many elements entered into its final productiveness. Behind the smooth instruction and guided learning were orderly steps resulting from well thought-out preparation. We pointed out the interdependencies of the special framework and the training staff, of the key trainers and the procedures writer, and many other interrelationships. What kept these dynamic parts of the system interweaving their efforts was a central instructional unit—combining technical, managerial,

11-2
Distribution of Responsibilities
For Training Activities

Activities: / *Responsibilities:*	Executive	Dept. Managers	Supervisor-Coach	Technical Expert	Personnel Staff	Training Staff	Planning Staff	Employees	Center Instruction Resources
Establish priority for learning									
Help in understanding the meaning of learning-training within an organization									
Advise and help managers in diagnosis, planning and execution of training									

Diagnose, plan and execute training-learning systems									
Review of subordinates' development of employees and recognition									
Contribute personnel, technical expertise to collaborative instruction									
Develop instructional skills									
Prepare learning-training materials									
Selection of supplementary external programs									
Feedback on progress in accomplishment of results									

Note: The activities outlined for the implementation of any training-learning system and the sharing of responsibilities will vary according to your plans.

and training expertise—which was backed by the Governing Board of the entire conversion effort. When problems and hitches arose in carrying out the plan, they were presented to the board; solutions were found and the effort progressed. When managers began to withdraw support, the Governing Board resisted these attempts.

A major characteristic of this successful training system (and it is true of other training-learning systems) is that the managerial, employee, and technical groups involved in the diagnosis and planning of what was required were also involved in the implementation. Thus they learned how to make the training system productive by applying and using it.

Measurement of Worth

We have said earlier that the training systems measure up when their initial purpose and use are known before they are initiated. Their objectives become the measure of worth. Therefore, the last phase of engineering the training system is to use the initial purpose and objectives as measures with which to evaluate its progress. A training system is worthwhile when it achieves the purpose(s) for which it was designed.

Who measures whether a training system is worthwhile? We have said in Chapter 9 that continuity of learning requires the participation of management both in the initial decision on the training objective and in the evaluation of how successfully the training system functions to achieve the needed objective. Measurement of worth also requires modifying, revising, and improving the learning experience so that it continues to become more productive.

Was the learning and training system effective? It was if the organization and its people learned what they needed to learn, *and* if that learning was utilized. Did it truly function in helping the organization and its people achieve the purpose for which it was designed in the first place? If so, it was effective and worthwhile. The impressive evidence of productive gains made by models discussed in this book was reviewed in Chapter 10. These models also suggest stimulating strategies for training and learning systems from which other organizations may benefit.

12

Organizational Models for Productive Learning

We have learned from comparative analysis of different training efforts that productive results depend upon an organized design to integrate learning with action vital to both the organization and the employee. Genuinely productive learning within an organization is not a matter of chance, nor is it solely a matter of good instruction, or of conscientious learners. What it requires is the understanding of what it takes in an organizational situation to make learning productive, and the ability and willingness to collaborate in making it work.

The elements of a favorable organizational environment and systematic instructional processes have been described separately in Chapters 2 through 10. In Chapter 11, we suggested how these elements could be engineered so that training-learning efforts can function to achieve purposes critical to the organization and its people. In the Appendix, five case studies from contemporary training practices in business and government organizations describe how they have incorporated learning with action to solve actual problems. In these cases you have the opportunity to see how organizations have engineered these critical elements to produce the desired results.

The models for productive learning must be designed to fit the needs of a particular organization. There is no one ideal model. What counts is that the model should be built to suit the organization's most pressing problems; it is necessary to learn what the organization, or its managers, or its employees need to learn in order to stay in business and improve their operational effectiveness. Organizations capable of continuous renewal and of adapting to future change do examine their learning and instructional processes. The comparison of affirmative examples of successful training-learning strategies has shown elements common to all that make the difference between productive and nonproductive learning:

1. Top leadership lifts the quality of thinking and points learning in productive directions by integrating learning with mainstream activities. Top leadership pulls together autonomous departments so that they learn how to function as parts of a whole team to achieve common goals.

2. Special frameworks and structures are interspaced in the regular organizational structure and provided with sufficient authority and combinations of expertise to engineer the productiveness of learning.

3. Managers make knowledge more productive. They develop their subordinates and thereby strengthen their own capabilities, establishing work goals, reviewing progress, providing feedback to subordinates, and recognizing productive contributions. Managers learn through participating as leaders and instructors in problem-solving groups and in collaborative instructional processes.

4. Work and work systems spark learning, particularly when changing requirements are seen as opportu-

nities to help employees learn to adjust to the changes. Job enlargement and restructuring are linked with training and learning processes that assist the worker's confidence in expanding his capabilities.

5. Individuals are aware of and desirous of learning; they are involved in planning and helping to shape learning and training experiences. The learning process functions to help people consciously adapt to changes.

6. Personnel systems are linked with growth and development processes. Instead of merely providing expedient and easy to administer personnel processes, the systems of recruitment and staffing, job and salary administration, and performance appraisal are seen as contributing to the development of productive behavior and utilization of knowledge.

7. Training-learning processes provide high relatedness, time and space flexibility, and instructional procedures that emphasize learning through the fulfillment of responsibility. The design of learning processes makes more certain the incorporation and use of what is learned and the engineering of the work environment to enhance, not impede, the utilization of knowledge.

8. Continuity of learning is provided through comparing the initial estimate of expected worth with the measurement of its accomplishment of the desired results, and the revision and improvement of the processes.

Organizations that are succeeding in making learning productive have rejected the traditional assumptions about training and learning within organizations. They have recognized that the old notion of two-way instructor-student relationships must give way to building more interrelationships, because many factors within organizational life aid or constrain the learning process and affect its outcome and productivity. They have found that efforts to superimpose training as separate course entities fall short of achieving their goal: the effective use of the new techniques and concepts. The completion of courses has never been a guarantee that new ideas and concepts will be incorporated in work. And unfortunately, efforts merely to increase courses and the number of employees participating in them often lead to lack of acceptance and legitimation of the training program. Unless the participant has the experience to test his knowledge and build his confidence in applying what he has learned, neither he nor the organization benefits.

Organizations successful in their learning efforts have questioned the traditional instructional and learning processes within the organization. They have devised new patterns based on their recognition of the following basic issues:

1. The training-learning processes are extended through and adapted to the organization of which they are a part, relating to the critical purposes and requirements of the organization's goals and the employees' learning needs.

2. Training and learning are functional toward accomplishment of work tasks and solution of problems; the purpose of training is more than the acquisition of knowledge and more than change in behavior, since these are only part of action to achieve the purpose.

3. The environmental influences of the organization can be engineered so that they work positively for the productiveness of learning.

The purpose of this book was—through comparative analysis of contemporary training and learning practices—to show elements common to successful engineering of productive learning. If an examination is made of the assumptions on which the present instructional and learning practices are based, it will be seen that ways can be opened up to gain productive results from training efforts. As the substantial benefits realized from new learning patterns described in this volume are considered, the reader may want to consider whether similar situations or problems exist in his organization. The question is: How can a learning and training system function to help you accomplish this task and solve problems critical to your organization and its people? If your organization is concerned with:

1. the problem of lower productivity, the weakening of employee performance, and the precariousness of growth—We have discussed examples of how organizations have used the learning process to release human potential, to control forces that impede progress, and that join autonomous parts of an organization in working toward common goals.

2. the development of manpower for present and future staffing needs—We have discussed examples of how organizations have prepared people for career advancement through work learning progression plans, contributing both to organizational productivity and strengthening the capabilities of its people.

3. keeping up with technological change—We have given examples of how organizations have used a training-learning system to: (1) help workers adapt to changing technological work systems that impose new requirements on their jobs; and (2) provide workers the assistance in learning new skills qualifying them for transition and transfer from obsolescent to needed work.

4. the lack of results from traditional management development courses—We have given examples to show that productive results in strengthening managers are gained from problem-solving groups, team-building expe-

riences, organizational development, and helping managers to perform their role in development of their subordinates, thereby developing themselves.

5. the influences of turbulent social changes upon efforts to produce the necessary goods and services—We have given examples in this book to show how organizations have used learning and training experiences to develop the quality of work life that upgrades and redirects efforts toward working together. New social patterns of learning are helping both organizations and people adjust to and live with technological change.

Since organizations are microcosms within which many of the present and future social changes will be experienced, the productive results as described in this book can help us to learn how to realize the potential resources which each organization contains within itself for its own growth and renewal and for the utilization of the capacities of all its members. Learning can function as a powerful force when appropriate training and learning processes are designed and a supportive learning environment is engineered.

Appendix A

TEAM EFFECTIVENESS PROGRAM (TEP)
Western Electric

Integration of Learning and Training with Action Needed To Solve Real Problems on the Job

This case illustrates: (a) integration of managerial team training with action needed to solve organizational problems, and (b) manpower development through linking recruitment and selection with systematic training and upgrading. Basically the Team Effectiveness Program as developed by Western Electric involves several levels of management, concerned with the same service or production goals, to concentrate as a team on solving a problem critical to each member of the team and to the organization. The group which learned and used team techniques for problem solving selected the problem of better utilization of skills currently available, as well as the recruitment, training, and upgrading of additional skills.

Background

Western Electric is one of the largest industrial employers in the United States with some 200,000 employees. It is the manufacturing and supply unit of the Bell Telephone System. Western Electric has over the years committed itself in many progressive ways to the continuing education and development of its work force. With a corporate headquarters in New York, Western Electric has service and product operations located throughout the United States. Training and development programs are handled by both corporate and local units. In the Personnel and Labor Relations Division at the New York headquarters, a Training Staff develops and field-tests training programs, and provides assistance to service and product regions.

The corporate training staff was recently centralized in its new Corporate Education Center near Princeton, New Jersey. The engineering and management training programs were previously conducted at eight different locations. With a resident staff of 75 training people and 125 visiting instructors, of whom two-thirds are engineering and technical instructors, the Center presents over 300 courses in engineering and in business management. In addition to the Corporate Center programs, others are developed and maintained by Western Electric's service regions and manufacturing locations.

As a result of the evaluation of various training programs, the Corporate Training and Development staff was concerned as to actual application and use of what participants had learned, specifically in the area of management development. There was some uncertainty as to the payoff from traditional management development programs that used simulated off-the-job situations to help managers learn how to solve problems. To make training more experience-based, a Team Effectiveness Program was developed which integrated learning with action needed to solve existing problems on the job.

The program as conceived by Western Electric's corporate training staff is described as follows:

I. Definition: The team effectiveness program or process is a team building effort designed to help the organization become more effective at identifying and resolving current and future organizational problems by making better use of the human resources available to it.

II. Goals:

A. Short term: The training group is to solve a problem critical to the organization. This solution can be reflected in written action items, recommendations, procedural changes, dollar savings, improved efficiency.

B. Long term: The participants learn through group interaction and work on the real problems and the application of managerial and team building theory of how to solve their problems. This learning is assimilated and used in future problem-solving efforts.

C. The broad goal: It is hoped to make the overall operation more effective by getting managers more involved in problem solving and bringing about actual improvements as a result of identifying barriers, finding what can be done, and actually accomplishing the improvement. The opportunity to confront interpersonal barriers would hopefully bring about more coordination as the result of learning how to get conflicts out in the open and reach agreement.

III. Steps:

A. The manager looks at his organization and determines whether:

1. there is a major organizational problem;

2. the present decision-making process needs to be improved;

3. the manager is willing to take an active role in team-building effort; and

4. there is a lack of commitment to organizational goals in his organization.

B. The manager calls in members of the Corporate or Regional Management training staff to discuss his perceptions of his organization and to explore the advisability of conducting TEP.

C. The TEP group is tentatively selected with the following conditions necessary for group makeup:

1. At least three or four levels of supervision are included.

2. The reporting relationship must be present; that is, if a department chief participates, his assistant manager and some section chiefs of his should be included.

3. The TEP training group is an entity in itself; that is, all members are in one manufacturing sub-branch, or members of an organizational task force reporting to one manager.

4. The group numbers approximately 12.

D. With his organization, the manager discusses embarking on a team effectiveness program. The training staff may be called upon to describe TEP and its implications. The group, with the manager, makes the decision about starting TEP.

IV. Progress of TEP: Since the spring of 1966, more than 500 management and engineering personnel have participated in Team Effectiveness Training sessions, including groups representing manufacturing, service, engineering, and headquarters staff. Groups have been organized at eleven different company locations and included representatives from four and five levels of management.

Locally Administered Training

Training and development programs are also developed and administered at Western Electric's service regions. For example, the Service Division West—Pacific Region, which is responsible for the service, engineering and installation of central office telephone equipment for the Bell System in four western states, has within its regional staff three training groups: Management Training, Management Development, and Technical Training. The case study in this instance deals with the program offered by the Management Training group. In 1966 the top managerial team of the region authorized a local management training program. It was staffed with line managers who were assigned on a rotational basis to the Management Training Department. Its first efforts were directed at providing a series of Management Workshops which covered communications, financial management, and performance appraisal training for managers in the more traditional manner. Later the corporate training staff instructed trainers from the Pacific Region in the Team Effectiveness Program and provided materials for their use in implementing this new program. The Pacific Region training staff then let it be known to managers that it could provide consultant and trainer assistance to managers interested in the use of this program.

Need

The manager of the San Francisco Bay Installation Area, Western Electric Pacific Region, wanted to build a management team that would develop and utilize their people, getting them to work together to achieve a more effective organization. The San Francisco Bay Installation Area was very much a part of the large San Francisco Metropolitan Area and was shaped partly by the influence of its environment and the kinds of people available for its work force. It presented to the manager, who was interested in change and renewal of the organization, a challenge more difficult than building a new organization from scratch, for the culture of this group represented a wide range of values and goals and fairly fixed patterns of getting the work done.

The manager received the offer of the Management Training staff to set up a TEP training group to help managers recognize and overcome obstacles that prevented the best utilization of its members in reaching objectives of the group. He had participated in similar training groups which he had found worthwhile. He saw the possibility of this program as a helpful experience for his managers, an experience that would help them to identify, analyze, and solve together a real problem, and thus bring about improvement in their operations.

Diagnosis and Plan

The manager discussed the possibility of a Team Effectiveness Program with the coordinator of the Regional Management Training group. As they analyzed the situation, the following needed to be done:

1. Determination by the group of barriers that blocked their effectiveness.
2. Decision by the group on a problem critical to the unit's work.
3. Managerial encouragement of individual initiative and growth and of willingness to accept responsibility.
4. Opening up of communication and the attainment

CHART A-1

San Francisco Bay Area Installation TEP Group Organization Chart Showing Levels, Reporting Relationships

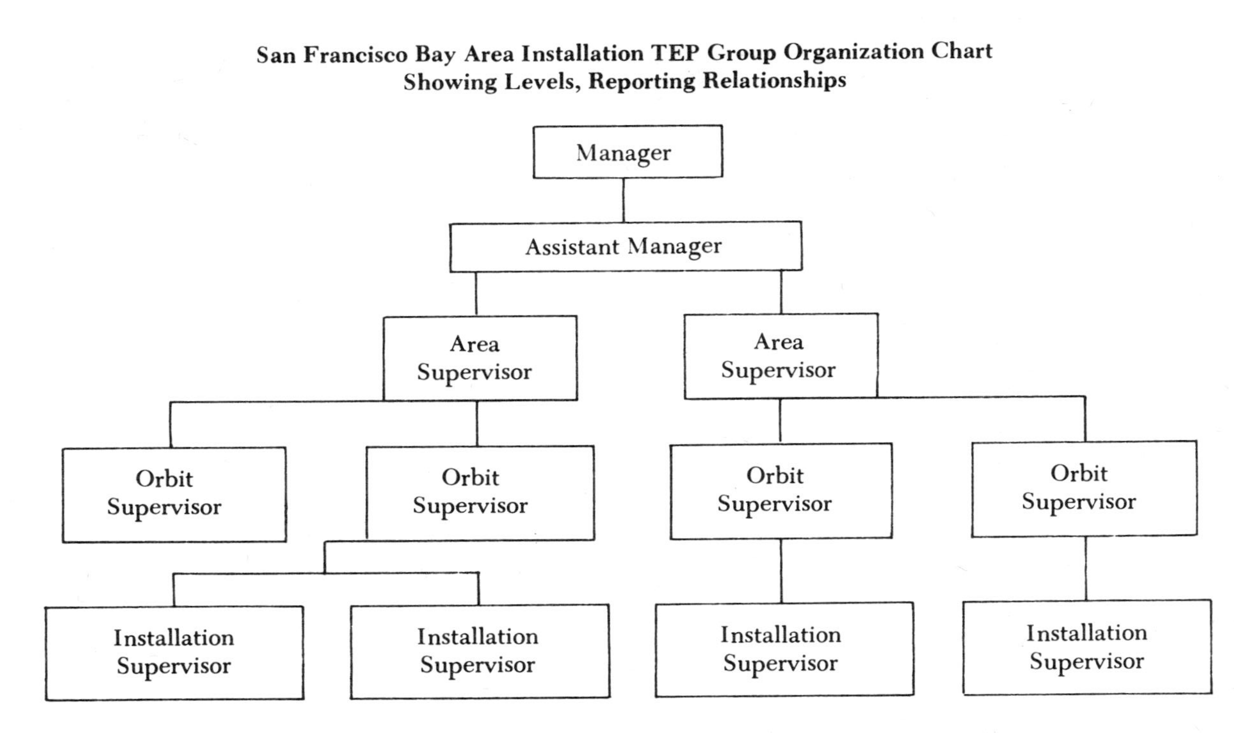

of greater trust, confidence, mutual understanding, and respect; inducing different levels of management to listen to each other; and removing the lower level managerial fear of speaking up.

5. Bringing about change in the way managers meet and continue to meet problems.

The plan they made included:

1. The establishment of team effectiveness training with representatives of five supervisory levels, including the top manager, meeting regularly for three hours once a week for ten weeks.

2. Conducting a series of anonymous interviews by the Regional Management training staff with the participants to get their views on the most critical problems facing their organization.

3. Analysis of the interview information by the training staff, a summary of which would be given to the entire group as a background for their choice of the problem upon which they would work.

4. Group work on resolution of the problem, concurrently with learning how to work as a team, discussion of techniques of group action and learning aids and hindrances to their progress.

5. Assistance by the trainer as an external consultant, at times providing theoretical explanations of group action, and at other times pointing out to the group what was going on, getting it to look at group member actions and their consequences.

Action

1. At the request of the manager of the San Francisco Bay Installation, the Regional Management training staff set

up a Team Effectiveness Program. The manager arranged for a group of twelve to participate, including himself and eleven managers of four lower levels of supervision (*see* Chart A-1).

2. About two weeks prior to the first session the members of the training staff conducted individual anonymous interviews with the participants to obtain their views on the organization, particularly to sense problems that interfered with getting the job done the way they would like to see it done. Prior to the group's first meeting, the training staff analyzed the information for frequency and commonality of data.

3. The training staff submitted to the group at its initial meeting a summary of those problems which seemed of greatest concern to the group:

a. How can we better utilize the abilities, potential, and skills of all members of our group to improve our decision-making process?

b. In what ways can we reduce the conflict between our individual needs and the needs of the organization regarding:

1) goals and objectives?
2) authority and responsibility?
3) training, development, and utilization of personnel?

c. How can we better plan, schedule, and coordinate our activities:

1) among ourselves?
2) with interfacing organizations?

4. The group continued for the next several meetings to work toward a selection of the problem upon which they would work. Leadership was shared among the group as determined by the group. The training staff helped the group by presenting explanations of group techniques and by observing and intervening at times to point out what was happening:

a. Presentation of theoretical explanations of group techniques and provision for analysis and practice:

1) Observation of different roles played by members during the group process such as task function (initiating, informing, clarifying, summarizing); maintenance function (harmonizing, encouraging); individual functions (such as blocking, dominating, etc.).

2) Leadership styles such as explanation of a theory of reality-oriented leadership (developed by the Management Research and Development Staff, Western Electric). This gave participants an understanding of and practice in relating three factors: the manager, his subordinate, and the situation. This helped the manager learn to use the most effective style in relation to his capabilities and those of his subordinates, and to the specifics of the situation. They also learned the degree to which different styles provided for various degrees of sharing in decision making, which in turn was related to the capabilities of subordinates.

3) Other techniques on group problem solving, group member impressions, feedback processes, and defensive/supportive climate.

b. Observation and intervention to call attention to critical incidents in the group process:

1) The training staff's contributions were related to the group process, not the content of their discussions. Comments concerned how the group was accomplishing its task.

2) For example, they intervened in the discussion when the group did not listen to an idea proposed by one of its members. This helped the group realize

that "we didn't give him a chance." Or when the group got off the track, the question "What are you doing here?" enabled the group to adhere to the subject at hand. Thus they contributed to the progress and the development of the group through getting it to observe its own action.

5. The group realized their organization faced an increase in its work loads, recruitment difficulties, increased movement of personnel between jobs, and more turnover. It finally decided that its major problem was the development and utilization of its work force, that it needed to make people more useful more quickly, to reduce turnover, and to utilize its current resources and skills more effectively. A final statement of the agreed-upon problem read: "To meet our 1970 work load requirements through: (a) improving our method of utilizing skills available; (b) hiring, developing and maintaining additional skills."

6. In addressing itself to the portion of the problem "improving our method of utilizing skills available," the group established a subcommittee to work on updating a skills inventory, involving job supervisors in periodic reviews of skill requirements, and sharing skills within the area supervisor's organization.

7. In addressing itself to the other portion of the problem, "hiring, developing and maintaining additional skills," the group looked into: (a) the appropriateness of the wage scale for the first two levels of newly hired installers; (b) the equitableness of credit for practical training as compared with academic credit given; (c) the desirability of lengthening the basic job skills training and the degree of involvement of supervisors in the hiring and training process such as establishing contact with the new hires; (d) the feasibility of follow-up questionnaires to new employees concerning their initial training; (e) the adequacy of contacts with local community resources for recruitment purposes and for publicizing installers' jobs.

Results

The Team Effectiveness Program brought about actual improvements as a result of identifying the problems and working out solutions. As a consequence of their learning to work together it brought increased self-confidence to employees and an awareness of the effectiveness of team work as a tool to get results.

Hiring, training, development of new skills:

1. There was an increase in the involvement of supervisors in the hiring, interviewing, and selection program. A better "high school relations" program was set up. Arrangements were made for supervisors to talk with school counselors and to give more time and thought to interviewing new installers. Publicity on work opportunities was improved and a more accurate picture of the job was developed.

2. The one-week basic training course for newly hired installers was increased to two weeks with provision for the trainee's prospective supervisor to meet with the trainee during the second week of training. Three members of the TEP work group monitored the new course.

3. An evaluation questionnaire was developed by managers which obtained comments of the new hires that was helpful in the improvement of the basic training course.

4. A request was made to corporate headquarters for an improved entrance wage schedule and for giving credit for practical training on an equitable basis with credit for academic training.

Utilization and development of skills of employees on rolls:

5. An Index Progress Record system was established to provide for systematic recording of the work assignments given to each installer by his supervisor as a basis for determining his qualifications for advancement.

6. Supervisors were required to review periodically the progress records of the installers under their supervision so that the supervisors would vary the kinds of work assignments, thus adding to the depth and scope of the installers' qualifications. The periodic review would also serve to encourage both supervisor and his subordinate installers to consider the need and potential benefit for additional training courses. Such periodic reviews provided for more systematic interrelationships between learning through work experience, training courses, and upgrading.

7. Provision was made for the sharing of skills within area district organizations.

Feelings of group on team effectiveness program:

8. The group generally felt it had made fuller use of existing know-how, talents, and resources, and that most aspects of their task had been accomplished. As a result interest and motivation were increased and the group decided to continue in a post-conference activity, since the group believed it had just begun to work collectively on problems and felt that it could make significant contributions.

9. The group had some reservations as to whether channels of communication had been fully opened, although it was aware that lower levels of supervision could and did play an important part in higher decision making. It was felt that it was still difficult for supervisors to disagree with the thinking of their bosses or to originate new ideas that had not been previously checked out with the

boss. There was still reticence and fear to speak openly in a hierarchical structure such as this group.

10. There were some feelings of doubt as to whether all members were willing to "pick up the ball," so to speak, even when the opportunities to take action were there. This was attributed to the uncertainty as to what they had power to do and the fact that most people do not think in problem-solving terms.

11. There was a breaking down of the individual or vested interest in certain units and a gradual buildup of interest in the goals of the entire organization.

Summary and Analysis

In summarizing the experience with the Team Effectiveness Program, we should keep in mind that it illustrates on one hand a team training effort to solve a real problem of the firm, and on the other hand the development of a more systematic program for hiring, training, and utilizing their people resources, which was the problem they selected for their team effort.

1. The Team Effectiveness Program illustrates that *the influence of the man at the top* makes a considerable difference in the learning and application of that learning in an organization. Leadership and participation of the man at the top was illustrated throughout the entire development and implementation of TEP. At the corporate headquarters of Western Electric, the President was a leader in the establishment of programs to develop managerial skills. The General Manager of the Pacific Region endorsed the program. And, in this example, we have seen that it was the top manager of the San Francisco Bay Installation group who from the beginning sensed a need for such a program and arranged with his managers and the regional training staff to initiate it. This influence comes not from the top man's ordering the program, not from the sense that he is the top authority, but rather from the fact that he *paved the way* for the group to get started; and by his involvement in the work of the group he not only felt the *value* of the effort but *set an example* for the lower level managers.

2. This case illustrates that the *management of training by managers themselves* makes a difference in the effectiveness of that training. For one thing, managers by their own participation in and willingness to learn demonstrated to lower level managers their estimation of the value not only of this program but of learning and development. Instead of *sending lower level supervisors* to training with the inference that it was the lower level supervisor who needed to improve, this was a family type group in which the higher level supervisors learned to appreciate the problems of the lower levels and built mutual interest and understanding as well as willingness to help the subordinates develop.

It is interesting to notice that the solution found by the team of managers to the problem of utilizing both new and current skills required managers and supervisors to become more involved in systematic hiring, training, and upgrading of installer personnel. For example, supervisors under the devised plan would make contact with new employees during their second week of basic training. Another example was the provision for periodic review by managers of their arrangements to assign installers a sufficient variety of work and schedule adequate participation in correlated training courses to qualify them for upgrading.

3. The Team Effectiveness Program demonstrates the principle that the *collaboration of those having the knowl-*

edge and functional abilities makes a considerable difference in the effectiveness of the learning and particularly in its application and interweaving with everyday operations. In this instance, the group was constituted of four managerial levels below the top manager, the subject matter experts in the installation function, and the Regional Management Training Staff with training expertise. This framework provided a structure with a built-in coordination of all the elements needed to bring about learning and its application to the improvement of work—in this instance through finding and taking action on better ways of utilizing and developing its manpower. In this respect, it provided a sharp contrast to programs that turn over to the training staff the job of management and supervisory development and thus confuse the responsibility for direction, control, and coordination of the effort.

Analysis of this is significant from an organizational perspective as well as the process of learning. To explain this, let us look more closely first at the organizational influence. The team that made up the TEP group had the knowledge and capabilities of the problem and the need; *it also had collectively the power to take action and thus apply what it was learning* through its fact-finding groups and the discussion of recommended steps for improvement. This is not very often a characteristic of learning programs. They may seek to simulate the real situation through case studies, role playing, problem solving, but the transfer and payoff possibilities remain precarious. Also, one notes that this structure of learning provides not only for actual accomplishment, but it automatically raises the status of training from an adjunctive or peripheral activity to a high priority and brings it into the mainstream of action. With the group's combination of knowledge, authority, and the functional responsibility, it moved and it acted. It organized itself into subgroups to better use its own capabilities, and once it had reached a decision it had within its own makeup all those whose operations were affected by the decision and the changes being made; thus it paved the way for coordination and did not have to face later the problem of getting agreement.

From the other standpoint—its significance in the learning process—it is important to notice that this type of team group learning process provided the attributes for true learning that made intelligent action possible. Such a learning process was useful in helping members of the organization learn to work together: its initiation was based on a firm foundation of need and group desire to participate; its content was of interest and relevant to work; its methods helped them learn by doing; it built upon their experience; and they were given information on their performance.

4. This case illustrates a principle discussed earlier (Chapter 11, Engineering the Training System), that the *way in which a learning program is initiated* makes a difference in its effectiveness. In this instance, the Team Effectiveness Program had been developed and field-tested by the corporate training staff after they had determined there was a need for this type of training. The regional training staff, after it had prepared itself to offer the program, then described it to the managers in the Pacific Region of Western Electric. The manager, in this instance, of the San Francisco Bay Installation Area, who saw the possible worth to his managers, discussed and verified the conditions and problems with his subordinate managers and with the staff trainer. It was only after there was an understanding and acceptance of the program that it was initiated.

5. The various aspects of the *structure* of the TEP

sessions made these effective as a learning process. In general, the structure evolved from the group, rather than being forced upon the group. Since the progress made by the group toward the selection of its task and the solution of the task determined the content of each session, there was no pre-ordering of the sequence of discussions.

(a) *Objectives*: The group was well aware of its objective—to solve a problem critical to the organization. They were not only well aware but interested in this objective, since their interviews had provided the facts from which they as a group would select their major problem. They also were motivated by this learning experience, since they knew it was to be used in achieving their objective.

(b) *Content*: The group found that the content was highly relevant to installation problems and to the people with whom they worked. The content consisted, furthermore, of topics bearing on their own choice, hence they had a high interest in it. The introduction of theoretical explanations about managerial styles and contributions to group processes was felt to be part of the solving of the actual problem, and thus these explanations were not regarded as academic and irrelevant.

(c) *Design, sequencing, and timing:* Except for the very broad design of the program, the sequence of units and the timing of their discussions were in the hands of the group. The fact that it took more than the first session to arrive at a decision as to what its task would be—in other words, what was the most important problem for the group to solve—shows there was no artificial control. Actually, the learning of the next step the group needed to take in order to proceed toward a solution was what governed the sequence of its topics.

(d) *Methods*: "You learn to participate by participating" might well describe the method of learning, and as such it influenced the effectiveness of the training. The group also learned to coordinate their functions by coordinating them. Even when there were theoretical presentations made about group processes, the group became involved in their application through participation in exercises designed to give them insight as to what was going on in the group. Learning about one's self was aided by the use of videotape recordings and feedback which mirrored for each group member his behaviors in a group effort such as this.

(e) *Interweaving of learning and work*: The effectiveness of this learning experience was strongly influenced by the bringing of training into the real world of work and operations. Probably this is the single most distinctive feature of TEP: the fact that it does not leave up to chance that there will be a transfer and application of learning, but rather plans the training of a group not only to apply what has been learned to the work situation but also build it in the action process. This was seen in, first, the way the group learned about team processes and then had the opportunity to apply this to their contribution to the group's more successful functioning; and second, the problem selected for solution—that of the better utilization of people's skills—was resolved by more systematically relating the experience and training to qualify installers for upgrading.

6. The *linking of training with other personnel processes* finds an excellent example in the solution achieved by the TEP training group. The managers became aware of and took action to insure the systematic integration of hiring, training, and upgrading. They set up a skills index progress report to insure that managers kept track of specific work assignments of installers, thus providing opportunities for installers to gain experience which would qualify them for advancement and motivating them to enroll in training courses that would facilitate promotion.

7. The TEP experience illustrates the influence played by *feedback to the group* on how the group handled its task and learned to work as a team. One of the keys to effective learning is the learning by experience based on information given to an individual or a group on performance. It was this knowledge of results, and the avoidance of any moralizing or corrective teaching, that helped the group make changes in its behavior. Thus they developed ways of handling problems and finding solutions.

8. This case provides an excellent example of the importance of involvement and participation of all levels of management in the training program. The feeling of worth and satisfaction of the accomplishments of the group was a *direct* influence. Another aspect was the interweaving of work and training. Normally managers look upon training as competing with work, as somehow detracting from productivity. In this instance, the interrelationships of the group learning and the action taken to make improvements and increase organizational effectiveness made them regard the learning program as worthwhile. The insecurity and fear sometimes felt by managers, because they regard their subordinates as threats to their own interests, were replaced by open communication through working together.

Appendix B

MANPOWER PLANNING AND DEVELOPMENT PROGRAM
Chase Manhattan Bank, N.A.

Changing Organizational Conditions to Improve Manpower Development Through a New Training Systems Concept

This case represents a strategy for meeting staffing requirements by organizational teamwork, resocialization of management, and job redesign to provide conditions for a modern training systems concept integrating work and learning.

Background

The Chase Manhattan Bank, N.A., is one of the world's largest banks, providing complete financial services in its 152 branches in metropolitan New York and other branches scattered throughout the world. Chase Manhattan has given continuing attention to meeting and solving critical urban problems, especially in New York City, in which it does so much of its business. It has initiated programs designed to upgrade the skills and living standards of lower income citizens in that area. One example is the Business Experience Training program (BET), which provides part-time jobs for high school students from minority groups in slum area schools with high dropout rates. These students are provided a work-study program with a part-time paying job as long as they remain in school, and a full-time job after graduation. The Job Opportunities in Business program (JOB), for young men and women mostly from minorities and dropout categories, provides four weeks of instruction in basic educational skills. This is followed by technical job training and entry into first-level positions, with continued assistance in further educational experiences.

Need

By the late 1960's the Chase Manhattan Bank had gained considerable experience with its programs that provided orientation and entry training of the minorities and the disadvantaged. Though this experience prepared the Bank for a new labor force that was gradually emerging in New York City, several warning signals suggested the need for a revised look at some basic assumptions and practices relating to manpower selection, placement, training, and development. These warning signals included high turnover, declining performance, and low internal development of new hires.

Diagnosis and Plan

The Community Banking Department of Chase, comprising its vast branch office network, was quick to recognize that its future viability largely depended on its ability to develop its human resources. Enlisting the aid of Corporate Training Services staff, Community Banking management was determined to design a systematic integrated framework that would make a positive impact on the problems of turnover, performance, and development. Underlying this determination was the belief that such problems require a focus on the total organizational situation, particularly the climate of the organization, and the effect of its day-to-day conditions and managerial practices on the employee.

1. *Supervisory attitude.* Supervisors felt that low development rates were primarily due to the fact that most of their new hires were marginal high school graduates incapable of being trained. They also felt that if they were given the "right" kind of people they could improve performance of these hires. To determine the actual limitations of the new hires' capabilities, the Training Services Staff developed a self-instructional unit, administered pretests, training, and post-tests to groups of the marginal new hires. These groups showed marked improvement, and it was concluded that the problem was more the *lack of systematic opportunity to learn* than the *lack of ability to learn.*

2. *Technological change.* The introduction of computer operations to the bookkeeping department had changed the flow of work and the job content. As a result, the main functions of the bookkeeper job changed from one that required a good deal of skill and imagination to one that consisted of routine secondary duties, such as filing and mailing checks, which provided little knowledge of bank functions and did not help qualify entrants for more complex jobs.

3. *Training plans.* There were no well-defined plans

for the indoctrination of new hires to their work, for helping them to learn their responsibilities, or for qualifying them for more complex jobs.

4. *Organizational framework.* It was not clear who was responsible for the development of subordinates. Responsibilities were assigned broadly to branch administration, the branch banks, various staff components at the Head Office, managers and supervisors at the branches. Unit heads were usually working supervisors and did not feel that they were directly responsible for helping their employees to learn and develop. Neither were they held accountable for such development.

5. *Perception of work by new hires.* A considerable number of new hires were placed in file clerk jobs that seemed remote from actual banking operations. The monotony of continual filing made them feel their positions were of inferior status. The behavior of others toward them—abrupt demands for information—resulted in breakdowns in communication. The result was that the branches had begun to reflect what could be described as a socially stratified system. The young and inexperienced, particularly, uncertain of themselves and the opportunities available to them, perceived few means for progressing within the system.

The Manpower Planning and Development Program provided for:

1. Organizational changes such as: (a) the decentralization of responsibilities to branches for the development of their personnel and control of the processes leading to their advancement; and (b) clarification of managerial roles and responsibilities for the development of human resources as well as for production and cost reduction.

2. Restructure of jobs and rewriting job descriptions for positions, particularly those whose work had lost meaning because of new technological systems.

3. Establishment of a job progression structure with clear lines of advancement as shown on schematic diagrams making visible to those interested in career promotion those jobs in their organization to which they could hope to work for promotion.

4. A personnel inventory system to coordinate staffing need with employees available for advancement.

5. Training systems that designed development processes which pulled together a variety of learning experiences both on and off the job and geared the employee for advancement.

Action

1. Schematic diagrams outlining job progression routes were drawn. Taking visual form in a "career map," these Development Plans charted various paths to positions of increasing complexity and responsibility. Each branch was provided its own reproduction with color-coded boxes indicating existing positions within that branch. At a glance, an employee could check the next immediate step in his progression.

2. The adoption of the program led to a number of actions. A central Manpower Planning and Development Committee was created as a framework—a sort of special organizational structure—interlocking the various components of the head office and the branches with staff groups in planning, implementing, reviewing, and revising the program. Made up of two representatives from each of the five branch groups, it bridged communication gaps between executives at the group and branch levels, the branch personnel, and staff specialists. It reviewed the new training systems, explained them to the branch personnel, and watched for day-to-day problems in the program. It devised ways to in-

CHART B-1

THE UNIT TELLER SYSTEM
Chase Manhattan's Training-Learning Progression

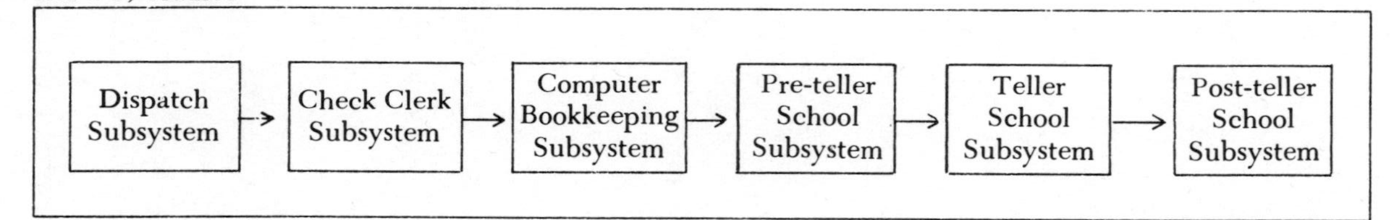

Each subsystem consists of:

1. Study of programmed self-instructional unit.
2. Work experience to practice knowledge and skills learned.
3. Instruction by supervisor or designated coaches.
4. Measurement:
   a) Evaluations of work performance
   b) Tests of knowledge acquirement
   c) Self-evaluation by employee

Time required is flexible:

1. Total: Maximum, 57 weeks; minimum, 9 weeks.
2. Each subsystem: As trainee demonstrates competence in a subsystem, he advances to the next subsystem.

volve operations people, the branch executives, and the group executives. It analyzed turnover and development records and educated its members on the comparative development rates of the different branches. It made visits to branches to obtain overall acceptance of the program.

3. Restructuring was commenced on jobs in areas with the highest turnover and the lowest development rates and on jobs affected by the introduction of computerized processes. Such jobs were analyzed for changes in responsibilities as well as in the relation of duties as preparation for other jobs. Jobs were standardized for all branch operations, thus opening up larger ranges of opportunities. Schematic charts were revised to show which jobs prepared employees for advancement and the higher level jobs to be obtained. For example, the Computer Unit Teller Training System was divided into sub-systems: Dispatch, Check Clerk, Computer Bookkeeping, Pre-Teller School, Teller School, and Post-Teller School. As the trainee demonstrated competence in a sub-system he advanced to the next sub-system. See Chart B-1. Also the supervisor's job was revised to make it much more than that of a working supervisor; it would now require supervisors to assume responsibility and accountability for the development of subordinates.

4. Managerial roles and responsibilities for training new hires were defined, and the roles of full-time coaches were established. A resocializing of middle and lower management required their development of subordinates, provided them the opportunities to guide and assist their subordinates, and recognized accomplishments of managers who successfully developed their subordinates. Monthly, the bank managers reported the number of various types of development, such as number of advancements and number of potentials. The new system took a look, on a monthly basis,

at the comparative records of development, hence the utilization of advancement of people.

5. Training systems were established to provide the opportunities for learning and progressing from one phase to the next in the Computer Unit Teller groups, where the turnover rates were highest. Self-instructional study materials were developed and combined with other training methods, such as orientation, on-the-job instruction, coaching, testing, and work evaluation. Each system was divided into several phases or subsystems. The supervisor-trainer was provided a guide for each phase which correlated the assignment of unit of work learning tasks with assignment of study units. Advancement was dependent upon performance evaluations and successful completion of the study programs. The training systems were linked with the restructure of the jobs and the inventory forecast system.

For example, the system for the Computer Unit Teller, completed in December 1969:

a. Made it possible for a new hire or staffer to qualify for a series of job assignments that progress to a Unit Teller job: Dispatch, Check Clerk, Computer Bookkeeper, pre-Teller School, Teller School, and Post-Teller School.

b. Provided flexible learning periods allowing individuals to move as rapidly as they were able to complete study materials and successfully apply what they had learned to performance on the job.

c. Organized each phase into tasks for which training schedules were prepared with approximate target dates for ratings and progression, dependent upon the trainee's performance and tests. Guidance was provided on the administration of materials and suggestions were made relating to on-the-job instruction and off-the-job training opportunities as well as pre-school preparation and post-school follow-up.

d. Provided objective instruments by which supervisors could measure knowledge acquired and work performed.

Results

1. A drop in turnover rates and increase in development rates resulted in improved performance. By December 1969, 174 trainees had completed their programs and had been placed in permanent quota assignments; 113 more were in the process of being trained. The number being developed from within the organization increased more rapidly than the number of hires from outside.

2. There was an increase in the number of branches volunteering to train new hires for the computer unit teller training system for the entire Community Banking Department.

3. Promotional opportunities were increased. Personnel were made aware of career development opportunities through job progression and of the specific jobs for which they could plan to train, and they could discuss their plans with their supervisors and with visiting representatives from the Manpower Planning and Development Committee.

4. There was a larger pool of qualified people to fill openings throughout the branch system; the inventory system made it possible to give consideration to all people with potential for promotion.

5. Branch managers and supervisors, in assuming their newly clarified roles, exercised responsibility and took an interest in the development of their employees. Recognition was given managerial effort in this respect through the

"Monthly Report of Your Manpower Inventory Planning and Development Program."

6. The opinions of the new hires toward their work became more favorable. A survey questionnaire in 1970 showed that 70 percent now believed that if they did good work and proved they had the needed qualifications they would have an excellent chance for advancement. A year before the majority of new hires had felt just the opposite, reporting that they felt they had no chance.

7. The Manpower Planning and Development Committee acted as a special advisory unit, giving leadership to the five branch groups, reviewing progress, considering and implementing changes, opening up communication channels both to and from the branches and their employees.

8. The training programs became more effective. Training time was cut in half and coverage of training material was increased; quality of performance and tests of self-instructional materials showed increased effectiveness.

Summary and Analysis

This case study describes an organization's strategy for integrating manpower planning and development with training systems to meet their staffing requirements by cutting down on turnover and increasing the development of their present employees. It involved the establishment of organizational teamwork, resocialization of management, and job redesign to provide conditions for a modern training systems concept integrating work and learning.

The strategy was first to diagnose the problem of turnover and lack of internal development. This was done with sufficient thoroughness to prove that new hires, even though marginal high school graduates, had the ability to progress when there were planned opportunities to learn and to apply knowledges and skills on the job. The diagnosis in fact revised the thinking of managers who previously had concluded that the new hires were incapable of learning. Managers not only had new insights from the credibility of the demonstration, but also learned more about their own roles and responsibilities in helping to develop their subordinates.

It was significant that the design of the program planned for constructive action to meet several different elements contributing to the problem: lack of definitive plans for training; uncertainties of managers as to their responsibilities; failure of the organization to place a value on managerial development of employees; demotivating aspects of the nature of the work; negative attitudes toward the entrance jobs that provided no line of advancement; and lack of inventory and planning for staffing and development.

The recognition that the problem of internal development of staff was related to many different parts of the organization's structure led to the establishment of a special framework—a center for the direction, guidance, control, and coordination of the program. It was not turned over to one staff group, such as the training branch, for unilateral action. A central Manpower Planning and Development Committee was established to represent everyone involved in this program. It provided visible leadership; it constantly reviewed the operations of the training systems; it took an active part in communicating the program and its benefits to bank personnel; it listened to the reactions and problems of the program and became involved in coordinating the work of all those participating in some phase of the program. This Committee acted as a task force interlocking the roles of various staff groups, the training specialists, and the position design technicians. The Committee, as well as the program which it administered, linked the training and instructional expertise of staff groups with the managerial and technical expertise of the branches. The training and the technical experts put knowledge and skill fundamentals for the Computer Unit Teller training series into learnable units. Supervisors and coaches were given guidance in how to assist their personnel in the learning and application of these skills. The Committee also requested them to give their suggestions for improvement of the coaching system, the linking of the pre- and post-experiences with the learning provided by the central teller school.

An important aspect was the recognition of the impact of urban environmental conditions, such as the labor market, on an organization. Action was taken to keep both the bank's systems and the thinking of its managers open to the impact of changing conditions, the need for changes in managerial values and priorities, and the urgency of action in the development of bank personnel. The bank, through its Committee, established requirements for positive leadership and support of internal development of employees. It further provided help in the form of job restructuring, establishment of lines of advancement, and sequenced learning systems. It also made certain that branch managers and their supervisors realized their accountability. The Committee provided a monthly report of manpower development rates by branches to encourage recognition and reinforcement of positive action.

Recognition was given to the impact of technological systems on the nature of certain jobs as well as the social structure. Action was taken to restructure jobs, parts of which had been taken over by computers. This restored interest and motivation. It provided the challenge to master certain basic banking processes that qualified employees for advancement.

The attributes of the training systems—particularly the

Computer Unit Teller series—are in marked contrast to many of the day-to-day improvisations called "on-the-job" training:

1. Initiation of the training was based on organizational as well as individual employee needs, as verified by the training staff's diagnosis.

2. Structure of the training provided clear objectives to managers, supervisors, and participants as to what would be learned, how it would be used on the job, and to what higher level jobs it would provide the basis for advancement.

3. The content of the self-instructional materials, on-the-job instruction, and class training paralleled the work phases and their steps.

4. The flexibility of scheduling allowed for adjustment to meet each individual's situation and abilities.

5. Instructors and coaches selected from technically qualified people were assigned full time, eliminating the dilemma of competition between getting the work out and giving guidance to new hires.

6. Participants were in the program because of their own choice of a career that progressed from an initial entry job such as the computer clerk to a top supervisory position, and eventually to the position of officer.

7. Training was linked with the evaluation process; instruments for rating both performance and learning of study materials were based on related phases of the work-learning process.

The increased visibility of the benefits of the Manpower Planning and Development Program influenced management's attitude toward and confidence in the development process. This was a result of involvement of management in planning, participating, instructing, coaching, and evaluating, and the overall leadership and coordination by the Central Committee. Just as learning was not an adjunct but closely integrated with work and daily operations, so were managers and supervisors involved in managing the learning process rather than treating it as an administrative detail to be handled by other personnel.

From the standpoint of the new hires as well as employees who had felt themselves without chance of advancement, this program brought an attitude of usefulness; it helped them to learn their current assignments as well as to prepare for the next phase; and it gave them a feeling of accomplishment in being able to learn and apply the learning to their work and their career plans.

Appendix C

ORGANIZATIONAL GROWTH AND DEVELOPMENT
Raymond Corporation
Changing Managerial Practices through
Integration of Learning with Action
To Solve Management Problems

This case illustrates the strategy of bringing about organizational growth through the learning process which, under the leadership of the man at the top, brought members of the organization together in new structures where they learned to work out solutions to problems together and, as a result, made more effective contributions to organizational productivity.

Note: The Raymond Corporation has often been cited as an example of successful "organizational development." Here it demonstrates how the learning process functions to bring about an awareness of the need and will to change, provide knowledge upon which to base change, and create opportunities to practice and develop confidence and skill in teamwork.

Background

The Raymond Corporation in Greene, New York, manufactures material handling equipment, electric industrial forklift trucks, and automated systems. It was founded in 1840 and acquired by the father of the current president in 1922 when it was primarily a job shop and small foundry operation. Following the depression, the company got its start in the material handling field through some early inventions in the handlift truck field, after which its sales grew from a quarter of a million dollars per year in 1940 to 5.7 million in 1956.

The authoritarian style of management during the father's control of the firm, mixed as it was with family paternalism, resembled a sort of benevolent dictatorship. Responsibilities were delegated, but authority was not. The father worked hard and expected everyone else to do likewise. Managers were supposed to remember how things had been done, or what the top man wanted. There were no written policies, no guidelines.

When Mr. Raymond became the president and general manager, he decided that the "scientific management" approach could best bring about needed growth. He wanted to develop a management team and to use modern management methods. He improved policy statements and clearly defined organizational guidelines and systematic procedures. Responsibilities were clearly delegated and authority was assigned as well as accountability for action. Despite the improvements in the organization, however, managers still did things the way they always had done them. Not only was there no real evidence of change, but profit, as a percentage of sales, dropped from 5.8% to 5.5%. The president was seriously concerned as to whether this small company could grow and compete successfully with large organizations in the material handling field.

Need

The Raymond Corporation was in need of a force to vitalize the company if it was to survive among the giants in the field. Scientific management had not succeeded in moving the company ahead. Despite his efforts, the president was not getting creative decisions or the best contributions and ideas from his top managers. Managers had the feeling that the president had pretty well made up his mind regarding problems upon which he asked their advice; therefore, they responded to his requests for their opinions with information that they thought would support his decisions.

In 1963 during Mr. Raymond's participation in a president's management workshop, a sensitivity type of training, he learned some things about managerial styles and their influence on utilizing people's skills to improve productivity. He also learned something about his own managerial style. He saw the need for helping his managers learn managerial styles and the techniques of team work. He also saw the need for providing opportunities to apply and use new concepts once they had been learned through integrating training with the action needed to solve real problems on the job.

Analysis and Plan

Mr. Raymond sought the help of a professional management consultant to help in the analysis of obstacles to organizational effectiveness, to design a plan to eliminate such obstacles, and to build positive supportive forces. Managers needed to learn alternative ways of managing their jobs and their people, the consequences of these different styles, how to assess their own style, and how to listen to others' assessment of their style. They needed to learn how to honestly criticize ways of doing things in their organization, to discern problems that interfered with growth and productivity, and how to get constructive team action. Managers must also be provided the opportunity to apply what they would learn, and to gain confidence by application and practice in day-to-day action.

To gain support of the entire organization, there was also the need to provide learning experiences for all members, if not immediately, at least on a long-range basis.

The consultant set up a plan which provided a variety of actions to meet these needs:

1. Measurement of communications between members of the organization, starting with survey and interview of the evaluations and feelings of managers, including the president and his top managers, of each other's managerial style and its effectiveness.

2. Identification of the parts of the system that needed to change.

3. Off-site conference for the top team of managers to share the results of the communication questionnaires and to bring into the open any feelings and problems not yet expressed; an analysis during this conference of each individual's management style.

4. Group decision by the top managerial team on the goals and direction of organizational growth and development.

5. Continuing learning and training processes for the middle and lower level managers and other members of the work force.

6. Provision for the carry-over of the team building learning experiences into work applications; training through on-the-job problem solving.

Action

Top Team Learning

Through questionnaires and interviews, the top managers analyzed their own managerial styles and also those of their peers and their boss, the president. As part of this preconference process, the president had also participated in the analysis of his management style as well as that of the others. The consultant interviewed the top levels of management about their perception of the way peer managers operated.

The top managers and the president met in a three-day off-site conference. They first listed problems which they felt blocked the organization's effectiveness; they discussed what caused these problems and what actions might be taken. The consultant presented the analysis of each member's managerial style, including what the man himself had written, what his peers had written, and what his boss, the president, had written. This provided a way to open up misunderstandings, gaps in information, and blocks to effective work relationships. Managers, during this session, learned for the first time about their own and others' managerial styles. They recognized their interpersonal problems and that change was needed to eliminate practices that were constraints on the organization's effectiveness. Feeling the worth of this type of lab experience, the top team decided to embark on a similar program for the entire organization.

Grid Lab Learning

The first Grid Lab was conducted by a consultant from Scientific Methods, Inc., the firm that had developed the Blake-Mouton Managerial Grid. With a feeling of confidence resulting from their own learning experience, the top management team initiated managerial grid training for the entire organization. During the last seven years, ten labs have been held, using their own managers as trainers, moderators, observers, and consultants. Participants consisted of corporate officers, middle managers, and first-line supervisors. In addition, about one-third of the office and factory workers have participated, representing many occupational levels. Attendance was required of the professional and managerial employees; it was voluntary for other employees. Managers and supervisors encourage participation, but do not tell their employees they must attend.

During the 50 hours of required pre-work and the 50 hours of classroom work for the first phase, participants learn by actual experience the problems of management, the value of team work versus individual action in organizational work, and the effect an individual can have on other members of the work team.

The Grid Labs enabled participants to understand different styles of managing and their consequences. They learned to organize themselves as teams, discovering and experiencing effective techniques to accomplish their goals. They learned the need for effective direction, decision-making, getting ideas from the group, and evaluation in an atmosphere of openness so that work processes could be improved. Thus they saw and felt the worth of learning.

Training to Use Team Concepts

Follow-up sessions were arranged for the members of the lab session to provide training through practice and application of techniques learned in the lab sessions. From these sessions, task forces and special teams were formed which worked on problems of the organization or units of it. They formed temporary structures superimposed, as it were, on the regular organizational structure. Each member of such a group remained in his regular organizational spot, but he also functioned temporarily as a part of the task force to accomplish a certain task or solve a special problem. Leadership was not fixed but shifted to different people, depending upon who had expertise in that area.

Top Managers' Follow-up Sessions

The top management team also continued to hold follow-up meetings. They worked on problems needing team attention by the top group. They continued to open up communications between departments. Annually they held a self-audit and planning meeting.

Periodic Surveys

Periodically all members of the organization were surveyed on the results of their lab experiences and their effect on work operations, as well as those of their superiors and their peers and subordinates.

Selection of Chief Coordinator

As the labs continued and the use of the newer team techniques became a reality in day-to-day operations, the president hired a personal assistant to help implement, coordinate, and maintain the various team building activities and projects.[1]

Results

To what extent has managerial and employee learning and application of new concepts of work operations borne fruit? Following are the results.

Successful Learning and Use of Team Skills

Personnel learned in the labs how to function as a team and the value of this process to corporate achievement. And they were able to carry over into day-to-day operations the use of these team skills, with resulting improvement in managerial practices. For example, when a major change was under consideration, such as the design and manufacture of a new product, a group was assembled of the responsible people concerned with the project, where in an atmosphere of openness differences were aired, conflicts were dealt with, and problems in interpersonal relations were anticipated. Working "family teams" learned how to solve problems together as a group. For example, one task force reviewed the entire compensation policy and developed a new salary program for the hourly work force, using the same criteria that were applied to management people.

Upward Mobility

Results were measurable in terms of increased capacities, work performance, and subsequent upward mobility. Of the 282 persons who have had Grid Lab training, 259 are still with the company. Of these 259, nineteen have been promoted to group leader or specialist positions; eighteen have been promoted to managerial positions; six who were already managers have been promoted to higher management jobs; and fifty-seven others in office and labor jobs have had promotions or transfers within their job classification.

Increase of Internal Trainer and Consultant Skills

The use of managers as trainers enabled the company to become less dependent on outside consultants and to increase self-directed team activity. Managerial skills in team building have been developed to the point where line managers have acted as consultants, trainers, observers, and moderators for the labs that followed the initial one.

Managers have made the development of their people a fundamental part of their jobs. Awareness of the need to plan and follow through on learning and training operations has convinced managers that this is a part of their job. According to one manager, "This is our job. We are responsible to know what our people need and how to help them develop."

Use of New Organizational Structures

Successful results from team-building action increased managerial confidence in both temporary and permanent changes in organizational structure. Formation of temporary systems of working family teams or task forces was superimposed on the regular structure. On the other hand, divisions were actually reorganized. For example, the vice-president of the engineering division reorganized his work into projects under the direction of project engineers. A product-planning group of three members was formed to which the product planning function was delegated. Task forces or product-management groups were created that crossed divisional lines for their representation. Middle managers were able to make decisions and take action at any step, from the early research stage to the creation of the final product. Changes in organizational structure opened up communication channels, and communications between and across levels improved, conflicts were surfaced and settled, and work operations functioned more effectively.

Evidences of Increased Productivity

Increased productivity was evidenced in the number of product changes, increased sales, and rate of profit growth. Seven product changes were brought out in the first year and a half following the initiation of this program. This was a decided contrast to the record for the previous three years during which there were no changes. The organization met its profit and sales goals at a rate twice as high as that before the organizational learning process was started. Sales increased from $7.6 million to $30 million. Net income rose from $520,000 to $1.2 million and earnings per share from 72c to $1.22. Not only that, but this small company successfully competed with the industrial giants in the same field. Raymond's rate of growth over the past five years has ranged from 10% to 15% more than the growth rate of the industry as a whole.

Summary and Analysis

Man at the Top

This case illustrates that the influence of the man at the top makes a difference in the effectiveness of learning within his organization. The initial push came in this instance from the young president of the firm who involved his top management team as well as himself in learning about their managerial styles, as seen by themselves and others. He provided both leadership and support, involving himself in the learning process and in continuing participation, thus enabling his team to give a sense of direction to the entire organization. This differed from merely providing support to a staff-initiated program.

In the words of the president, "I have tried to illustrate that it has taken me as president about ten years of concentrated effort to change the culture of our company, and we haven't made it all the way yet. How long would it take to change, and in fact is it really possible to change, if the president isn't the leader in the change? When my father was chief executive officer and I was president, he often got faster action by asking a question than I did by issuing a direct order."[2]

Managerial Practices

Throughout the development and change resulting from actions of the Raymond Corporation, we can see the importance of managerial practices in relation to learning and growth of the organization. Its managers were the mediums through which this program was planned, developed, and continued. Learning was a function of managerial practices in two ways: (1) managers must learn and use new concepts and techniques of working together; and (2) the practices of managers make a great deal of difference in what learning takes place in the other elements of the organization and by other groups of people in it.

The analysis of the influence of managerial practices on learning tells us much about the integration of training with the day-to-day operations:

a) Managerial convictions about training depend largely on how well managers understand the program and feel its worth. By participating in the processes, managers saw and felt its benefits. When the managers in this firm understood training because its values became visible and their convictions were based on productive results, then they became leaders in the further development and continuation of the program. Their active roles as consultants, observers, trainers, and moderators added to their confidence and understanding.

b) Managers changed in the way they handled the development of their employees. Instead of regarding subordinates possessively and fearing that any investment of time and sharing of knowledge with employees might be lost through their promotion, managers saw that their responsibility to the organization as a whole required that they develop their people so they could be upgraded and contribute more to the organization's effectiveness. Hence, higher priorities were given to the tasks of coaching, guiding, and developing subordinates.

c) Learning in an organization is heavily conditioned by behavior of those who manage. People learn by what they see and how they are treated. The examples set by managers in this case influenced the attitude, interest, and accomplishment of their subordinates. Workers knew that their bosses were making the effort to learn and to apply new concepts about team work. Therefore, there was new significance in actions taken by their bosses. Also changes were seen in their treatment, such as more open communications, the way discussions were held, the manner in which work was assigned, the interest evidenced in the learning and growth activities of their subordinates. Employees learned much from observation of their superiors' behavior.

How Learning and Training Are Initiated

The Raymond Corporation's program for organizational change illustrates that the way the training process is initiated strongly influences how well it achieves its objective. In this case, the group of managers who initiated the program understood its purpose and wanted it. Also they were willing to participate. The top managers and Mr. Raymond mutually agreed that they needed to learn together how to work to achieve common goals. Everyone understood what they planned to do and no one was forced to participate.

The top man participated with his managers, all of whom had a voice in the organizational development training. They continued as participants in different roles, such as instructor, moderator, and observer. Thus they were able to carry through the initial planning. In this case, through their own experience and awareness, managers saw the need for learning to work together.

The fact that higher level managers participated in and understood the team-building process provided a stimulating example to participants. It also made the managers knowledgeable about the program and helpful in informing their subordinates about participation. Employees were not sent by managers. Participation was not forced, and in the final analysis, each participant made his own decision to go and thought out in advance what he hoped to accomplish by taking part. In discussing attendance at these sessions, one manager said, "You can lead your employees, but you can't make them go. However, none have turned down an opportunity."

The Structure of the Learning Process

Analysis of various aspects of the structure of this learning program will show us the difference they make in its effectiveness.

Objectives. Individuals saw and felt the objectives of the program: to learn to work with one another as a team, to gain a better direction of work toward organizational goals, to learn how to consider each team member's ideas in order to arrive at the best decision, and to apply these concepts to their work situations. Knowledge of these objectives did two things: it helped individuals direct their own learning; and it stimulated their interest because they knew they would use it.

Content. The content was vital and real, not academic and abstract. It is correct that some concepts introduced were abstract, but they were made quite real by experiencing the events and interactions these concepts described, such as the frustrations or successes that hindered or helped the group's progress. They learned the effect that one individual could have on another, and the value of teamwork in day-to-day relationships. This was highly relevant to their work; it was absorbing and it was vivid and real. Therefore, it was learned—and retained.

Design. The design and sequence of this learning process was not left to chance or improvisation. Learning sequences were well programmed. The early study materials and first group exercises formed a foundation upon which were built more complex exercises and more difficult concepts.

Methods. This was not a telling and listening process. Methods were participative. They required participants to be involved in active processes, to think in new ways, to take new steps, and to work together in new ways. Individuals were stimulated to think; they were placed in situations from which they could not escape without thinking.

Integration with work. Instead of assuming that learning of principles and techniques automatically are transferred to work situations, this process provided for carry-over of learned principles to real problem solving. A training process was thus built into this program which brought about actual use and practice; the development of skills through day-to-day practice prevented the dissipation of learning.

Integration of the program into day-to-day operations was an extremely important influence on the effectiveness of the program. First, learning and training became part of the mainstream of planning and action. When a problem needed a solution, a task force or "family group" was formed that cut across divisional lines and reached down through several levels. Thus constituted, such groups worked together for the best solution and put it into action. Second, the visibility of the process and its benefits greatly raised the status and estimate of value of this program. Third, the usefulness of learned principles in their application to the organization's operations motivated both managers and employees. The continuation of the Grid Labs and the participation of those completing the sessions made people want to learn principles and techniques they knew they would have good opportunity to use.

Continuing feedback. Groups learned to look critically at how they functioned. Information was given to group members on how they handled the group exercises in reaching decisions and comparing their techniques. They learned what they had accomplished, or did not accomplish. They learned the reasons for success or failure. People do learn from experience, provided they understand their experiences and learn to look at them critically.

Learning Linked with Personnel Processes

This case illustrates the reinforcement provided a learning program through linking it in a consistent way with personnel procedures. This is seen in two ways: when people know their superiors support them in moving up in the organization, and when they learn that the personnel system makes it possible for those who demonstrate growth and development activities to receive promotions. This is what makes learning worthwhile to employees.

Managerial Perception of Worth

Fundamental to the effectiveness of learning in this case was the fact that managers saw the program as worthwhile. Managerial confidence grew from their first experience as participants through successful applications to their continuing participation in training roles. A new norm for managers had been established, and they were recognized for their leadership in the program for organizational change. They did not see the management of training as lost time but as part of their job. They did not regard this learning effort as useless. On the contrary, the benefits of increased productivity, better team work, new products, increased sales, and the increased capacities of their employees—this was solid and visible evidence of value.

Employee Perception of Worth

This case illustrates the importance of the way in which employees feel that learning is worthwhile. In this instance, employees found they had a real stake in learning: in the labs, in team and task forces, and in other learning activities. Peers whom they trusted found and expressed the worth of team exercises. Employees knew they were free to move within the firm, and that they would receive support, provided they showed their ability to advance. The investment and effort put forth in learning was recognized and rewarded. Employees felt the interest and support of supervisory encouragement. They knew their ideas counted. As Mr. Raymond put it, "We involved people in how to make changes. They had a chance to influence the direction."

Appendix D

MANAGEMENT: LEARNING AND PERFORMING ITS TRAINING ROLE

Internal Revenue Service, Western Region Incorporating the Training Function in the Managerial Role through Collaborative Instructional Processes and Organizational Development

This case represents a strategy that requires management to make knowledge more productive through the establishment of a collaborative instructional process and the engineering of an organizational environment favorable to learning.

Background

Among federal government organizations, none have met a greater challenge to change than the Internal Revenue Service. And change it has from a rather slow-moving, traditional organization to a highly effective and much respected public servant with a very sensitive mission, whose watchword is courteous, intelligent, and efficient assistance from workers who are vigilant and well trained. This year approximately 72.4 million personal returns will be filed with a $102.3 billion intake on individual returns. The leaders of the Internal Revenue Service have deliberately set out to build a strong organization through developing the strength of their people. The successful operation of the greatest wealth-gathering machine in human history has been accompanied by a change in its image and that of its employees. There has been continual development of its people to meet the challenge of change, to monitor increasingly complex rules to an entire nation, and to match the skills of tax and law specialists of large corporations and wealthy individuals.

Backing this tremendous transformation is the dynamic build-up of people through an extremely well organized development program based on sound growth principles—sound from the standpoint of learning theory and from the design of favorable organizational conditions that have created a positive learning environment. Internal Revenue has learned what it needed to learn and what its people needed to learn. It has gone about its business in a professional way with excellent results.

The Internal Revenue Service of the United States Treasury Department is administered through seven plus regions. Of these, the Western Region, which is the subject of this case study, covers the ten states of California, Nevada, Oregon, Arizona, Utah, Idaho, Montana, Alaska, Hawaii, and Washington. It has a work force of approximately ten thousand. These employees represent a wide range of occupations such as: accountants, lawyers, auditors, collection officers, investigators, appellate conferees, data processing technicians, clerical, and administrative management types.

The Western Region through the development of its people has itself grown in effectiveness and productivity. It has succeeded in establishing the managerial role for developing people and integrating learning with work; and with managerial leadership it has made its training, growth, and development highly successful.

Need

The Internal Revenue's Western Region was aware of the need to develop its people so that they could make their strongest contribution to the organization. The Western Region was also aware that it must improve the practices of its managers with respect to their development of people. There was need for increased training and educational opportunities and resources, particularly related to the policies, procedures, and principles of the Internal Revenue Service. Needed were managers with the understanding, willingness, and ability to incorporate new knowledge, concepts, and ideas into their operations. To develop and update their employees, the Western Region needed to improve both its instructional resources and to build organizational conditions and the climate that would encourage development.

Diagnosis and Plan

In order for management to learn its training role and to manage the development of its people, there needed to be: (1) strong top management leadership holding managers accountable for the development of their employees; (2) a collaborative instructional process by which managers could contribute their technical and managerial expertise, make personnel available to prepare and administer instructional experiences, and furnish information on training requirements; (3) initiation of training-learning efforts based on firm objectives for their use and with content and instructional qualities appropriate for the achievement of the objectives;

(4) development of managers through team building, involvement in course development and instruction, and the application of new practices in the development of subordinates through mutually established work goals, feedback from progress reviews, and recognition of work accomplishment.

As the result of the preceding diagnosis, the following plan was developed:

1. Top leadership would establish learning as a mainstream activity with high priority for managerial action and would follow through on managers' development of subordinates.

2. A collaborative instruction process would be established to which all components of the region would contribute their managerial and technical expertise as well as their personnel on part-time assignments to develop and present instructional experiences. A Regional Training Center would provide an organizational framework in which professional training personnel would be augmented by temporary assignments of needed expertise to develop courses and give instruction in them. Thus the Center would be an instrument of the organization and would make it possible for members of the organization to share in the development and transmission of needed knowledge and techniques throughout the organization.

3. A strong and capable training staff separate from the personnel department would report *directly* to the Regional Commissioner, providing counsel and advice to his leadership in the training and development of his workers, the Training Director acting as part of the top management team.

4. Managers would participate in a variety of development experiences, would contribute know-how and personnel to share in the support of the Regional Training

Center, and would manage the integration of learning in the day-to-day development of their subordinates by extending the instruction from the Regional Center to their people and by providing coaching guidance to their subordinates in their work.

5. The qualities of learning programs would make them worthwhile both to participants and to the organization through the appropriateness of their content, instructional procedures, flexibility, and instructors.

6. Development and growth would be established as part of the personnel processes, such as: selection and pretraining of potential leaders; appraisal of managerial performance in light of success in application and utilization of what has been newly learned, with preference in career advancement for those participating in course development and instruction and showing ability in developing their subordinates.

Action

1. The Regional Commissioner of the Western Region established a Training Task Force representing all functions, operations, and components of the region to make recommendations for a sound development and growth program. The Commissioner with the help of the Training Officer and staff then developed policies and started action programs. District directors and their training officers followed suit. Concern for the development of human resources earned top priority for training and development matters.

2. An organization structure was established which provided the basis for coactive efforts in training (see Chart D-1, p. 284). First, a training committee was organized at the regional level, representing all parts of the organization, to recommend overall policy, programs,

CHART D-1

COLLABORATIVE STRUCTURE FOR TRAINING-LEARNING ACTIVITIES
Internal Revenue Service: Western Region

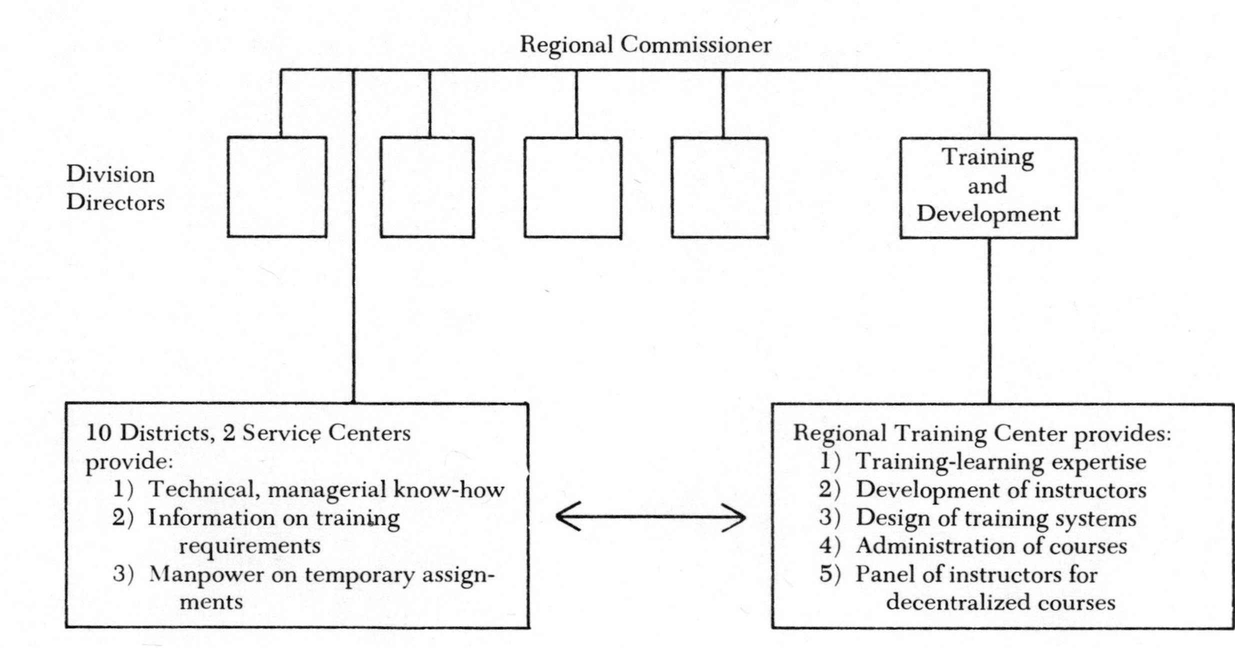

and actions. Participating in the committee were divisional directors who were responsible for their people's growth and development. Second, a training staff was established as a separate department with direct access to the Regional Commissioner, who personally provided training leadership. Third, a Regional Training Center was established as the major instrument of the organization to share in the development and transmission of knowledge and techniques needed throughout the region. A small permanent nucleus of training professionals was augmented by contributions of personnel from the organizational components. Such temporary "training" personnel were actually on a full-time basis while assigned instructional duties. Assignments were sometimes for short periods during which such temporary additions learned how to develop and present instructional materials, and then returned to their regular jobs. They were retained on a "panel of trainers" from which they could be called to present the course(s) for which they had been groomed. Panels provided instructors for such functions as Audit; Collection; Alcohol, Tobacco and Firearms; Intelligence; and Administration.

3. Managers acquired know-how and confidence in their ability to manage training as well as to prepare and present instructional materials. They managed the development of their employees through target setting, progress reviews and feedback, and recognition of work accomplishment. They supplemented such development on the job by securing instructors from the Regional Training Center and arranging for local sessions. When managers were rated by their superiors, special attention was given to accomplishment in the development of subordinates. Those managers and technicians who participated in course development and instructional work were given special consideration for career advancement in recognition of their contribution to training

programs. The large percentage of current managers literally "grew up" as excellent technicians through on-the-job and formal instruction routes.

4. The Western Region initiated Organizational Development Seminars under the leadership of the Regional Commissioner and the technical direction and support of the Regional Training Director. Impetus to this program has been given by the attendance of executives at the Federal Executive Interagency Training Program at Charlottesville, Virginia (discussed previously in Chapter 2 and Chapter 6,) which provides an understanding of the benefits of organizational development. For example, the Director of the Western Service Center, Ogden, Utah, attended the Federal Executive Institute. He felt it was important that the Western Region Service Center increase its concern for the human side of the organization in addition to its concern for productivity. He was fully aware that Internal Revenue Service Centers have tended to be highly concerned with the mechanics of processing returns and the quantitative measures of production. The question was: Could its managers be given more insight and ability to help people improve their contributions to the Center's effectiveness?

The Western Service Center—with the help of the Western Region Training Director—held its first Organizational Development Seminar in March 1970, in which the Director of the Service Center and the staff from the Region and the Service Center acted as instructors. Other top managers participated as trainers, instructors, and moderators in the seven seminars that followed. The Organizational Development sessions consist of forty hours of pre-course work and forty hours of learning individualized management practices and building team skills. These sessions also prepared the participants for the transfer of their techniques to their work problems. The participants were organized in work groups during the sessions, which made it possible for them to continue their problem-solving activities at the original work site. A coordinating committee at the Western Region Service Center is now seeing that the work groups from eight organizational development seminars are continuing their productive activities.

Results

The strategies used to incorporate the training function in the managerial role have been successful. Managers have learned to manage the training and development of their subordinates. They participated in the development of knowledge critical to the organization. They contributed manpower to maintain the activities of the Western Region Training Center and the Panel of Instructors.

The results are seen in well-trained people who enable the Internal Revenue Service to continue to meet increasing challenges and develop the high level of competence it needs to monitor and audit the collection of internal revenue.

The image of the Internal Revenue has been changed, and citizens are given excellent service and assistance. In an area of great sensitivity the work force is able to do its job politely and firmly. The Training Center has increased its curriculum offerings to over one hundred courses, with some five hundred professional instructors available and over two thousand participants during a year. The quality of instruction is high and methods are constantly updated.

The results of the Organizational Development at the Western Service Center are equally impressive. All 325 supervisors who have participated in the training labs are now actively participating in work groups, bringing about continued improvements in operations through solving of problems, removing roadblocks, and increasing communication throughout the Center. One recent improvement has resulted in a 250,000 manhour return in one division alone. A recent conference of the directors of the Western Service Center illustrates the productive use of team building techniques. The group developed future goals and strategies to include the extension of Organizational Development for its technicians and clerks, and the involvement of all levels of supervision in a survey of relationships between supervisors and their subordinates.

Summary and Analysis

This case described an organization's strategy of helping managers to manage the training and development of their people through involving their managers in learning and application of those practices that develop people.

Leadership. The vitality of the leadership made a great difference in managers' contributions to the development of people. The Regional Commissioner provided the initial push by his personal involvement in setting up the training task force to examine the instructional processes and to make recommendations for action. Top managers expected subordinates to develop their employees and gave recognition to those who did.

Organizational framework. This case illustrates how the proper structural framework makes learning function effectively. The training staff had direct access to the Regional Commissioner. Instead of delayed and incomplete communication, the technical counsel of training professionals was immediately available. Line managers incorporated the training function as part of their overall role. They did this as part of their accountability to the Regional Commissioner. They provided personnel and their expertise to the Regional Training Center, and also shared in the benefits provided by the Center. They developed their subordinates through the setting of goals, through their feedback information on their employees' performance, and through recognition of work progress.

The full-time instructor concept does much for the internal regeneration of skills and abilities. Managers and technicians who participated in developing and presenting instructional materials also strengthened their own knowledge and confidence. Also, managers and technicians with experience have greater impact on students because their presentations "ring true" in the exchange of ideas. The fact that managers and technicians were relieved of their regular duties while they participated in instructional work upgraded the status of training, since training was not looked upon as a "secondary" duty or added burden but recognized as a part of work operations. Training was seen as requiring time, thought, and skill in order for the learning experience to be worthwhile.

The concept of collaborative instruction in this case made possible the sharing of knowledge developed by workers themselves from their daily experience. The curriculum was closely related to employees' needs, and since it was highly relevant and usable it was regarded as worthwhile.

The Regional Training Center acted not as a detached school but as a responsive instrument of the organizational components it serves, closely interrelated with the needs of those components. Backed by top leadership, the Center is not a precarious operation since it cannot be hampered by managerial self-interest which, as one person said, might find it inconvenient to support it. Thus it is not subjected to start-stop training situations, immobilization of training activity, dissipation of results, lowering of priority, loss of benefits, and the costs of added effort required to re-start training activity. The Center continues to grow stronger and more productive in organizational development.

Managerial practices. Managers established a working

climate that challenged employees to learn; it also provided them with help in their development. Managers learned to diagnose problems that could be helped through learning experiences. They secured instructional resources from the Regional Training Center as well as locating external training opportunities.

The Organizational Development seminars have helped managers to learn about their own styles of managing and how they affect others, alternate styles of managing, the importance of listening for dissent in order to arrive at the best decisions, and the importance of feedback as a learning experience. In fact managers learn while providing feedback on work progress, and are therefore themselves being developed.

Managers were encouraged in their efforts to develop their people because they received recognition of this factor in their performance appraisals and special consideration was given in their career advancement.

Qualities of learning experiences. The strategies used in this case made the learning efforts highly effective and worthwhile both to managers and individuals. The major breakthrough, as illustrated in this case, is the result of the strategy which incorporates the training function in the managerial role. The superior-subordinate relationship is the basis for all other training processes, because it is the primary channel through which learning is utilized on the job. The managers contribute to the functioning of the collaborative training center by loaning their personnel as instructors and through the application to the work of the knowledge transmitted from the Center.

The interrelationships of the managerial training role with the functioning of the Regional Training Center has built qualities of instructional resources that achieve learning objectives: content is appropriate and highly related to the purpose for which the training has been established; the instructional procedures are selected that will provide the most appropriate instructional procedures with a high degree of actual learning through experience and information on results; the flexibility provides timing and sequence that brings maximum learning; and the selection of instructors guarantees the use of those best qualified for the particular learning experience.

An intern in revenue agent work said, "Until I started to learn, I hadn't realized how strong the training program is here, especially the coaching. Upon return from a course you observe as you accompany agents; then you get your own case load and a trained man accompanies you. You do learn best by doing. The increase in responsibility is stimulating." In the Organizational Development seminars, the managers and supervisors from different parts of the organization work together in teams to solve problems. Through the efforts to arrive at the best solution as agreed to by the entire group, the individuals learn how to become good team members, how to get the best ideas from the group, and obtain group understanding of why a certain solution is the best for the group. By experiencing what goes wrong as the result of poor team work—such as the loss of time, failure to get all the ideas and contributions available from the group, and wasted motion—the groups learn to work out problems effectively together. Managers learn the worth of group decision-making, the value of listening to their employees through the actual experience of learning by doing. They continue in the teams formed at their Organizational Development seminars; however, these teams become continual team-building groups when they return to their own organization, working on the problem their group has selected until the solution is agreed upon by all and is put into action. This makes a reality of what has been newly learned and created as part of the mainstream of the organization's activities.

Appendix E

COOPERATIVE EDUCATION
WHITE SANDS MISSILE RANGE

Integrating Academic Study with Learning through Work To Provide Trained Scientists and Engineers

This case represents a strategy for integrating learning with work to meet an organizational problem—the shortage of scientists and engineers—through a cooperative education program alternating college study and work.

Background

The White Sands Missile Range is a part of the Army Material Command which is made up of the Army Test and Evaluation Command, Aberdeen Proving Ground, and the Army Electronic Command, Fort Monmouth, New Jersey. All of these commands are under the Department of Defense. White Sands has trainees under both the Test and

Evaluation Command and the Electronic Command. White Sands Missile Range was established July 9, 1945. Located in South Central New Mexico, it has two and a half million acres of deserts, sand flats, and bare mountains. An integrated testing range, it is responsible for the design, development, testing, launching of guided missiles and rockets for the Army, Navy, and the Air Force. Since its establishment it has played a vital part in the development of scientific technology. Its ranges were the scenes of the first atomic bomb explosion and much of the preliminary work for satellite space shots.

Following World War II the nation was seriously concerned about the problem of training and educating a sufficient number of scientists and engineers to enable this country to maintain leadership in the field of industrial and space technology.

Need

In the six-year period following the close of World War II, the White Sands Missile Range experienced difficulty in recruiting scientists and engineers. Its isolated location and the small output of professionals in these fields from nearby colleges were aggravated by a nationwide shortage. Military manpower was available, but the technical and scientific jobs required more professionals than the military personnel could provide. Other Army or federal agencies could not provide such personnel through reassignment and transfer. Civil Service jobs with their lower pay scales could not compete with the attraction of private industry.

Furthermore, the need, in addition to the quantitative aspects, meant provision for the development of a permanent cadre that could, after training in the early known techniques and systems, be able continually to create and develop innovations in rocket and missile technology.

Diagnosis and Plan

The White Sands personnel staff diagnosed their problem:

1. They needed personnel to supplement the professional and subprofessional staffs in their research, testing, and development activities.
2. They needed trainees with potential for professional development to fill scientist and engineer vacancies.
3. Students from nearby colleges could be used if some way were found that they could also continue work toward completion of their academic degrees which were required for professional jobs.
4. Work assignments that paralleled the full college program should provide job progression so that the development of these trainees would be challenged by increasingly difficult work assignments and projects.
5. Work assignments at White Sands should be related to the level and subject matter of their studies at college.

Work experience would be considered an integral part of the educational process, and learning would be considered an integral part of the work process. It would be advantageous for the students to alternate between periods of academic instruction at a college and the related experience on the job. This would make it possible for the students to provide the needed manpower, contributing to production as they learned. It also meant that the employer would contribute significantly to the students' education by making it possible for students to earn as they learned.

Plans in cooperative education were not new. The first plan, that of Dean Schneider of the University of Cincinnati for his engineering students in 1906, had been followed by others such as that of Antioch College, Boston's Northeastern

University, and the Drexel Institute of Technology. The record showed that graduates had done well both in their college work and in their part-time jobs, and had gone on to successful professional careers. Army's Frankford Arsenal in Philadelphia had participated in a cooperative education program, working with the Drexel Institute in 1949. Current estimates show that this work-plus-study plan is now in use in 300 American colleges and universities. Over 300 more are now under consideration. Congress is studying a plan for start-up grants to educational institutions for cooperative programs. The United States Army has 33 installations employing cooperative students.

Among the cooperative systems studied by White Sands were the following three:

1. The undergraduate student attends college full time during the regular school year and works at an installation or company during the summer months.

2. The student may attend class for half a day and work the other half. This is normally on a year-round basis, and the morning and afternoon groups exchange places on the jobs at the organization where they work.

3. The year may be divided into two equal six-month periods with one group of students attending college full time while the other group is working full time. The two groups exchange places twice a year at the start of the semester or summer session.

The first plan was the easiest to place into operation since it would involve no action by the participating college, which would consider the student as only having summer employment. The disadvantage of the plan was that the installation would have the benefit of the student's productive ability for only three months of the year and in most cases the trainee would have little opportunity to do more than observe engineering and scientific work. This uneconomical factor, together with a steadily increasing shortage of personnel who normally carry out subprofessional work—such as Engineering Aides, Draftsmen, Physical Science Aides—resulted in rejection of that plan.

The second plan, wherein students would work half a day, was eliminated for a practical reason—the location of White Sands Missile Range; since the student would have to spend approximately two hours traveling to and from work, this was considered impractical.

The third plan not only overcame the objections of the other two programs but had the advantage of increasing the student's earning during his undergraduate period.

Action

White Sands personnel staff coordinated the proposal with manpower, budget, and management officials at White Sands, as well as with Civil Service Commission representatives, and then secured approval of the Commanding General of the White Sands Missile Range.

The next step was to obtain the interest and agreement of a college to participate in the plan. A delegation from White Sands visited New Mexico's College of Agriculture and Mechanical Arts which had a fine engineering school and departments of mathematics and physics. (The University of Texas at El Paso later joined the plan.) It was pointed out that White Sands had much practical experience available in their labs, experimental shops, and in the field from which students could learn much. Furthermore, students would have the opportunity to work with many of the world's best space scientists, engineers, and physicists. It was explained that bright students could earn almost all of their tuition by working part time at White Sands. In addition, they could be promoted without competition to the next higher level of work outlined in their training plan. The college authorities met the problem of providing sufficient

TABLE A-1

White Sands Co-operative Work and Degree Program

	Year				
	1	2	3	4	5
Work Period					
August to January Rate of Pay (1/2 of Annual Rate)	$4621	$4621	$5212	$5853	$6548
Evening Credit Hrs.	3	3	3	3	3
Full-time Study					
February to July 18-week semester credit hours	18	19	19	19	19
6-week session credit hours	6	6	7	7	7

Total credit hours:

August-January Evening	15
February-July (18-week)	94
(6-week)	33

Credit hours required for B.S. degree in Engineering:

University of Texas	128
New Mexico State University	132

(*Note:* For a student entering the program in July after high school graduation, the plan requires five years to complete the program and earn the degree.)

time to earn credits for a degree and to work six months of the year by extending the school year to the full twelve months with no summer vacations, and extending the college program to five years, as a minimum for the college degree, as shown in Table A-1.

The personnel staff at White Sands next turned their attention to setting up the internal work structure to select areas that would provide challenging work assignments and managerial coaches in these areas with abilities for instruction and development of their workers and with interest in doing this. Specific jobs were structured and grades assigned, ranging from a GS-2 entry level to a GS-5 target level.

The college was then asked to screen students for interest in this program, as well as their achievements, demonstrated leadership, and professional potential. Students had to have a B average in high school or college and be in the upper third of their class. The College Coordinator then sent nominations for the vacancies to the White Sands Cooperative Education Coordinator.

Nominees were interviewed by personnel staff at White Sands and referred to the supervisors of job vacancies. Each applicant had an opportunity to see the kind of work and to discuss the job with various representatives at White Sands. If there was mutual agreement of the applicant and the organization having the vacancy, a commitment was made.

The training plans were designed to integrate work on the projects with learning experiences needed to qualify the trainee for advancement as well as related to his academic major. Supervisors followed these principles:

1. *The work assigned the trainee is designed to contribute to the productivity of the organization.* As one supervisor said, piecemeal bits of work are assigned, but the majority of the trainee's work is composed of projects which extend over days, weeks, or even months. The

trainee does not usually bear responsibility for meeting the major milestones of the branch's assigned tasks, but he is nevertheless expected to help meet its requirements, and, by knowing how his assigned project ties in with the organization goals, he is able to judge for himself the importance of the work assigned.

2. *Work is assigned which is commensurate with the trainee's academic background and interests.* This is explained by a supervisor: "For example, a trainee in electronic tracking systems development can expect to get training in laboratory procedures data analysis, tracking systems, computer programming, control systems."

3. *Provision is made for a training program as broad as the mission will allow.* As a supervisor said, "Our mission is usually sufficiently broad to allow the trainee to get experience in many areas. We believe that the broader the assignments and the less the supervision, the better the working relationships will be."

Personnel staff at White Sands established a records system on the development of each of the co-op students, which included an individualized training plan, continuing evaluations of performance and progress by supervisors and the co-ops, and academic progress furnished by the college co-op coordinator. At the close of the first six-month work phase, the co-ops were placed on leave without pay to return to college for the six-month phase of academic training. Upon completion of that, the co-op was eligible for advancement to the next higher grade at White Sands providing that his performance evaluations showed that he was qualified for promotion.

Results

As a result of the Cooperative Education Program, well-trained scientists and engineers were developed. Thus it helped the Army meet a pressing need—a shortage in this category of manpower. While they were qualifying themselves for scientific and engineer positions through their academic study and their work experience, co-op students were supplementing the work of professional and subprofessional staffs by filling lower level jobs such as engineering aides and physical science aides. The extent of their manpower contribution is shown by the following:

1. One of every six scientist and engineer jobs at White Sands is filled by a former participant in their Cooperative Education Program.
2. Nearly 80% of those completing the program (157 out of 207) have been employed by White Sands. The rest went to work for other government agencies or private industry, thus making a contribution of equal importance to the success of the missile and space program.
3. From the inception of the program to the present time, there were from 75 to over 200 co-op students participating each year. If this is multiplied by the eighteen years of the program's existence, some conception is gained of the manpower contribution of these semitrained low-cost employees to the productivity of the organization.

Some of the latent or unexpected consequences are of special interest in contributions to both the organization and the co-ops:

1. Progress made in a collaborative framework headed by the command itself and including manpower and budget staff, scientific expertise, and the personnel and training know-how.
2. Progress made in liaison with external agencies such as the federal Civil Service Commission and the colleges that participated.
3. Commitment of supervisors to achievement of results; managerial responsibility and accountability for

operational results in the training and development of co-ops; also visibility of the worth of the co-ops' contributions through their learning on the job.

4. The co-op students made significant contributions saving thousands of working hours and tens of thousands of dollars:

a) An "altitude chamber" to test Air Force balloons under the conditions of wind and weather and climate that the balloons would meet in the upper air.

b) A computer program that solved an immense set of linear equations dealing with the propulsion system of a certain missile.

c) A very high-speed motion picture camera to catch the launching phases of a missile in actual flight from which resulted pictures that could be translated in the lab to scientific data impossible to get by any other means.

5. The foundation for formulation and maintenance of career plans that related work experience to the completion of requirements for professional degrees.

6. The contribution of earned salaries to the self-support of students in their college educational costs.

Summary and Analysis

The consequences—both intended and latent—are significant to those interested in effective learning programs as part of organizational operations because they provide a clue as to day-to-day conditions that acted as determinants in this case. In addition to a solution to manpower shortage in the scientific and engineering fields, there were other accomplishments that caused the organization, its managers, supervisors, the students, and the colleges to see its worth.

It proved, for one thing, that an active learning process

integrated into day-to-day operations can make a significant difference in: (1) the effectiveness with which the organization meets its production goals, and (2) the feeling of satisfaction on the part of individuals as to their work accomplishments and opportunity to progress. The training, growth, and development of the co-ops were visibly worthwhile. It raised the importance and thus the status of the function of learning.

An active learning process integrated with work makes a significant difference in the return on the investment in human resources:

1. There was better utilization of manpower. Redistribution of functions helped scientists and engineers accomplish their more complex functions when assisted by the co-ops. As one supervisor put it, "I would not trade one co-op for ten other workers."

2. The job structure providing for progression for co-ops made certain "a place to go." The challenge of working toward the next plateau was created. In the words of one of the co-ops, "It links learning with moving ahead." The training agreements providing the evidence of effective qualification through learning on the job made it possible for the White Sands personnel staff to receive permission from the U.S. Civil Service Commission to agree to "non-competitive promotions"; that is, the co-op student could be promoted to the next higher level without having to compete with all others within that organization who might qualify. This ruled out uncertainty as to how and when one might move ahead.

3. The learning process integrated with work proved itself to be stimulating because: (a) Objectives of the work projects and assignments were understood as well as were the long-range goals; purpose was present as well as the continuing job progression. (b) Self-awareness of the need for

learning in order to accomplish their assignments was developed. (c) The content of the learning and work operations was challenging; it was seen as vital and important, and even the menial tasks were seen in relation to the whole. (d) Learning and accomplishment of the work were self-directed; the co-ops were delegated responsibility to learn and to do, to solve problems and complete projects. (e) Job progression and graduation were contingent upon what they learned and what they accomplished in application and use of their learning on the job. (f) Their coaches were interested in them. As described by several co-ops, "His [the supervisor's] interest in my work and encouragement of learning motivate me to work for him." "Makes me feel a definite part of the organization. . . . I attend all meetings." "He asks me questions and assigns me projects that make me learn." "He takes the time to point out results of my work."

4. Students were stimulated to greater understanding and interest in their academic work. Learning on the job helped to lessen the gap between academic theory and the practice provided by real work. In the words of one co-op: "It overcomes the disillusionment about college." And another said, "You can't get these labs and field work in schools."

5. Students were helped to decide upon careers *during*, not *after*, graduation from college. The interaction of work and courses assisted them in making choices. As one of the co-op students said, "It provides a searching period before graduation." And another: "It avoids the traumatic experience of looking for a job and finding something you can succeed in after you graduate."

As a strategy, this model for the integration of learning into operations has been worth its salt. The organizations learned how to provide conditions for increased effectiveness in learning on the job. The productive results—trained and competent scientists and engineers together with significant contributions to the work—were visible. The White Sands Missile Range, the universities, managers, and the co-ops recognized the *work that had been accomplished as the result of the learning opportunities,* as well as the *educational advances* that had been made as the *result of the work experience.* The personnel staff had collaborated to develop a work-learning process by which recruitment, job restructuring, and training progression qualified co-ops for their promotion. Learning incorporated with work became a stimulating, natural process. The coach-supervisor provided both challenge and approval for learning integrated with work experiences. The coach-supervisor understood his task in the development of the co-op students. His empathy encouraged their learning, his delegation of responsibility caused their self-directed learning, and his recognition of creative contributions helped them to progress further.

Appendix F

A Note to the Presidential Task Force[1]

Dr. Marvin H. Berkeley
Corporate Personnel Director
Texas Instruments, Inc.
Dallas, Texas

. . . Development cannot be externally forced on the individual; it must spring from the person's inner desire to grow, initiative to begin, and persistence to achieve.

The governmental institutions wherein development takes place bear the responsibility to their employees to foster those conditions, as a natural part of the working environment, whereby the need for self-development becomes obvious, personal efforts are enhanced, and appropriate talent and achievements are rewarded.

'Most' professional and technical growth occurs on the job itself, especially where personal developmental goals become clarified, are meaningful, and are complementary with the operational goals of the government. If we accept these three premises, then it follows that a complete evaluation of education and training must consider the operational systems wherein goals are set and achievements rewarded. Unless we deliberately plan to evaluate the internal systems, there will be a tendency to focus on education and training programs external to the job. Such programs are extremely important for development, but they are not ends in themselves. They must be evaluated on the basis of whether or not the added skills and know-how of the graduates did indeed contribute to better job performance in the most economical and effective way. In other words, external programs are supplements to the 'major' developmental influences on the job, and the latter should be a principal focus of study.

How then might we proceed to evaluate the day-to-day systems and practices and their influence on the developmental process? This is complex indeed, but it is far-reaching. It will require follow-on research and analysis long after the Task Force has completed its mission. I believe, however, that we are obligated to pave the way. A few areas in the form of evaluative questions are as follows:

1. How are the operational goals first broadly set, and then shared and shaped with those chiefly responsible for their attainment?

2. How are the progress reviews discussed between those directly responsible and among the many indirectly concerned?

3. How are postmortems carried out and the benefits therefrom transferred to related projects?

4. How are personal carrer opportunities described and broadcast, and how are job inquiries processed?

5. How are personal developmental plans and problems discussed, and how are they related to the operational environment?

6. How are the more outstanding performers identified, transferred into alternate assignments for growth, rotated into different environments for breadth, and eventually accelerated into more responsibility?

7. How are the marginal performers identified, counseled with on their problems, transferred into more appropriate assignments, or eventually demoted into less responsibility they are able to handle?

8. How are employees encouraged to improve their work methods and to reach for higher standards of performance, and how are they rewarded for achievement?

9. How are specific managers and whole departments evaluated against the criteria of staff development and the general upgrading of their respective work forces?

10. How are the job-related attitudes of employee groups determined, appropriate and feasible actions taken, and results fed back to those concerned?

President Johnson has stated that the primary objective of the Task Force is 'the elevation of the performance and perspective of our careerists.' He has requested the Task Force to recommend 'the best modern methods of development' through 'creative and innovative approaches.'

The foregoing comments suggest that performance elevation and perspective can and do depend heavily on the daily institutional environment of government and that creative and innovative (and practical) approaches are readily available if we will evaluate the influences on the job as rigorously and as critically as we will evaluate the programs of education and training external to the job.

Appendix G

PARTICIPANTS IN THE SURVEY OF TRAINING PRACTICES

Western Electric

Service Division-Pacific Region:

- J.H. Moore
- W.K. Robinson
- L.P. Whittier
- W.R. Kugler
- W.F. Breslen
- V.A. Frost
- Barbara Robles
- J. Greenbaum
- J.W. Cullen
- R. Boggs
- G.W. Hildebrand
- R.S. Van Sant
- L.R. DeVore
- C.A. Roberts
- J.T. Parano
- James Etheredge Jr.
- Ingrid Liberski
- Leslie Canez
- Harry Shipley
- Robert Kehoe
- John Miller

S.F. Bay Installation:

- J.B. Martin
- T.W. Stewart
- R.G. Olson
- G.W. Gookin

Corporate Office, New York:

- Arthur G. Foster
- Matt Lynaugh
- P.J. Patinka
- K.J. Verostick

Training Center, Princeton, New Jersey:

- J.I. Thiesmeyer
- T.G. Bentson

Raymond Corporation

- George G. Raymond, Jr.
- Robert T. Cline
- Richard Thurber
- Donald W. Coulson
- Harold Maider
- Cy Youngs
- Donald Wright
- Jack Lyles
- Mary Nowalk
- Inez Pollard
- Ron George

Chase Manhattan Bank, N.A.

Albert S. Woodhouse
Ben Roter
Mark Loftin

Western Region, Internal Revenue Service

Regional Office:
Joe Davis
Paul O'Rourke
Brent Thorne
Vikki Renneckar
Mary Del Carlo
District Office, San Francisco:
Herbert Futrell
Charles Kingman
Howard Johnson
Jack Wood
Carl Chiara
Robert Toso
Paul Krug
Ogden Service Center, Utah:
Robert Terry
Lynn Peterson
Fred Berry
Mike Jones
Maxine Bills
Eula Stringfellow
Dick Nelson
Eli Yearsley
Barbara Sanders

White Sands Missile Range, New Mexico

Roy Autry
James Patton
Michael Brady
Carl Clifft
William Scharfenberg
Elizabeth Mayfield
Mary Maestas
Harvey Lassiter
Guy T. Calafato
Roy Cano
Joe Deare
Harold Lambeth
Bea James
John Nance
Gus Bigelow
Joe Peckum
Ball Chin
Stanley Hawkinson
Fernando Casas
Creed Dye

Notes

Chapter 1

1. Elias H. Porter, *Manpower Development: The system Training Concept* (New York: Harper & Row, 1964).

2. David King, *Training within the Organization: A Study of Company Policy and Procedures for the Systematic Training of Operators and Supervisors* (Chicago: Educational Methods, Inc., 1965).

3. Avice M. Saint, "Learning in an Organization" (unpublished doctoral dissertation, University of California, 1969).

Chapter 2

1. John W. Gardner, *Self Renewal, The Individual and the Innovative Society* (New York: Harper & Row, 1963), pp. 78-79.

2. Elliott Jacques, *The Changing Culture of a Factory* (London: Tavistock Publications, 1951), pp. 289-290.

3. Alfred P. Sloan, *My Years with General Motors* (New York: Doubleday, 1964), pp. 431-444.

4. *Ibid.*, p. 434.
5. *Ibid.*, p. 435.
6. Peter F. Drucker, *The Effective Executive* (New York: Harper & Row, 1967), pp. 89-91.

Chapter 3

1. Warren Bennis, "Organizations of the Future," *Personnel Administration* (September-October, 1967), pp. 7-9.
2. *Ibid.*

Chapter 4

1. Marvin H. Berkeley, "A Note to the Presidential Task Force," contained in *Self and Service Enrichment through Federal Training* (Selections from Studies, Reports and Papers Submitted to the Presidential Task Force on Career Advancement). Distributed by U.S. Civil Service Commission, Washington, D.C., 1967, pp. 91-93.
2. Robert J. House, "*Management Development: Design, Evaluation, and Implementation*" (Bureau of Industrial Relations, Graduate School of Business Administration, University of Michigan, Ann Arbor, 1967) chap. 1. Management Development: What, How, Why? pp. 9-19.
3, Douglas McGregor, *The Human Side of Enterprise* (New York: McGraw-Hill, 1960), p. 204.
4. Earl R. Gomersall and M. Scott Myers, "Breakthrough in On-the-Job Training," *Harvard Business Review* (August, 1966).
5. McGregor, p. 203.

Chapter 5

1. Burton R. Clark, *Educating the Expert Society* (San Francisco: Chandler Publishing Co., 1962), chap. 2.

2. Peter F. Drucker, "Management's New Role," *Harvard Business Review* (November-December, 1969), pp. 52-55.

3. Elias H. Porter, *Manpower Development: The System Training Concept* (New York: Harper & Row, 1964).

4. David R. Francis, "Bell System Seeks Jobs that Fit People," *Christian Science Monitor*, May 10, 1968.

5. Richard A. Nenneman, "Workers Need Job-Change-Aid," *Christian Science Monitor*, Nov. 26, 1971.

Chapter 6

1. Anselm L. Strauss and Norman H. Martin, "Patterns of Mobility within Industrial Organizations," *Organizational Careers, A Sourcebook for Theory*, Barney G. Glaser, ed. (Chicago: Aldine Publishing Co., 1968). Chapter 25.

2. Margaret Mead, "Thinking Ahead," *Harvard Business Review* (November-December, 1958), p. 34.

3. John Holt, *What Do I Do Monday?* (New York: E. P. Dutton & Co., 1970), p. 25.

4. Eugene E. Jennings, *Routes to the Executive Suite* (New York: McGraw-Hill, 1971).

5. Although the Presidential Task Force on Career Advancement in the Public Service recommended the establishment of this advanced study center, which opened early in 1968 at Charlottesville, Virginia, the idea spanned the terms of four presidents—Truman, Eisenhower, Kennedy, and Johnson—and is now endorsed by a fifth, President Richard Nixon.

6. Gene W. Dalton and Paul H. Thompson, "Accelerating Obsolescence of Older Engineers," *Harvard Business Review* (September-October, 1971), pp. 57-67.

7. Peter F. Drucker, "What We Can Learn from Japanese Management: Decision by 'consensus,' lifetime employment, continuous training, and the godfather system

suggest ways to solve U.S. problems," *Harvard Business Review* (March-April, 1971), pp. 110-122.

8. Margaret Mead, "Youth Badger Savants: Report on intellectual summit conference on mankind's values in a scientific age," *Christian Science Monitor*, Oct. 9, 1969.

Chapter 7

1. Eugene E. Jennings, *Routes to the Executive Suite* (New York: McGraw-Hill, 1971).

2. André Fonsny, "Training within the Company: A Study of Management Training Practices in Three Industrial Enterprises," *Management International* (1963), pp. 46-51.

3. Douglas McGregor, *The Human Side of Enterprise* (New York: McGraw-Hill, 1960), p. 87.

4. Herbert H. Meyer, Emanuel Kay, and John R. P. French, Jr., "Split Roles in Performance Appraisal," *Harvard Business Review* (January-February, 1965), pp. 123-129.

5. Gene W. Dalton and Paul H. Thompson, "Accelerating Obsolescence of Older Engineers," *Harvard Business Review* (September-October, 1971), pp. 57-67.

6. R. A. Nenneman, "Cause of Engineers' Obsolescence Tackled," *Christian Science Monitor*, Jan. 18, 1972, p. 7.

7. See note 5.

8. Peter F. Drucker, "What We Can Learn from Japanese Management," *Harvard Business Review* (March-April, 1971), pp. 120-122.

9. Felician F. Foltman, "Xerox Corporation: A Case Study in Retraining," in *Management of Personnel Quarterly*, I, No. 5 (Bureau of Industrial Relations, University of Michigan, Autumn/Winter, 1962), pp. 8-20.

Chapter 8

1. Robert F. Mager, *Preparing Objectives for*

Programmed Instruction (Palo Alto, Calif.: Fearon Publishers, 1962).

2. Edgar H. Schein, "The First Job Dilemma," *Psychology Today* (March, 1968), p. 31.

3. Robert F. Mager, "Learner-Controlled Instruction," unpublished study, Varian Associates, Palo Alto, Calif. I owe a great debt of gratitude to Dr. Mager for giving me a copy of this piece of research which demonstrates the benefits of introducing learner-controlled techniques into their factory engineering training program. The effective development of auto-instructional programs was shown to depend upon the development of behaviorally stated objectives. It demonstrated that learner motivation in an instructional situation is a direct function of the amount of apparent control the learner can exert over the situation.

4. Richard Beckhard, *Organizational Development, Strategies and Models* (Reading, Mass.: Addison-Wesley, 1969), p. 27.

5. Robert F. Mager and Kenneth M. Beach, Jr., *Developing Vocational Instruction* (Palo Alto, Calif.: Fearon Publishers, 1967).

6. Robert F. Mager and Peter Pipe, *Analyzing Performance Problems, or "You Really Oughta Wanna"* (Belmont, Calif.: Fearon/Lear Siegler, Inc., Education Division, 1970).

Chapter 9

1. John W. Gardner, *The Recovery of Confidence* (New York: W. W. Norton & Co., 1970), p. 34.

2. Jerome S. Bruner, *The Process of Education* (New York: Vintage Books, Division of Random House, 1960, by the President and Fellows of Harvard College), p. 17.

3. John W. Gardner, *Self-Renewal The Individual and the Innovative Society* (New York: Harper & Row, 1963), p. 12.

4. Peter F. Drucker, "What We Can Learn from Japanese Management," *Harvard Business Review* (March-April, 1971), pp. 116-18.

5. Douglas McGregor, *The Human Side of Enterprise* (New York: McGraw-Hill, 1960), pp. 213–14.

Chapter 11

1. Walter R. Mahler, *Diagnostic Studies and Surveys: Powerful Tools for the Training Director,* Cassette Recording of presentation at American Society of Training and Development, 1970 National Conference, published by CREDR Corporation; also write Walter R. Mahler, Mahler Associates, Inc., 10-B Midland Park Center, Midland Park, N.J. 07432., for a copy of his presentation on "Diagnostic Surveys—A Tool for Change Making," presented to New York Metropolitan Chapter of ASTD, 1969.

2. Robert F. Mager and Peter Pipe, *Analyzing Performance Problems, or "You Really Oughta Wanna,"* (Belmont, Calif.: Fearon Publishers/Lear Siegler, Inc., Education Division, 1970).

3. Harold M. F. Rush, *Behavioral Science, Concepts and Management Application,* Personnel Policy Study No. 216, 1969 National Industrial Conference Board, Inc., New York, 1969; and The Conference Board in Canada, Montreal.

4. Kamla Chowdhry, "Management Development Programs: Executive Needs," *Industrial Management Review* (School of Industrial Management, MIT, Spring, 1963), p. 31.

5. *Ibid.*

Appendix C

1. Harold M. F. Rush, *Behavioral Science, Concepts and Management Application,* Personnel Policy Study No.

216, 1969 National Industrial Conference Board, Inc., New York, 1969; and The Conference Board in Canada, Montreal, p. 121.

2. George Raymond, "The President's Role in OD," *What's Wrong with Work?* (National Association of Manufacturers, New York, 1967), p. 21.

Appendix F

1. *Self and Service Enrichment through Federal Training* (Selections from Studies, Reports and Papers Submitted to the Presidential Task Force on Career Advancement). Distributed by U.S. Civil Service Commission, Washington, D.C., 1967. pp. 91-93.

Index

About the Author

Avice M. Saint, Ed.D.

Dr. Saint has devoted the past 30 years to personnel and training activities. At present she is training and development officer for a U.S. Army facility, a lecturer at Golden State University, and a consultant in organizational learning and training.

Her past experience includes working with a number of large-scale organizations on research related to the training of employees, and holding staff and operating positions in the personnel management field in this country and abroad. She also has taught at the University of Maryland.

Dr. Saint was educated at the University of California, Berkeley, where she earned her Ed.D. degree.

A member of the American Society of Training Directors, and the American Society for Training and Development, she has taken part in numerous panels and conferences.